Zara Yaqob, Walda Heywat
The *Hatata Inquiries*

The *Hatata* Inquiries

Two Texts of Seventeenth-Century African Philosophy from Ethiopia about Reason, the Creator, and Our Ethical Responsibilities

Written by Zara Yaqob and Walda Heywat
Translated and edited by Ralph Lee
with Mehari Worku and Wendy Laura Belcher
In Cooperation with Jeremy R. Brown
Preface by Dag Herbjørnsrud

DE GRUYTER

ISBN 978-3-11-221411-4
e-ISBN (PDF) 978-3-11-078192-2
e-ISBN (EPUB) 978-3-11-078198-4

Ralph Lee ORCid ID: 0000-0002-9698-810X
Mehari Worku ORCid ID: 0000-0003-1082-8752
Wendy Laura Belcher ORCid ID: 0000-0003-1734-4136
Jeremy R. Brown ORCid ID: 0000-0001-9606-4866
Dag Herbjørnsrud ORCid ID: 0000-0003-1356-0368

Library of Congress Control Number: 2023943594

Bibliographic information published by the Deutsche Nationalbibliothek
The Deutsche Nationalbibliothek lists this publication in the Deutsche Nationalbibliografie;
detailed bibliographic data are available on the internet at http://dnb.dnb.de.

© 2025 Walter de Gruyter GmbH, Berlin/Boston
This volume is text- and page-identical with the hardback published in 2024.
Cover image: Adobe Stock Image by Picturellarious, "Looking Out of the Famous Daniel Korkor Church in the Tigray Region" of Ethiopia
Typesetting: Integra Software Services Pvt. Ltd.
Printing and binding: CPI books GmbH, Leck

www.degruyter.com

Contents

Dag Herbjørnsrud
Preface —— IX

Maps and Figures —— XV

Simplified Spellings of Geʿez Words —— XIX

Abbreviations —— XXIII

Chronology of Events regarding the *Hatata Inquiries* —— XXV

Wendy Laura Belcher
Introduction to the *Hatata Inquiries* —— 1

Wendy Laura Belcher and Jeremy Brown
Manuscripts of the Texts —— 9

Wendy Laura Belcher
The Authorship of the *Hatata Inquiries* —— 17

Wendy Laura Belcher and Ralph Lee
Translation Principles —— 55

Ralph Lee with Mehari Worku and Wendy Laura Belcher
Translation of the *Hatata Zara Yaqob* —— 61
Part I: My Life (1600–1632) —— 61
Introduction —— 61
Chapter 1: My Birth —— 61
Chapter 2: My Schooling —— 63
Chapter 3: My Days of Persecution —— 64
Chapter 4: My Fleeing into the Wilderness —— 66
Part II: My Inquiries —— 67
Chapter 5: My Inquiry regarding Wickedness —— 67
Chapter 6: My Inquiry regarding the Existence of a Creator —— 69
Chapter 7: My Inquiry regarding the Truth of Different Religions —— 70
Chapter 8: My Inquiry regarding Falsehood —— 73
Chapter 9: My Inquiry regarding Jewish, Islamic, and Christian Laws about Sexuality and Bodies —— 75

Chapter 10: My Inquiry regarding Jewish, Islamic, and Christian Laws about Food —— 79
Chapter 11: My Inquiry regarding Religious Agreement —— 81
Chapter 12: My Inquiry regarding False Doctrine and God's Established Order —— 83
Chapter 13: My Inquiry regarding Death —— 85
Chapter 14: My Inquiry regarding Intelligence and the Truth of the Bible —— 87
Chapter 15: My Inquiry regarding the Efficacy of Prayer Against Sin and Enemies —— 90
Chapter 16: My Inquiry regarding Work and Happiness —— 94
Chapter 17: My Inquiry regarding Nature and the Feebleness of the Human —— 95
Part III: My Life (1632–1693) —— 97
Chapter 18: My Becoming a Scribe after the Return of the Orthodox Faith —— 97
Chapter 19: My Getting Married and Starting a Family —— 99
Chapter 20: My Surviving Wicked Enemies, War, and Famine —— 101
Chapter 21: My Patron Dying and My Teaching His Sons —— 105
Chapter 22: My Son, His Wife, and Their Children —— 106
Chapter 23: My Writing This Book —— 107
Coda: The Completion of the Book —— 108

Ralph Lee with Mehari Worku and Wendy Laura Belcher
Translation of the *Hatata Walda Heywat* —— 111
Prologue by the Scribe —— 111
Part I: Inquiries —— 111
Chapter 1: On the Importance of Performing Inquiries —— 111
Chapter 2: My Inquiry regarding the Risks and Benefits of Inquiry —— 113
Chapter 3: My Inquiry regarding the Goodness of Creation —— 114
Chapter 4: My Inquiry regarding the Nature of Spirits and Souls —— 115
Chapter 5: My Inquiry regarding Religious Faith —— 117
Chapter 6: My Inquiry regarding Questions of Faith and God's Care —— 119
Chapter 7: My Inquiry regarding Loving One Another and Cooperation —— 121
Chapter 8: My Inquiry regarding Humanity as the Ruler of Creation —— 122
Chapter 9: My Inquiry regarding the Consequences of Violating the Established Order of the Creator —— 124
Chapter 10: My Inquiry regarding the Suffering of the Innocent and Reincarnation —— 125
Chapter 11: My Inquiry and Prayer regarding Temptation and the Testing of the Faithful —— 127
Chapter 12: My Inquiry regarding Prayer and the Prayerless Human Soul —— 129
Chapter 13: My Inquiry regarding Justice, Self-Preservation, and Neighbours —— 130

Part II: Advice —— **132**
Chapter 14: Loving Your Neighbour —— **132**
Chapter 15: Accepting Other Cultures —— **134**
Chapter 16: Honouring One's Parents and Elders —— **135**
Chapter 17: On the Importance of Learning —— **136**
Chapter 18: Hard Work and Its Fruits —— **137**
Chapter 19: The Management of Wealth and Drinking —— **138**
Chapter 20: Food and Fasting —— **139**
Chapter 21: Cleanliness, Clothes, and Homes —— **140**
Chapter 22: Charity and the Lazy —— **141**
Chapter 23: Slander, Adultery, and Theft —— **142**
Chapter 24: Celibacy, Marriage, and Sex —— **144**
Chapter 25: Divorce and Remarrying —— **148**
Chapter 26: Winning Your Spouse's Love —— **149**
Chapter 27: Children and Abortion —— **151**
Chapter 28: Raising Good Children —— **151**
Chapter 29: Living with the Customs of Your Time —— **153**
Chapter 30: Trust and Caution —— **155**
Chapter 31: Pride and Anger —— **156**
Chapter 32: The Abuse of Authority —— **156**
Chapter 33: Rewards for Good Deeds —— **157**
Chapter 34: Embracing Death Joyfully —— **158**
Coda: Some Final Words —— **159**

Jeremy R. Brown, Ralph Lee, and Mehari Worku
Appendix 1: Chart of Differences between Abb 215 and Abb 234 of *Hatata Zara Yaqob* —— 161

Jeremy R. Brown and Wendy Laura Belcher
Appendix 2: Scribal Intervention in Abb 215 and Abb 234 —— 189

Contributors —— 193

Bibliography —— 195

Index —— 205

Dag Herbjørnsrud
Preface

This volume makes fully available to global audiences two texts of early African philosophy. Ralph Lee and Mehari Worku, working with Wendy Laura Belcher, have translated and annotated the remarkable *Hatata Inquiries*, composed in highland Ethiopia in 1668 and around 1693 by the critical thinker Zara Yaqob and his student Walda Heywat. These autobiographical and philosophical investigations into the necessity for independent thought and ethical action have never been as timely as they are today.

Unfortunately, these two African texts have frequently been excluded from histories of philosophy. This is partly due to challenges to their authenticity (about which, see Belcher's persuasive introduction) but also due to Western prejudices. The exclusion of African and non-European philosophy from the canon of philosophy is no surprise. During the heyday of European colonialism in the early 1800s, central Western philosophers began to define philosophy so narrowly that only the thinking of white Europeans met the definition of 'true' philosophy (Park 2013). The rest, outside of 'the West', were dismissed as irrational thinkers, lesser beings to be colonized and civilized. This colonial mindset remains, directly or indirectly, embedded in philosophical studies, as demonstrated by an even cursory glance at reading lists of university philosophy courses worldwide, especially in Western Europe and North America.

As a leading scholar of Chinese philosophy bluntly concluded in 2017, 'Philosophy as it is practiced professionally in much of the world, and in the United States in particular, is racist. . . . To omit all of the philosophy of Asia, Africa, India, and the Indigenous Americas from the curriculum and to ignore it in our research is to convey the impression—whether intentionally or not—that it is of less value than the philosophy produced in European culture, or worse, to convey the impression—willingly or not—that no other culture was capable of philosophical thought. These are racist views' (Van Norden 2017).

This attitude has impoverished philosophical studies. For instance, it was not until recently that the first two works of the eighteenth-century African philosopher Anton Wilhelm Amo were translated from Latin and became commonly available in the US and Western Europe (Amo 2020; 1968). Born around 1703 in Axim in what is now Ghana, Amo moved to what is now Germany and grew up in a wealthy European family (Lochner 1958; Abraham 2004). In 1729, Amo defended, likely orally, the law thesis 'On the Rights of Moors in Europe', based on a study of Roman law (now lost)—possibly the first thesis in Europe arguing against the enslavement of Africans. In 1734, Amo defended his inaugural dissertation *On the*

Impassivity of the Human Mind at the University of Wittenberg, and in 1738 he finished his *Treatise on the Art of Soberly and Accurately Philosophizing* (Amo and Nwala 1990). He then began teaching philosophy at the University of Jena before he, in 1747, chose to take a ship back to Ghana, where he continued his philosophical work.

Even though Amo wrote his theses in Latin, in the heart of Europe, where they were known as a vital contribution to Cartesian discourse, his work was erased from the European canon after the early 1800s. In his own time, in the early German Enlightenment of 1733, the rector of the University of Wittenberg, Johann Gottfried Kraus, declared about Amo that he came from a continent, Africa, that had 'great ... fertility in human natural aptitude, devotion to letters, or religious teaching' and that had produced 'a great many very eminent men' (as translated in (Amo 2020, 191)). Kraus then praised such African thinkers as Terence of Carthage, Tertullian, and Augustine, stating that 'liberal learning' in Europe only became possible due to Africans who 'crossed from Africa into Spain' with books by 'ancient writers'. He concluded that all European scholars 'owed a debt to Africa'.

However surprising such a non-colonial way of thinking might seem today, this was a rather typical worldview before the 1750s and the development of 'scientific racism' during the late Enlightenment. To find another example, we need look no further than the English thinker Thomas Hobbes, a contemporary of Zara Yaqob and Walda Heywat, and his main work, *Leviathan* (1651). Hobbes matter-of-factly writes that philosophy began in Asia and Africa long before the discipline spread to the Greeks: 'Where first were great and flourishing *Cities*, there was first the study of *Philosophy*. The *Gymnosophists* of *India*, the *Magi* of *Persia*, and the *Priests* of *Chaldæa* and *Egypt*, are counted the most ancient Philosophers; and those Countreys were the most ancient of Kingdomes' (Hobbes 1968 [1651], 186).

Indeed, attributing the origin of learning to Africa was even more common among the ancients. For example, the Greek rhetorician Isocrates, Plato's senior peer, wrote that 'all men agree' that the Egyptians 'introduced philosophy's training' for 'their soul' (as translated in (Isocrates 1966, 115, Ch. 11.22). Recent research supports this view, as it has found that the ancient Egyptian text of the *Book of Thoth* 'forms a source of the Platonic text' *Phaedrus* (Poetsch 2021, Abstract). After all, in this dialogue by Plato, Socrates also states that it was the Egyptians who 'invented numbers and arithmetic and geometry and astronomy, also draughts and dice, and, most important of all, letters' (as translated in (Plato 1947, 561, 274d). In addition, twenty-first-century scholarship has demonstrated how even the term 'philosopher' (Greek: *philosophos*, 'lover of wisdom') seems to stem from an ancient Egyptian language and its term *mr-rḫ* ('mer-rekh', 'lover of wisdom'), as attested in the *Book of Thoth* (Jasnow and Zauzich 2005, 13; Rutherford 2016; Herbjørnsrud 2021a). In other words, philosophy is not a European invention.

Meanwhile, contemporaneous but separate philosophical traditions were active outside early modern Europe. For instance, in the 1530s, the Spanish friar Bernardino de Sahagún crossed the Atlantic and began a five-decades-long study of the thought systems of the Nahua people of Mesoamerica in today's Mexico. Writing decades before the birth of Descartes, Spinoza, and the modern European philosophical tradition, Sahagún noted that the Nahua (misleadingly known today as 'the Aztecs') had devoted philosophical scholars (*tlamatinime*, 'knowers of things')—both women and men. These thinkers taught girls and boys to consider the world's existential questions in dedicated schools (*calmecacs*), where the students enrolled from the age of eight. Sahagún wrote admiringly that, like the Greeks, it was 'the custom' of the Nahua to hold in 'high esteem' whatever was 'wise, eloquent, virtuous, and courageous' (as cited and translated in (Portilla 2002, 116). His bilingual work in both Nahua and Spanish, written after a detailed co-operation with Nahua scholars from 1540 to 1585, covers some 2,400 pages and 2,000 illustrations (by Nahua artists) over 12 books; one of which is dedicated to *Rhetoric and Moral Philosophy* (Sahagún 1969).

Even cherished views that Europeans alone developed scepticism and rationality have been disproven. Atheism and the critique of religions predate Europe and even Greece. Some 2,700 years ago, Indians had entire schools of thought developed to such. The atheist Lokayata and Carvaka schools were not just a crucial part of Indian discourse; they influenced the ancient Greeks and Epicurus (for example, via the Greek philosopher Pyrrho [365–270 BCE]), who travelled to India) and the early modern Europeans (for example, via the Jesuits, who from the 1580s reported on the philosophical and religious discussions at the court of the Mughal emperor Akbar the Great, where the atheist Carvakas participated) (Gokhale 2015; Herbjørnsrud 2020).

The Chinese also were active in developing philosophy schools, including one that 'advanced the earliest form of consequentialism' (Fraser 2002). The philosopher Mo Zi (400s BCE) founded the Mohism school, which advocated a radical altruism of 'universal love'. In it, people 'would view other people as they view themselves' and thus combat the tragedy that 'the strong inevitably dominate the weak, the many inevitably plunder the few, the rich inevitably ridicule the poor' (as translated in (Mo Zi 2013, 77)).

Neither were anti-slavery polemics the invention of enlightened Europeans. In the early 1600s, the Timbuktu scholar Ahmad Baba (1556–1627) argued for an end to 'racial slavery', the enslavement of Black West Africans, by rejecting the 'Ham theory' that intelligence and skin colour were correlated. 'In this respect [of intelligence], there is no difference between races', Baba concluded (Barbour and Jacobs 1985; Cleaveland 2015). Before Baba, in his *Introduction* (Al-Muqaddimah, 1377) to his Universal History, the North African scholar Ibn Khaldun (1332–1406) stated that peoples' intelligence and character had nothing to do with their skin colour, an insight sadly lost to Hume, Kant, and the pseudo-scientific 'race studies' of the 1800s and 1900s (Abdullahi and Salawu 2012). This conclusion is in line with Khaldun's argument, written down five centuries before Darwin, that all humans are one, as there is 'a gradual process of creation' from apes: 'The higher stage of man is reached from the world of monkeys, in which both sagacity and perception are found, but which has not reached the stage of actual reflection and thinking. At this point we come to the first stage of man' (as translated in (Gribbin and Gribbin 2022, 10)).

Thus, this English translation of the Ethiopian *Hatata Inquiries* is part of a larger, rewritten canon that helps us to counter colonial narratives of the history of ideas and philosophy. Scholars, students, and the public now have access to the vast riches of a more global intellectual past. Through these texts, they will better understand highland Ethiopian intellectual history and its written tradition of many centuries.

Far from being a backwater outside the sweep of global history, Ethiopian scholars were in dialogue with scholars throughout the old world, including ancient Greek authors, the Desert Fathers and Desert Mothers of Egypt, the medieval sages of Syria, Byzantium, and Arabia, and the early modern linguists and historians of Europe. Zara Yaqob and Walda Heywat often quote from the Bible, which was translated into Geʿez by 600 CE. Walda Heywat references the sixteenth-century Geʿez adaptation of the ninth-century Arabic book *The Sayings of the Philosophers*, composed by the ninth-century Arab scholar Hunain Ibn Ishaq, who in turn cited Socrates, Plato, and Aristotle and relayed stories dating to fifth- and fourth-century BCE Egypt (Sumner 1974; Pietruschka 2005). Both Ethiopian authors would have known of the sixth-century Geʿez translation of the third-century Egyptian *Physiologus*, a literary work on the natural world (Weninger 2005). Both would have known the fourteenth-century Geʿez adaptation of *The Life and Maxims of Skendes*, purportedly the work of the second-century Greek philosopher Secundus (Weninger 2010; Perry 1964). They were part of the early global exchange of ideas.

The *Hatata Inquiries*, as texts questioning religion and the status quo, were not unique in Ethiopian intellectual history (as laid out in Belcher's introduction). The fourteenth-century Ethiopian monk Ewostatewos (1273–1352) led a radical movement 'in complete defiance of the rest of the Ethiopian Church' (Taddesse Tamrat 1972, 211), and his words are preserved in his hagiography (Fiaccadori 2005). The fifteenth-century followers of Abba Estifanos (known as Stephanites) were persecuted for arguing that monarchs had no 'natural or divine property' but rather 'the government belongs to God' and that monarchs should 'obey the law and govern according to the law' (as cited and translated in (Mennasemay 2010, 11)). Their values, theories, and arguments are also preserved in texts. In other words, the *Hatata Inquiries* stand in a long history of critical thinking in Ethiopia. For all these reasons, they deserve to take their rightful place in the global canon of significant philosophical texts and can now do so with this vital new translation.

Maps and Figures

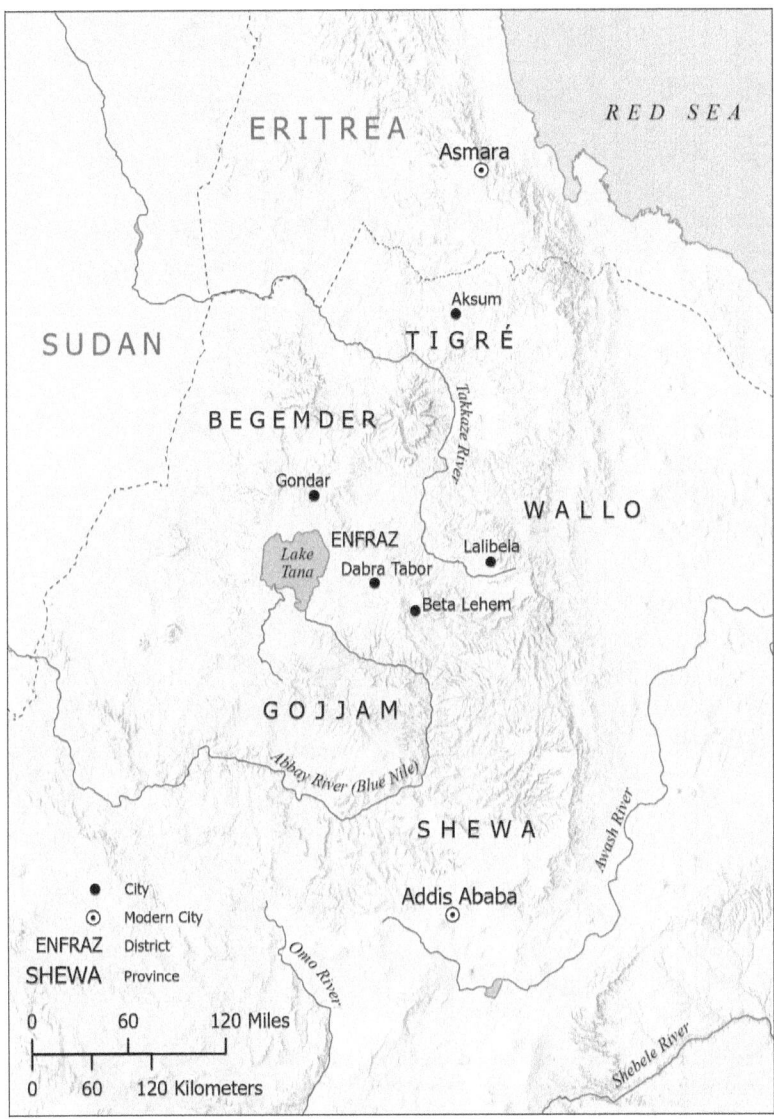

Map 1: Map of highland Ethiopia. The author Zara Yaqob was born near Aksum, in Tigré Province. Later, he travelled south to the Takkaze River and across to the Amhara region and the districts of Begemder and Enfraz. There he lived for the rest of his life. The author Walda Heywat was born there and also lived there. The Italian priest Giusto da Urbino lived farther southeast, near Dabra Tabor, which is near in Beta Lehem. Map designed by Tsering Wangyal Shawa.

https://doi.org/10.1515/9783110781922-204

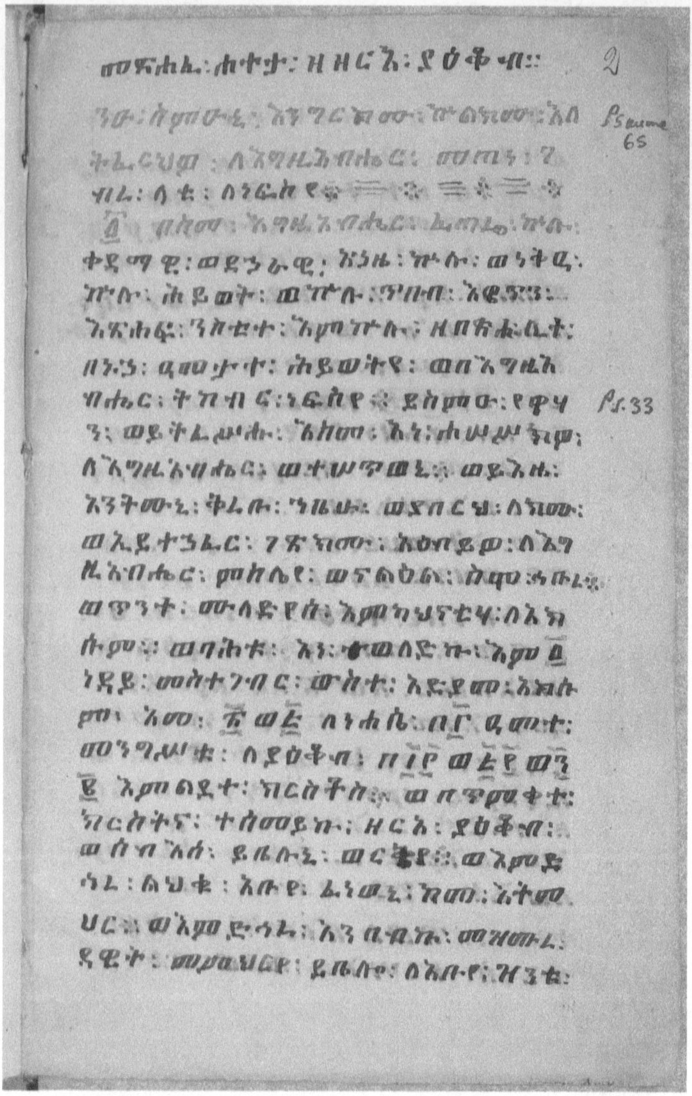

Figure 1: Paris, Bibliothèque nationale de France, Éthiopien d'Abbadie Manuscript No. 234, folio 2r. This image is of the opening folio of the *Hatata Zara Yaqob* in a manuscript produced in the months before February 1853. The Italian Roman Catholic priest Giusto da Urbino, who lived in Ethiopia in the 1850s, was the scribe of this manuscript. He was new to writing the Geʿez script, so his handwriting was rough and he frequently corrected his own work. He used his own system, not the standard Geʿez methods and proofreading marks. To learn more, see the Manuscripts of the Text section. A colour digital copy of the manuscript is accessible online at https://gallica.bnf.fr/view3if/ga/ark:/12148/btv1b52518435d, last accessed on 14 June 2023. Reprinted by permission of the Bibliothèque nationale de France.

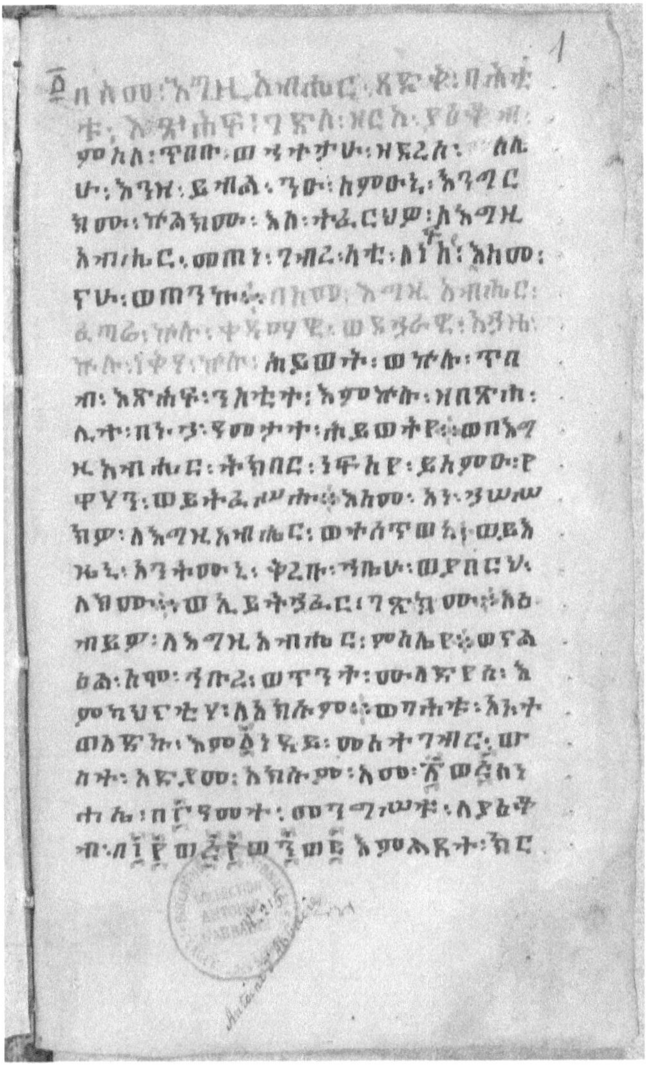

Figure 2: Paris, Bibliothèque nationale de France, Éthiopien d'Abbadie Manuscript No. 215, folio 1r. This image is of the opening folio of *Hatata Zara Yaqob* in a manuscript produced in the months before April 1854. The scribe, Gabra Maryam, does not appear to have been a highly trained church scribe, as his handwriting was rough and the text has many corrections. The scribe uses the methods and proofreading signs typical of Geʿez manuscripts. One such correction is visible in the sixth line from the top. The letters ፍ and ፀ have been correctly added to ለነሰ to make it ለነፍሰየ. The ፍ is in Gabra Maryam's handwriting, correcting his own work; the ፀ may have been added by him or someone else. To learn more, see the Manuscripts of the Text section. A colour digital copy of the manuscript is accessible online at https://gallica.bnf.fr/view3if/ga/ark:/12148/btv1b525184250, last accessed on 14 June 2023. Reprinted by permission of the Bibliothèque nationale de France.

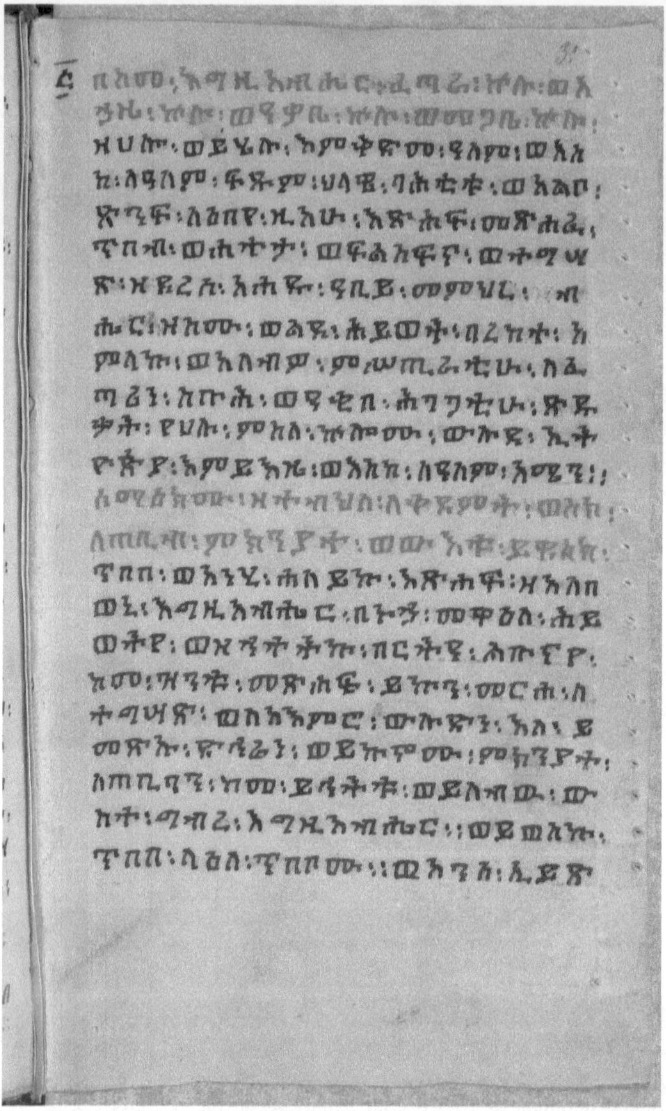

Figure 3: Paris, Bibliothèque nationale de France, Éthiopien d'Abbadie Manuscript No. 215, folio 31r. This image is of the opening folio of *Hatata Walda Heywat*, copied by the scribe Gabra Maryam in the months before April 1854. To learn more, see the Manuscripts of the Text section. Accessible online at https://gallica.bnf.fr/view3if/ga/ark:/12148/btv1b525184250, last accessed on 14 June 2023. Reprinted by permission of the Bibliothèque nationale de France.

Simplified Spellings of Geʻez Words

Simplified	Original
Afonso Mendes	አፎንስ Ǝfons, head of the Catholic Mission in Ethiopia from 1622 to 1632
Aksum	አክሱም Aksum, ancient city in the northern Tigré region
Amhara	አምሐራ Amḥara, Ethiopian people and central Ethiopia region
andemta	አንድምታ andəmta, word for textual exegesis
Begemder	በጌምድር Bägemdər, lake district in the Amhara region
Beta Israel	ቤተ እስራኤል Betä Ǝsraʾel, Ethiopian Jews
Beta Lehem	ቤተልሔም Betä Ləḥem, Ethiopian town in the Amhara region, where the priest Giusto da Urbino and the scribe Gäbrä Maryam lived
Betsega Habta Egziabher	በጸጋ ሀብት እግዚአብሔር Bä-Ṣägga Habtä Ǝgziʾabḥer, the son of Zärʾa Yaʿəqob
Destaye	ደስታየ Dästaye, second grandson of Zärʾa Yaʿəqob
Enbaqom Qala Wald	ዕንባቆም ቃላ ወልድ Ǝnbaqom Qalä Wäld, sixteenth-century Ethiopian-Yemeni abbot and author
Enfraz	እንፍራዝ Ǝnfraz, lake district in the Amhara region
EOTC	Ethiopian Orthodox Täwaḥədo Church
Eseteye	ዕሴትየ Ǝsetäyä, eldest granddaughter of Zärʾa Yaʿəqob
Estifanos	እስጢፋኖስ Ǝsṭifanos, fifteenth-century founder of the EOTC reformation movement of the Däqiqä Ǝsṭifanos (Stephanites)
Ewostatewos	ኤዎስጣቴዎስ Ewosṭatewos, fourteenth-century Ethiopian religious leader and saint
Fantaya	ፈንታየ Fäntayä (also called Wälättä Peṭros), Lord Habtu's noble daughter-in-law
Fasiladas	ፋሲለደስ Fasilädäs, king of Ethiopia from 1632 to 1667
fidal	ፊደል fidäl, name of the script used to write Geʻez and other Ethiopian languages
Gabra Maryam	ገብረ ማርያም Gäbrä Maryam, nineteenth-century scribe of Abb 215
Gabriel	ገብርኤል Gäbrəʾəl, biblical archangel
gadl	ገድል gädl, book about a saint's life, literally meaning 'striving', 'struggle'
Geʻez	ግዕዝ Gəʿəz, ancient liturgical and scholarly Ethiopian language
Gojjam	ጎጃም Goǧǧam, region to the south of Lake Ṭana
Gondar	ጎንደር Gondär, historical capital of Ethiopia, in the Bägemdər district
Habtu	Habtu, a wealthy man, Zärʾa Yaʿəqob's patron and Wäldä Ḥəywät's father
hatata	ሐተታ ḥatäta, word for 'inquiry', 'investigation', 'exploration'
Hatata Walda Heywat	ሐተታ ወልደ ሕይወት Ḥatäta Wäldä Ḥəywät, the second *Hatata*

(continued)

Simplified	Original
Hatata Zara Yaqob	ሐተታ ዘርአ ያዕቆብ *Ḥatäta Zärʾa Yaʿəqob*, the first *Hatata*
Kristos Samra	ክርስቶስ ሠምራ Krəstos Śämra, fifteenth-century Ethiopian woman saint
Matsehaf Bet	መጽሐፍ ቤት Mäṣḥaf Bet, EOTC school stage of studying exegesis
me'eraf	ምዕራፍ *maʿəraf*, the Divine Office, the prayers that believers pray each hour of the day
Medhanit	መድኃኒት Mädḫanit, Zärʾa Yaʿəqob's daughter-in-law
Metekku	ምትኩ Mətäkku, Wäldä Ḥəywät's other name
Michael	ሚካኤል Mikaʾel, biblical archangel
Nahase	ነሐሴ Näḥase, Ethiopian calendar month roughly corresponding with August
Nebab Bet	ንባብ ቤት Nəbab Bet, EOTC school stage of learning to read
Pawlos	ጳውሎስ Pawlos (Paul), sixteenth-century Ethiopian monk
Qeddase Bet	ቅዳሴ ቤት, EOTC school stage of studying liturgy
Qene	ቅኔ qəne, word for poetry and rhetoric
Qene Bet	ቅኔ ቤት Qəne Bet, EOTC school stage of studying rhetoric and poetry
Qwarit	ቋሪት Qʷarit, district in the west of Gojjam
Salus	ሠሉስ Śälus, Tuesday
samenna warq	ሰምና ወርቅ sämənna wärq (wax and gold), rhetorical mode of double meaning
Sanuy	ሰኑይ Sänuy, Monday
sewasew	ሰዋስው säwasəw (ladder), word for grammar
Shewa	ሸዋ Šäwa (also spelled Sewa in the HZY), region in southern Ethiopia
Sime'on	ስምዖን Səmʿon, sixteenth-century Ethiopian nobleman and author
Susenyos	ሱስንዮስ Susənyos, king of Ethiopia from 1606 to 1632
Ta'ammera Maryam	ተአምረ ማርያም *Täʾammärä Maryam, the Book of the Miracles of Saint Mary*
Takkaze	ተከዚ Täkkäzi, also spelled as ተከዜ Täkkäze and transcribed as Tekeze, a river in northern Ethiopia
Takla Haymanot	ተክለ ሃይማኖት Täklä Haymanot, nineteenth-century Ethiopian Catholic priest and author
Tana	ጣና Ṭana, huge lake in the Amhara region
Tesemma	ተሰማ Täsämma, other name of Wäldä Gäbrəʾel, younger son of Lord Habtu
Tewalda Madhen	ተወልደ መድኀን Täwäldä Mädḫən, fifteenth century author of a saint's life
Teqemt	ጥቅምት Ṭəqəmt, Ethiopian calendar month roughly corresponding with October
tergwame	ትርጓሜ tərgʷame, word for textual interpretation

(continued)

Simplified	Original
Tewahedo	ተዋሕዶ Täwaḥədo, word for 'oneness', used in የኢትዮጵያ ኦርቶዶክስ ተዋሕዶ ቤተ ክርስቲያን (Ethiopian Orthodox Täwaḥədo Church)
Tigré	ትግሬ Təgre or ትግራይ Təgray, region in northern Ethiopia
Walatta Petros	ወለተ ጴጥሮስ Wälättä Peṭros (also called Fäntayä), Lord Habtu's noble daughter-in-law
Walda Gabriel	ወልደ ገብርኤል Wäldä Gäbrəʾel, one of Lord Habtu's younger sons
Walda Giyorgis	ወልደ ጊዮርጊስ Wäldä Giyorgis, patron of a pre-Abb 234 HZY manuscript
Walda Heywat	ወልደ ሕይወት Wäldä Ḥəywät (also called Mətəkku), author of the second *Hatata Inquiry* HWH
Walda Michael	ወልደ ሚካኤል Wäldä Mikaʾel, first-born son of Lord Habtu
Walda Yosef	ወልደ ዮሴፍ, Wäldä Yosef, scribe of pre-Abb 234 HZY manuscript
Warqe	ወርቄ, Wärqe, Zärʾa Yaʿəqob's other name
Weddase Maryam	ውዳሴ ማርያም Wəddase Maryam, famous hymn devoted to Mary
Yaqob	ያዕቆብ Yaʿəqob (Jacob), common name
Yetbarak	ይትባረክ Yətbaräk, Zara Yaqob's eldest grandson
Yohannes	ዮሐንስ Yoḥannəs (John), seventeenth-century Ethiopian king
Yostos	ዮስጦስ Yosṭos (Justus, Giusto, Justin), name Giusto da Urbino went by in Ethiopia
Zara Yaqob	ዘርአ ያዕቆብ Zärʾa Yaʿəqob, also called Wärqe, author of the first *Hatata Inquiry*, HZY; this seventeenth-century Ethiopian author is not to be confused with the fifteenth-century Ethiopian emperor of the same name
Zema Bet	ዜማ ቤት Zema Bet, EOTC school stage of studying music and hymnody

Abbreviations

Abb 215	Bibliothèque nationale de France, Antoine D'Abbadie Collection, Manuscript No. 215. Contains both philosophical texts: *Hatata Zara Yaqob* and *Hatata Walda Heywat*
Abb 234	Bibliothèque nationale de France, Antoine D'Abbadie Collection, Manuscript No. 234. Contains only *Hatata Zara Yaqob*.
BNF	Bibliothèque nationale de France (National Library of France)
Chap	Chapter
EAe	*Encyclopaedia Aethiopica*
EOTC	Ethiopian Orthodox Tewahedo Church
HWH	*Hatata Walda Heywat*
HZY	*Hatata Zara Yaqob*
Litt Ed	Littman's edition of the *Hatata Inquiries* (Littmann 1904)
LXX	Septuagint, an early Greek translation of the Old Testament, the basis of the Ge'ez Old Testament
MS	Manuscript, handwritten document
MS A	Abb 234
MS B	Abb 215
NT	New Testament
OT	Old Testament
PEMM	Princeton Ethiopian, Eritrean, and Egyptian Miracles of Mary (PEMM) project
Sum	Sumner's book on the *Hatata Inquiries* (Sumner 1976)

Chronology of Events regarding the *Hatata Inquiries*

Some of the seventeenth-century dates below stand for historical events confirmed in many sources. Others are stated in the *Hatata Inquiries* or calculated based on information in them; those appear indented.

1557 Jesuit Catholic missionaries arrive in Ethiopia
    1600 First *Hatata Inquiry* author, Zara Yaqob (called *Warqe* at birth), is born on 28 August near Aksum in the region of Tigré during the reign of Yaqob I (Note: he was *not* born in 1599)
1607 Susenyos becomes king of Ethiopia
    1608 Zara Yaqob begins school around the age of seven
1612 King Susenyos converts to Catholicism
    1613 Zara Yaqob completes his studies in poetry and rhetoric in a district outside of Aksum
1621 King Susenyos forbids the teaching of Ethiopian Orthodoxy and publicly professes Roman Catholicism
    1623 Zara Yaqob completes his biblical interpretation studies
    1623 Zara Yaqob returns to the district of Aksum to begin teaching, during a period when the Jesuits were having an increasing influence over the church and education
1625 Jesuit missionary and mission head Afonso Mendes arrives in Ethiopia at the age of 46
1627 King Susenyos begins persecuting those who refuse to convert to Roman Catholicism
    1627 Zara Yaqob's disciple Walda Heywat (also called Metekku), the author of the second *Hatata Inquiry*, is probably born this year but perhaps one to seven years earlier
    1630 Zara Yaqob flees from Aksum south to the Takkaze River and then heads south toward the Shewa region after his enemy lies about Zara Yaqob to the king, saying he is a rebel
    1630 Zara Yaqob lives in a cave in the Amhara region for two years, spending his days in prayer with the Psalter and theorizing
1632 King Susenyos rescinds the edict forcing conversion to Roman Catholicism
1632 King Susenyos dies, and his son Fasiladas becomes king
    1632 Zara Yaqob abandons his solitude, walks further south into the Amhara region, arriving at the Begemder district and then the Enfraz District, where he stays for the rest of his life
    1632 Zara Yaqob gains a patron, Lord Habtu, the father of his future disciple Walda Heywat
1633 King Fasiladas banishes the Jesuits, and Afonso Mendes leaves
    1634 Walda Heywat begins 59 years of study with Zara Yaqob
    1635 Zara Yaqob marries Hirut, Lord Habtu's servant
    1638 Zara Yaqob and Hirut's son is born on Monday, 18 October, and named Betsega Habta Egziabher
    1642 A great famine begins and lasts for two years in Enfraz
    1645 Zara Yaqob's patron Lord Habtu dies
    1640s Lord Habtu's first-born son Walda Michael marries a noble woman named Walatta Petros (also called Fantaya)
    1658 Zara Yaqob's son marries a woman named Medhanit
    1660 Zara Yaqob's first grandson Yetbarak is born, one of five sons (including Destaye) and four daughters (including Eseteye) born to Zara Yaqob's son and his wife Medhanit
1667 King Fasiladas dies, and his son Yohannes I becomes king

Chronology of Events regarding the *Hatata Inquiries*

1668 Zara Yaqob writes his *Hatata Inquiry* at the age of 68 in the first year of the reign of Yohannes I

1693 Zara Yaqob dies at the age of 93

1697 Zara Yaqob's wife Hirut dies

170? Walda Heywat writes his own *Hatata Inquiry* (HZY) in his seventies or eighties, sometime between 1693 and 1717

171? Walda Heywat writes his coda to Zara Yaqob's *Hatata Inquiry* (HWH) when he is 'very old', sometime between 1707 and 1720

1700s and 1800s Copies of HZY and HWH circulate secretly as heretical texts

1847 The Italian priest Giusto da Urbino arrives in highland Ethiopia in December

1848 Giusto da Urbino takes up the study of Ge'ez language and literature

1852 Giusto da Urbino writes to his patron Antoine d'Abbadie in May, saying that he has been working on a Ge'ez grammar and dictionary

1852 Giusto da Urbino writes to d'Abbadie in September, saying he has come across an unusual philosophical text, HZY, written in the 1600s, but has not been able to purchase it

1853 Giusto da Urbino has been able to purchase HZY and sends a copy to d'Abbadie in February, copied on paper by himself (Abb 234); the colophon mentions HWH but does not include it

1854 Giusto da Urbino sends a copy of HZY and HWH to d'Abbadie in April, copied on parchment by the Ethiopian scribe Gabra Marham (Abb 215)

1855 Giusto da Urbino is expelled from Ethiopia

1856 Giusto da Urbino dies in Sudan in November

1902 D'Abbadie's collection of Ge'ez manuscripts (including Abb 234 and 215) arrives at the BnF

1903 The 'Oriental' section of the Archaeological Society in Paris dedicates a meeting, in September, to Boris Turayev's Russian article on HZY entitled 'Ethiopian Freethinkers of the Seventeenth Century'

1904 Enno Littmann publishes an edition and translation into Latin of both HZY and HWH

1905 Boris Turayev publishes an edition and translation into Russian of HZY only

1916 Carlo Conti Rossini publishes an article in Italian expressing doubts about the authorship of the *Hatata Inquires*

1920 Conti Rossini publishes an article in Italian arguing that the *Hatata Inquires* were written by Giusto da Urbino

1934 Eugen Mittwoch publishes an article in German arguing that the *Hatata Inquires* were written by Giusto da Urbino

1936 J. Simon publishes an article in French critiquing Mittwoch but agreeing that the *Hatata Inquires* were written by Giusto da Urbino

1955 ZaManfas Qeddus Abreha translates the *Hatata Inquires* into Amharic

1961 Amsalu Aklilu publishes an article arguing for Zara Yaqob's authorship

1965 Lino Marchiotto completes an Italian translation of the *Hatata Inquires* for his doctoral thesis, which concludes that no decision can be made about authorship but also condemns the tone of the European scholarship on them

1968 Alemayyehu Moges publishes his dissertation on HZY, using philology to argue against Giusto da Urbino's authorship and for Zara Yaqob's authorship

1976 Claude Sumner publishes an English translation of the texts and collates detailed evidence against Giusto da Urbino's authorship and for Zara Yaqob's authorship

2007 Luam Tesfalidet completes her thesis in German, arguing against Giusto da Urbino's authorship and for Zara Yaqob's authorship
2012 Kidane Dawit Worku completes an English translation of HZY in his dissertation and argues against Giusto da Urbino's authorship and for Zara Yaqob's authorship
2013 Anaïs Wion publishes two articles in French, arguing for Giusto da Urbino's authorship and against Zara Yaqob's authorship; the articles are translated into English and published in 2021
2017 Getatchew Haile publishes a chapter arguing against Giusto da Urbino's authorship and for Zara Yaqob's authorship
2022 *In Search of Zara Yaqob* conference held at Oxford University
2024 *Hatata Inquiries* translated and edited by Ralph Lee with Mehari Worku, Wendy Laura Belcher, and Jeremy Brown and published by De Gruyter

Wendy Laura Belcher
Introduction to the *Hatata Inquiries*

This book introduces and translates two texts of African philosophy written in Ethiopia in the 1600s in the ancient African language of Geʻez (Classical Ethiopic). They are essential parts of the global history of philosophy.

Despite their importance, the texts lacked rigorous, accurate, and fluid translations into English, ones that took advantage of recent scholarship on the texts and their digitization.[1] Our book now provides that as well as information useful for different audiences. Undergraduates and the public now have many footnotes that explain the texts' cultural and religious context. Scholars now have a more comprehensive translation, one that uses the two editions of the one text. They also have a sophisticated scholarly apparatus that explains philological issues and notes the texts' many intertexts. Finally, we corrected some errors in earlier editions and translations, including that of one author's birth and residence. As a result, we have put the study of these texts on firmer footing.

Our book is a collaboration among Ralph Lee, one of the leading scholars and translators of Geʻez literature; Mehari Worku, a scholar with deep training in the Ethiopian Orthodox Tewahedo Church (EOTC) educational system who is pursuing a doctorate in the United States; myself, Wendy Laura Belcher, a scholar of early African literature, especially in Geʻez; and Jeremy R. Brown, a palaeographer who specializes in scribal emendations in Geʻez manuscripts. Dag Herbjørnsrud, a historian of global philosophy, has contributed the preface about the texts' importance.

While these two texts are different from each other, they are both a joy to read. Sometimes exuberant, sometimes curmudgeonly, these texts delight in surprising the reader. They fiercely celebrate what is human and criticize pious cant. They put desire above asceticism, love above sectarianism, and the natural world above its uses. They advocate for the rights of women and of animals, plead for religious and cultural tolerance, and condemn slavery and warfare. They give advice on how to be happy in life, work, and marriage. They offer ontological proofs for God and explore the nature of being, as well as the human, ethics, and the divine. They ask epistemological questions about what we can know and how we know it, while establishing

---

[1] The late Canadian professor Claude Sumner published a translation into English titled *The Inquiries into Reason* (Sumner 1976). Published by a small publisher in Addis Ababa, it has long been out of print and has no clear copyright owner (the author is deceased). Further, the translations did not use both manuscript copies of *HZY*. Some other English translations exist (Dawit Worku 2012; Bailey 1921), but access to them is extremely limited, their translation is of only *HZY* and not *HWH*, and/or they did not use both manuscripts.

the right methods for evaluating evidence and discerning the truth. And they insist that we the reader must use our own reason to test ideas, rather than simply accepting others' beliefs because we were told we should. In every way, the two texts are remarkable examples of early written African thought.

Their Authors

According to the two texts, the author of the first is Zara Yaqob. He was born on 28 August 1600, near Ethiopia's ancient holy city, Aksum, as the son of a poor farmer (see Map 1). As an independent thinker, he was already having trouble with friends and family when the Ethiopian King Susenyos converted from the faith of his fathers, the Ethiopian Orthodox Tewahedo Church (EOTC), to the new faith brought by the Europeans, Catholicism. An old enemy denounced Zara Yaqob, and he fled at night, taking with him only his Psalter, which included the biblical Psalms and other hymns. In the anchoritic tradition of the church, he lived in a cave as a hermit, for two years. He there prayed with his Psalter daily and elaborated a theoretical and practical philosophy about the human condition and the divine. Then, the persecution stopped in 1632 when the new king, Fasiladas, restored the Ethiopian Orthodox faith. Although Zara Yaqob no longer considered himself a Christian, he took advantage of this political change to return from exile, ending up in a region along northern Lake Tana, where he became a scribe, married, and had a child and grandchildren. He wrote his *Hatata Inquiry* in 1668 and died in 1692 at the age of 93. We refer to his *Hatata Inquiry* as the *Hatata Zara Yaqob* or *HZY*.

In his mid-thirties, he began teaching his philosophy to his noble patron's younger son, Walda Heywat, born around 1627. Walda Heywat then wrote the second *Hatata Inquiry*. At some point, he also wrote the coda to the first one. By contrast to Zara Yaqob, he included little information about his life, only stating that he was Zara Yaqob's disciple and had studied with him for almost six decades. We refer to the second *Hatata Inquiry* as *Hatata Walda Heywat* or *HWH*.

Some have questioned whether these men were indeed the authors of the *Hatata Inquiries*. They argue that the texts are allonymous (authored by someone who falsely attributes them to another). All five of us involved in this edition believe that these two Ethiopians authored these texts. So, we treat Zara Yaqob and Walda Heywat as the authors throughout, explaining our many reasons for this in the Authorship of the *Hatata Inquiries* section.

Their Style and Content

In the first *Hatata Inquiry*, Zara Yaqob argues for putting one's own rational thoughts and investigations at the centre of one's life and actions. Zara Yaqob criticizes the different religious teachings (Christianity, Islam, and Judaism as well as Indian and South Arabian religions) equally, arguing that everyone insists on their own religion's truth simply because it is theirs. He questions whether holy books tell the truth, laments humanity's tendency to believe lies, and examines the proof for a divine creator. He stresses that when religion is not in accord with logic or nature— such as religious laws celebrating celibacy, polygamy, or the Sabbath—human beings, not God, invented such laws. He asserts the equality of men and women and argues against treating women as impure due to natural life-giving processes. He states that, unlike his family and friends, he is not a Christian, but he also eloquently argues for a first cause. In the long African tradition of using proverbs to underscore or make points, Zara Yaqob frequently cites from Amharic proverbs and the Ge'ez Bible, especially the Old Testament *Psalms*, which he memorized as a child. He opens and closes with chapters on the dramatic story of his life. The sentences in *Hatata Zara Yaqob* are a bit better structured and more systematic than in *Hatata Walda Heywat*.

The second *Hatata Inquiry* by Zara Yaqob's student Walda Heywat has a more confident tone, building on his teacher's text. His writing style is less personal (supplying no authorial biography) and more formal. He has pronounced ontological and phenomenological interests; for instance, he asks whether we can know that spirits exist and if animals have souls. *Hatata Walda Heywat* is didactic, a treatise on how we should live. He stresses what is morally correct, of use in society, and in accord with God's will. He is concerned with daily life, an elder advising the young about, for instance, proper clothes, beds, and windows. The *Hatata Walda Heywat* is very concerned with embodiment; for instance, he argues that husband and wife are one flesh, and that men should ensure that women have equal sexual satisfaction. He quotes other texts less often than Zara Yaqob, and when he does, they tend more often to be paraphrased (Sumner 1976, 131).

Their Philosophy

The exact ways in which these texts constitute philosophy has been the subject of much debate and we hope this volume will enrich that discussion. Although the texts are frequently held up as examples of 'rational philosophy', we do not find the narrow term particularly useful. The *Hatata Inquiries* are not examples of Western rational philosophy. Rather, as Peter Adamson cogently laid out in a conference on the *Hatata Inquiries*, they are in the Orthodox Christian philosophical tradition (Adamson 2022). Favouring reason over unthinking faith has always been the heart of this tradition. This tradition includes work in Greek, Syriac, Georgian, Arabic, Armenian, Coptic, and Geʻez, and was active from the 500s into the 1600s, stretching back to the Desert Fathers and encompassing the African and Levantine world. Its many gnomologic works—collections of edifying sayings, proverbs, anecdotes, and allegories—are often dismissed as 'wisdom literature' or 'popular philosophy'. Scholars have assumed that such works are not rigorous or sophisticated. Yet, Adamson argues, Zara Yaqob gives rich answers to the question of what a human being is: a toiling soul, a fleshly being, a creature with free will, and so on. In this tradition, a philosopher was precisely someone like Zara Yaqob, who spent time in a cave living apart from others and meditating on the human and the divine.

Fasil Merawi has also argued that comparisons with early modern Western philosophers (e.g., searching for similarities to Kant or Descartes) do not constitute productive encounters with these deeply religious texts, especially given their relational and affective, rather than technical, mode (Fasil Merawi 2022).[1]

Meanwhile, Dag Herbjørnsrud argues that it is important not to 'over-rationalize' the Western European philosophical tradition (Herbjørnsrud 2021b). Most Western philosophers cannot be described as rationalists, including Pythagoras, Plato, Augustine, Anselm, Aquinas, Schopenhauer, Kierkegaard, Nietzsche, Heidegger, and Sartre. Although people date the Western rational philosophical tradition to Descartes and Spinoza in the 1600s, even they fail to fit the broad definition well. Descartes dedicated his main work, in which he vehemently opposed atheists, to Catholic Church faculty. In that work, *Meditations,* he stated the work's religious purpose: 'to accept by means of faith the fact that the human soul does not perish with the body, and that God exists' (Descartes 1911 [1641], 1).

In the end, whatever type of philosophy they constitute, the *Hatata Inquiries* are definitively philosophy, concerned with epistemology, metaphysics, and phe-

---

[1] This was among the conference presentations at the international conference on the *Hatata Inquiries* held in 2022, titled *In Search of Zara Yaqob*, convened by Jonathan Egid, Lea Cantor, and Fasil Merawi at Worcester College, University of Oxford, on 29–30 April 2022. Speakers included Dr. Teshome Abera (Addis Ababa Science and Technology University), Prof. Peter Adamson (Ludwig Maximilian University of Munich/King's College London), Mr. Eyasu Berento (Kotebe Metropolitan University), Dr. Ralph Lee (SOAS), Prof. John Marenbon (University of Cambridge), Mr. Binyam Mekonnen (Addis Ababa University), Dr. Fasil Merawi (Addis Ababa University), Prof. Justin E. H. Smith (University of Paris 7—Denis Diderot), Prof. Neelam Srivastava (Newcastle University), and Dr. Anaïs Wion (Centre National de la Recherche Scientifique).

nomenology. The authors describe their quests to reason through to the deepest truths, recommending certain techniques for evaluating evidence while excoriating others. They reason through what we can know about God and how we can know it, rejecting the normative. They explain their methods for arriving at principles of ethical conduct and demonstrate the very openness they call for by exploring multiple ways of approaching the world, including those of various religions and cultures. Systematic, clear, and argumentatively vigorous, the *Hatata Inquiries* are superior examples of early modern theoretical and practical philosophy.

Their Religious and Educational Context

The *Hatata Inquiries* emerge from a rich cultural, religious, and educational context, reflecting Ethiopia's long tradition of original composition, intellectual questioning, and radical thought. These texts live squarely in the Ethiopian Orthodox Tewahedo Church (EOTC) modes of exegesis, commentary, and philosophical inquiry, as many Ethiopian scholars have argued (see, for example, (Eyasu Berento 2022; Merawi 2018; Amsalu Aklilu 1961)). That is because the authors trained in one of the longest running educational systems in the world, that of the EOTC (Binns 2016; Chernetsov 2005; Alaka Imbakom Kalewold 1970; Ephraim Isaac 2012). Understanding this system is important to understanding various aspects of the *Hatata Inquiries*, including its use of many quotations from memorized sources, its word play, and its question-and-answer format.

The EOTC educational system has five areas of study, which take at least twenty-five years to complete. First is the *Nebab Bet*, the house of reading, in which a student learns to read and memorize the Psalms and other set prayers (Habtemichael Kidane 2007b). Children learn to read around the age of four and are sent to *Nebab Bet* at the age of seven, where they memorize the entire Psalter in the four reading styles, three melodies, and two chanting forms. They must properly perform each Psalm in front of their teacher before going on to memorize the next one. This bone deep knowledge of the Psalter informs nearly every page of the *Hatata Zara Yaqob*, where memorized wording of the Psalms is constantly being deployed. As Mehari Worku put it in conversation, 'The Psalms must live within you for years—from participating in the liturgy and having all of the Psalms and the rest of the Psalter memorized to reciting them daily—to be able to recall them like this and deploy them with such mastery'.

The next stage is the *Zema Bet,* the house of music, in which they learn chanting and memorize hymns (Habtemichael Kidane 2014; Damon-Guillot 2014). Zara Yaqob did not linger in this stage, having no ear for music and being teased mercilessly for it. People devote more or less time to a particular house, depending on their interest and talents. So, as soon as he had learned its main principles, Zara Yaqob went on to the *Qeddase Bet*, the house of liturgy, in which students learn and memorize the various anaphoras for the Divine Liturgy for the Eucharist and the Horologium. This stage is most relevant for priests, who must memorize this material to perform the liturgy.

Few progress to the next stage, which is perhaps the most difficult, the *Qene Bet*, the house of poetry, in which they study grammar, style, and history; analyse the canon of poetry going back centuries; and compose original poetry (Meley Mulugeta 2010; Alemayyehu Moges 1970; Mulualem, Tamiru, and Kelkay 2022; Binns 2016; Kidane Habtemichael 2010). First, students learn *sewasew* (grammar), studying Geʻez verb conjugation, parts of speech, phrase structure, and sentence structure. Next, they listen to poetry, including that of students ahead of them. Then, they start to prepare short works of poetry and perform them for their teacher, who corrects them for melody and meter. Students at the end of this stage must be quick-witted, able to create poems on the spot, in the larger African tradition that came to inform rap in the United States. These students create sophisticated poems with double meanings, textual allusions, and rhymes. They often quote and adapt phrases from the lectionary, the Gospels, the Psalter, and the Synaxarium. Since these are public performances, a better student may snatch a line away by finishing it with other words. In the modern period, a famous scholar spent forty years studying qene in different schools to get all the nuances and melodies in every qene tradition in Ethiopia.

Being informed about *Qene Bet* is essential to reading the *Hatata Inquiries*. The *Hatata Zara Yaqob* displays signs of being authored by someone who studied in this EOTC stage and learned much about wordplay, poetic parallelism, and adaptation of biblical quotations for a specific rhetorical purpose. For instance, consider the repetition in this line in the *Hatata Walda Heywat*: ቃለ ሰብእ . . . ቃለ እግዚአብሔር . . . ቃለ ልቡና (qalä säb'... qalä Ǝgzi'abḥer... qalä ləbbunna; the *qal* of human beings... the *qal* of God... the *qal* of intelligence). The author is playing with a philosophically rich term in the Ethiopian tradition ቃል (qal; word, voice, meaning), using anaphoric parallelism to elaborate a multiplicity of meanings. Getatchew Haile once described such elegant turns of phrase in Geʻez literature as the author 'riding the language like a young horse' (Getatchew Haile 2018, 31).

The last stage is *Matsehaf Bet*, the house of exegesis, in which students learn to interpret scripture and texts (Habtemichael Kidane 2007a). Today, it takes a student many years to study the interpretation of the Old and New Testament (the first taking about four years, the second three years). Students must memorize great swathes of *andemta* (commentaries) on the Gospels. The andemta tradition originated around Gondar, the capital of Ethiopia from the early 1600s into the mid-1800s. The origin of the tradition appears to be primarily oral, although a significant amount of the material was compiled and written down by imperial decree around 1682 CE to resolve confusion over different approaches to interpretation, and to develop commentary in Amharic, the region's dominant language (Stoffregen-Pedersen and Tedros Abraha 2003).

While the authors may not have started this stage, they would be familiar with its pedagogical question and answer format. As Solomon Gebre Ghiorgis explains, 'discussion and asking questions is encouraged' in its schools and students are 'trained to think rather than believe'. As a result, 'they have been dissenters more often than not. Since they tend to rely on reason rather than on mere faith, they tend to be more philosophical than their counterparts—the priests. Indeed, it can be said that Ethiopian philosophy in its truest sense, i.e., philosophy based on the primacy of reason, originated in the kine school' (Solomon Ghebre Ghiorghis 1972, 10). Such ancient rhetorical practices exist in the EOTC tradition in part because it existed in relation to other ancient educational systems. For instance, philosophical texts from Egypt, Greece, and Persia were translated into Ge'ez as early as the 600s CE. Understanding the EOTC educational system is essential to understanding these authors.

Their Titles and Genre

The texts are popularly known by the title *Hatata*. But this word does not represent their title. It is the name of their genre in Ge'ez: the word 'hatata' means 'inquiry', 'investigation', 'exploration', 'examination', or 'scrutinization'. For ease of reading, however, we follow convention and use this genre term as part of their titles: *Hatata Zara Yaqob* and *Hatata Walda Heywat*. Then, to maintain the Ge'ez wording and keep its meaning at the forefront of readers' minds, we have chosen a reduplicative title for our volume, using both the Ge'ez and the English term to refer to these texts as the *Hatata Inquiries*.

This genre deploys a variety of rhetorics to investigate subjects. Some arise from the ancient *erotapokriseis* genre, popular in the EOTC educational system, of positing an imaginary junior person asking questions that the senior author answers. Another is the Ge'ez rhetoric of *samenna warq* (wax and gold), the art of creating a double meaning, one on the surface and another deeper (allegorical). Another is *tergwame* (interpretation), which includes three discursive modes, including *andemta* (exegesis).

Walda Heywat also names another genre. In his introduction to Zara Yaqob's book, he describes it as a *gadl*, which literally means 'striving', 'combat', and 'struggle' but is often translated as 'life story' or 'hagiography' because the word always appears in the titles of the lives of the saints (e.g., *Gadla Petros*). As Dawit Worku points out in his dissertation on the *Hatata Inquiries*, however, Zara Yaqob's *gadl* is neither a biography (being written by the subject himself) nor a hagiography. It 'is not telling the "saintly life" of the author'; rather, Walda Heywat uses the term because it is accurate for Zara Yaqob's '"striving" or "fight"' in order to discover the truth' (Dawit Worku 2012, 390).

Teaching the Hatata Inquiries

The *Hatata Inquires* contain a wealth of information about African and Ethiopian philosophy, religion, history, philology, and autobiography. They also provide a rich opportunity to teach students about how to read primary sources, test previous scholarly arguments, and form arguments in relation to an ongoing debate. A useful lesson plan and PowerPoint slides are online at https://wendybelcher.com/african-literature/hatata/ (last accessed on 14 June 2023).

Wendy Laura Belcher and Jeremy Brown
Manuscripts of the Texts

Two parchment manuscripts were used in composing this translation. No other manuscripts of the *Hatata Zara Yaqob* and *Hatata Walda Heywat* are known to scholars. This absence is not surprising due to their content and purpose. Before the printing press, 'heretical' literature like these works circulated only through private copies and went unpreserved in the archives of the day, monastic libraries. Private copies are far less likely to survive for centuries, residing as they do in individual homes. Also, works not used in church services tend to have few copies.[1]

These parchment manuscripts exist because the Italian Roman Catholic priest Father Giusto da Urbino sent them to France to the scholar and collector Antoine d'Abbadie in 1853 and 1854 (Abbadie 1859; Conti Rossini 1912). After d'Abbadie's death in 1897, the manuscripts were bequeathed to French institutions and ended up at the Bibliothèque nationale de France (BNF) in Paris in 1902. The BNF began providing free online access to the manuscripts (digitized from black and white microfilm) in 2019. In 2022, after we purchased digital colour copies of the opening folios, the BNF generously posted both manuscripts in full in colour.[2] This spectacular colour digitization made visible for the first time the many primary and secondary hand additions, edits, and erasures in the manuscripts, which previous scholars could not see due to working from the print edition or black and white microfilms.

These two manuscripts entered the scholarship with the names of BnF Éthiopien d'Abbadie MS 234 (35 folios) and BnF Éthiopien d'Abbadie 215 (78 folios). Their names are often shortened to MS 234 and MS 215 or Abb 234 and Abb 215. Below, we also call them MS A and MS B, respectively.

The two manuscripts do not contain both philosophical works. Rather, Abb 234 (MS A) contains only the *Hatata Zara Yaqob* while Abb 215 (MS B) contains both *Hatata Zara Yaqob* and *Hatata Walda Heywat*.

Giusto da Urbino was the scribe for Abb 234 (MS A). He produced it on paper, not the parchment typical of Ge'ez scribal practice, in the four months between September 1852 (when he wrote to d'Abbadie saying that he had *not* been able to

---

[1] Even a text as essential to Ethiopian identity as the *Kəbrä Nägäśt* (the founding narrative of Ethiopia's Solomonic dynasty) has only fifteen known manuscripts (Anonymous forthcoming 2025). By contrast, a text read aloud during church services, like the *Ta'ammera Maryam* (Miracles of Mary), have thousands of extant copies.
[2] See Abb 215 and Abb 234 at, respectively, https://gallica.bnf.fr/view3if/ga/ark:/12148/btv1b52518 4250/f7 and https://gallica.bnf.fr/view3if/ga/ark:/12148/btv1b52518435d/f7, both last accessed on 14 June 2023.

purchase the *Hatata Zara Yaqob*) and February 1853, when he shipped Abb 234 (MS A) to d'Abbadie. We can confirm that Giusto da Urbino was the copyist because the handwriting in Abb 234 matches that of his other documents. His handwriting in Abb 234 (MS A) is poor; he was not a trained scribe (see Figure 1).

Then, a year later, Giusto da Urbino commissioned an Ethiopian scribe to copy both *Hatata Zara Yaqob* and *Hatata Walda Heywat* onto parchment, producing Abb 215 (MS B). This scribe, whom Anaïs Wion later identified as Gabra Maryam (Wion 2021a, 9), gave the book a traditional leather stamped cover, choosing to omit a common feature—an embossed cross. Gabra Maryam completed it in the months before April 1854, when Giusto da Urbino shipped it to d'Abbadie.[1] Gabra Maryam's handwriting reveals that he was not a highly trained church scribe, although his handwriting is neater, more consistent, and better trained than Giusto da Urbino's (see Figures 2 and 3).

Their Origin and Transmission

We conjecture that these two manuscripts came about as follows (see the stemma of manuscripts in Figure 4). In 1668, the philosopher Zara Yaqob wrote *Hatata Zara Yaqob*. He may have written it down himself or had an amanuensis copy down what he said aloud.[2] Either way, this creation is the original (autograph) manuscript of *Hatata Zara Yaqob*. We call it MS α, using a Greek alphabet character. In philological practice, the Greek letter indicates that the manuscript must have existed but is no longer extant. If this manuscript still exists, we do not know where it is.

Then, at some point between 1693 and 1717, the philosopher Walda Heywat wrote *Hatata Walda Heywat*. Likewise, he may have written it down himself or had an amanuensis. Either way, this creation is the original (autograph) manuscript of *Hatata Walda Heywat*. We call this manuscript MS ω, using a Greek character because it is no longer extant.

---

[1] The copyist for BnF Ethiopic MS Abb 200 is clearly stated—*Däbtära* Gäbrä Maryam from Bet̠a Leḥem—and the hand is the same as that in Abb 215 (Wion 2021a, 9).

[2] At the opening of *Hatata Zara Yaqob*, Walda Heywat states that 'I shall write down' Zara Yaqob's story, which Zara Yaqob 'himself composed'. Three sentences on, Zara Yaqob states 'I, Zara Yaqob, write' this. Perhaps Walda Heywat wrote down on parchment what Zara Yaqob said aloud to him, or perhaps he copied what Zara Yaqob wrote on parchment.

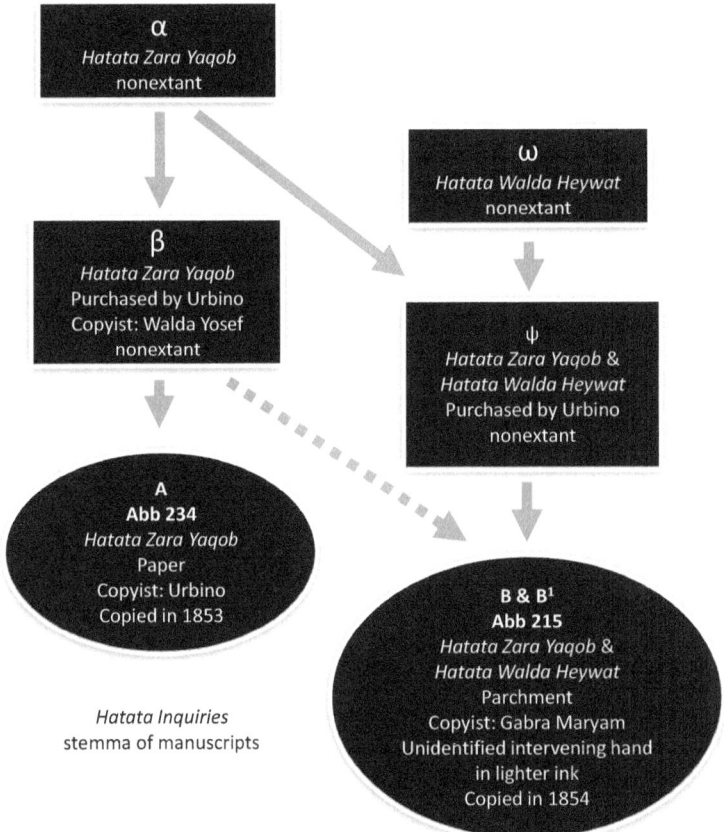

Figure 4: Manuscript Stemma. This manuscript stemma represents the likely history of the texts of the *Hatata Zara Yaqob* and *Hatata Walda Heywat*. The Greek letters (α and β, ω and ψ) indicate the no longer extant manuscripts that must have existed, and the Roman letters (A and B) indicate the two extant manuscripts, with B¹ indicating the intervening hand in MS B. The arrows indicate which manuscript served as the base for another manuscript. The dotted arrow indicates which manuscript served as the source for the intervening hand of B¹. See also Appendix 2.

At some point between the late 1600s and the mid-1800s, scribes copied these originals. Then, scribes copied those copies, including the scribes who eventually produced Abb 234 (MS A) and Abb 215 (MS B), the final manuscripts in our stemma. Philologists have a word for the manuscripts produced in between the first and the last: intermediate manuscripts. We do not know how many intermediate copies existed, but traces in Abb 234 (MS A) and Abb 215 (MS B) prove they existed, as explained below.

A scribe named Walda Yosef made one of these intermediate manuscripts, a copy of *Hatata Zara Yaqob*. We call this manuscript MS β, using a Greek character because this manuscript is no longer extant. Giusto da Urbino purchased it sometime in 1852 from a soldier who had been on campaign in the Lake Tana district (as translated in (Sumner 1976, 82)). We know the scribe's name because the scribe named himself in the text at the end of his manuscript (in the colophon). He also named his patron Walda Giyorgis there. This colophon is how we know that Walda Yosef's manuscript was not the original, as autographs almost never have patrons, being written down by the author. If it had unusually had a patron, it would have been Zara Yaqob himself.

Walda Yosef's manuscript served as the base for Abb 234 (MS A). That is, Giusto da Urbino produced Abb 234 (MS A) by copying *Hatata Zara Yaqob* as it appeared in Walda Yosef's manuscript β, including faithfully copying his colophon. We know that Walda Yosef was talented because Giusto da Urbino described MS β as 'in a beautiful style' (as translated in (Wion 2021a, 8, 6)). Giusto da Urbino decided not to send MS β to d'Abbadie because it was too 'big' and instead sent the copy he had made (Sumner 1976, 87, 82).

The chain of manuscripts for *Hatata Walda Heywat* is a little different. At some point, it began to travel with *Hatata Zara Yaqob*, appearing in the same manuscripts. It is possible that they always appeared together. That is, that Walda Heywat wrote down the original of *Hatata Walda Heywat* in a copy he made of *Hatata Zara Yaqob*. Either way, one of the intermediate manuscripts includes both works and we call it MS ψ, using a Greek character because it is no longer extant. Giusto da Urbino purchased it sometime in late 1853 or early 1854. This MS ψ was the base for Abb 215 (MS B). That is, the scribe Gabra Maryam produced Abb 215 (MS B) by copying *Hatata Zara Yaqob* and *Hatata Walda Heywat* from MS ψ. Giusto da Urbino described MS ψ as inferior in quality to MS β, stating that it was 'on bad parchment and in very irregular handwriting' (as translated in (Wion 2021a, 8, 6)).

In other words, neither of the extant manuscripts—Abb 234 (MS A) and Abb 215 (MS B)—is the original of either work. Even those who believe that Giusto da Urbino was the author of these two works do not believe that either extant manuscript is the original. For one, Abb 215 (MS B) cannot be Giusto da Urbino's autograph of *Hatata Walda Heywat* because the manuscript is not in Giusto da Urbino's handwriting and because he drafted his compositions himself, without an amanuensis, as evidenced by his work on a Ge'ez dictionary and translations. For another, Abb 234 (MS A) does not show traces of a composition process. Meanwhile, neither manuscript can be Zara Yaqob's original either. In terms of handwriting, Abb 234 (MS A) is in Giusto da Urbino's handwriting and Abb 215 (MS B) is in Gabra Maryam's handwriting. Finally, in terms of chronology, Abb 215 (MS B) was copied after Abb 234 (MS A), so it cannot be the autograph of the *Hatata Zara Yaqob*.

Their Corrections

An intriguing aspect of Abb 215 (MS B) is that someone made corrections to it in lighter ink (see Figure 5). The manuscript exhibits an extensive use of lines, circles, and dashes to mark text for erasure, typical of Ethiopian manuscript culture. Following philological practice, we label this intervening hand MS B[1] (see Figure 4). Some speculate that Giusto da Urbino handwrote these corrections into his scribe's copy, taking the opportunity to edit his own composition (Wion 2021b).

However, this is unlikely for three reasons. One, this hand is not an exact match for Giusto da Urbino's when compared with his known hand in Abb 234. While it may be his, it is not certainly his. Two, the intervening hand consists almost entirely of spelling and proofreading corrections (87 percent). That is, they are not inventive edits, changing the meaning. The proofreading corrections are made due to checking a third manuscript—likely Giusto da Urbino's first purchase, Ms β. Brown has documented that 73 percent of the words and phrases added in the margins or interlineally in Abb 215 align the text with that in Abb 234 (see Appendix 2 for this evidence). Another 14 percent are simple spelling corrections. The remaining 13 percent are minor substantive corrections (for instance, adding the word 'Mohammed' to Abb 215 even though it does not appear in Abb 234 because the phrase would be unclear and grammatically incorrect without this addition). Such clarifications are typical of scribal interventions in Ethiopian manuscript culture. Three, the intervening hand used traditional Ethiopian proofreading marks, which we know from Abb 234 that Giusto da Urbino did not use (see Figure 5 as well as Appendix 2 for an analysis of scribal intervention in Abb 215 and Abb 234). Most likely, Gabra Maryam used MS ψ as the base source for Abb 215 (MS B) and then had another Ethiopian scribe check his copying against Ms β.

The full colour digital copies of Abb 234 and Abb 215 transform our understanding of these texts. In some cases, they vitiate arguments made about them. Some of Getatchew Haile's arguments about authorship, based on his work with the black and white microfilms, are contravened (Getatchew Haile 2017) (see Appendix B). For instance, the microfilm made it seem like some lines were original, but the colour copy revealed that the flat lines are in a lighter ink, that is, later additions. Getatchew Haile had made an argument about dating based on a numeral: ፬ (4) (on Abb 234 f. 4r). However, the flat lines above and below the character did not indicate that it was a number. Rather, they were proofreading marks indicating that the Geʽez character o was wrong and should be omitted. The phrase was not ምዓኦአብአልተ (from the four wealthy people) but እምዐአብአልተ (from the wealthy people). This misinterpretation came about, first, because of the close resemblance of a fourth order ayin (o) and the numeral 4 (፬); second, because of Abb 234's untrained scribal hand; and third, because the manuscript's red ink was not visible in the black and white

Figure 5: Detail from Abb 215 f. 3r. The intervening hand is visible at the top, where a phrase—ወንቅትሎ ለንጉሥ (and let's kill the king)—is written in lighter ink and in a slightly different hand than the main text. The scribe has used the ancient *ancora* proofreading marks of ⊢ to indicate the words to be inserted and ⊥ to indicate where they are to be inserted (two characters from the end of line 5). This is a proofreading correction not an edit, as these missing words appear in Abb 234, and likely result from the proofreader consulting Giusto da Urbino's Ms β. In black and white, these changes are difficult to see; please consult the colour copy online https://gallica.bnf.fr/view3if/ga/ark:/12148/btv1b525184250, last accessed on 14 June 2023.

copy (the flat lines above and below numerals are always done in red ink in this manuscript).

More important, the colour digital copies reveal serious deficiencies in Enno Littmann's edition. He stated that he had included all emendations and notations in his edition and translation (Littmann 1904, 2). He definitively had not. As just one example, Littmann failed to notice that a phrase about masturbation was censored on folio 28v of Abb 215. The closeup makes visible that someone erased and scratched out several words (see Figure 6). By consulting the same sentence in Abb 234, and detecting the first four characters in Abb 215, we can perceive that the missing phrase is about masturbation. Littman's editorial choice to dismiss Abb 234

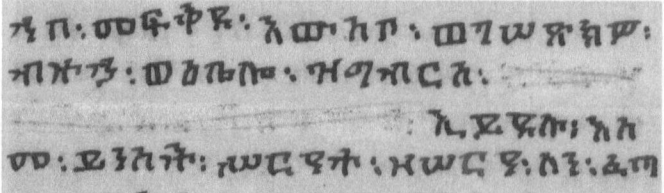

Figure 6: Detail from Abb 215 f. 28v. Words have been erased (making the background a bit lighter) and then also scratched out with two lines. The beginning of the phrase, at the end of the second line, is just visible: ከዐወ ዘ... These are the first four characters of a phrase that appears in Abb 234: ከዐወ ዘርአ (spilling his seed). In black and white, these changes are difficult to see; please consult the colour copy online at https://gallica.bnf.fr/view3if/ga/ark:/12148/btv1b525184250, last accessed on 14 June 2023.

as a dependent, copied manuscript, one with no value for the reconstruction of the original, is here revealed as particularly unfortunate. Consulting Abb 234 would have aided him in seeing this omission.

Their Relative Quality

Unfortunately, translators have followed Littmann's edition in ignoring Abb 234. The mistaken emphasis came about, Getatchew Haile argued, because a European had copied Abb 234 on paper while an Ethiopian scribe had copied Abb 215 on parchment and the latter was thus seen as more authentic (Getatchew Haile 2017, 56). But Getatchew Haile believed that not only should editors and translators have consulted Abb 234, they should have prioritized it. Abb 234 was 'closer to the original copy' (MS α) than Abb 215 (Getatchew Haile 2017, 54) because a principle of philology is that 'the shorter version [of a work] . . . is closer to the original than the longer one' (Getatchew Haile 2017, 57). That is, works tend to accrete words, phrases, and sentences over time, rather than losing them. We agree with Getatchew Haile that Abb 234 and Abb 215 are each a copy of 'a slightly different version' of *Hatata Zara Yaqob*, and that Abb 234 is likely closer to the original. Our manuscript stemma in Figure 4 is inspired by his observations.

As a result of our research on the manuscripts' relationship to each other, we have followed Abb 215 in the body of our translation of *Hatata Zara Yaqob* but noted any differences from Abb 234 in a footnote, documenting it with an English translation. In no other translation of the *Hatata Zara Yaqob* can scholars instantly see what both manuscripts have. We have also provided two appendices on the topic. Appendix 1 is a chart of the differences between Abb 215 and Abb 234, documented in Ge'ez and with an English translation. Appendix 2 is a statistical analysis of the intervening hand's changes. This will improve scholars' ability to directly compare the differences and make arguments accordingly.

The variations between Abb 234 and Abb 215 (excluding scribal interventions) defy simple grouping into clear categories. Instead, we will note some general differences between the two manuscripts of the single text HZY. For a further discussion, see the Manuscript Philology section.

First, Abb 215 clarifies vague wording in Abb 234. For example, Abb 215 includes the prepositional phrase 'to school' to make explicit where someone's education is taking place. Abb 215 clarifies why Egyptians acted the way they did by adding the phrase 'on account of their faith'. Abb 215 frequently adds questions to bring the point home, such as 'And from where did I come?', 'Can human deliberation improve on the work of God?', and 'For how much more I have understood while living alone in a cave than I understood when I lived with scholars?' Appendix 1 documents dozens of additional examples of clarification.

Second, Abb 215 more clearly defines the boundary between Zara Yaqob's followers and other religious groups, more negatively depicting Jews, Christians, and Muslims. Abb 215 adds material about Christian and Muslim fasting, scoffing at 'those who keep the Christian fasting laws' and those who would suggest that God told Muslims that during Ramadan they could eat at night not during the day. Abb 215 also expands upon the critique of EOTC feasting and fasting in Abb 234. Abb 215 adds polemical statements that the books of (the Jewish) Moses represent 'detestable wisdom' and that 'Mohammed's instruction cannot be from God'. Abb 215 expands a Catholic accusation against the Coptic Christians for denying 'the orthodox faith' by specifying that they deny 'the orthodox faith of Peter's See'. Perhaps Walda Heywat edited the work of his teacher Zara Yaqob, altering it to take a stronger stance against outsiders now that the community of Zara Yaqob's disciples was established.

Finally, Abb 215 has a different opening and closing than Abb 234. This is because Abb 215 includes both the HZY and the HWH (unlike Abb 234) and must explain the role of Walda Heywat.

Wendy Laura Belcher
The Authorship of the *Hatata Inquiries*

Some have questioned whether Ethiopians wrote the *Hatata Inquiries* in the 1600s, arguing instead that a European missionary in the 1850s invented them both wholesale.[1]

As translators and editors, Ralph Lee and I have spent several years deep in these two texts, feeling our way, word by word, sentence by sentence, chapter by chapter, through their language, concerns, and styles. Mehari Worku and Jeremy R. Brown joined us later and spent many months doing the same. From these extended encounters, we are all confident that two Ethiopians named Zara Yaqob and Walda Heywat composed these two texts. In this, we stand with dozens of other scholars, including the late Getatchew Haile.

Below, I present a history of the authorship debate, then lay out the case for European authorship, followed by the case for Ethiopian authorship. I will regularly be deploying legal language in the sections below—speaking of the 'case', 'evidence', the 'defence', and the 'prosecution', and so on. I do so not because I believe that the texts are accused human beings, or should be treated with hostility, but because legal language helps us to see the shortcomings in previous argumentation for the European authorship of the *Hatata Inquiries*.

This debate about authorship is part of what makes the *Hatata Inquiries* wonderful teaching texts, aiding those seeking to teach the problem of authorship and authenticity when reading primary sources. They supply incredible teaching moments for the very debate they inspire, and the debates about the debate, and that makes them a valuable part of the conversation about African studies methods.[2]

---

[1] I am grateful for feedback on this section on the authorship debate, and many wise suggestions for improvement, to Samantha Kelly, Alessandro Bausi, Dag Herbjørnsrud, Jonathan Egid, the anonymous peer reviewers as well as my co-editors Mehari Worku, Jeremy Brown, and Ralph Lee. Special thanks to Naomi Murakawa and Marcia Shenk for writing companionship.
[2] For a lesson plan on teaching the *Hatata Inquires*, see https://wendybelcher.com/african-literature/hatata/, last accessed on 14 June 2023.

https://doi.org/10.1515/9783110781922-003

The History of the Debate on Authorship

How did the authorship of the two *Hatata Inquiries* come to be questioned?

In June 1903, the Russian scholar Boris Alexsandrovich Turayev visited Paris and became fascinated by the *Hatata Inquiries*, which had only become publicly accessible the previous year, at the Bibliothèque nationale de France. His report on the 'Ethiopian Rationalist of the Seventeenth Century' electrified scholars and spurred a meeting of the Oriental Section of the Archaeological Society on September 25, 1903. Turayev then published his translation of the *Hatata Zara Yaqob* into Russian in St. Petersburg in January 1905 (Turayev 1905), just a few months after the German Orientalist Enno Littmann published his edition of the two texts and his translation of them into Latin (Littmann 1904) and, later, German (Littmann 1916).[1]

As soon as scholars began to discuss the *Hatata Inquiries* as works of African thought, they attracted European sceptics. Imbued with deeply racist ideas about African capacities, European scholars began by insisting that Africans could not have written such profound works and then dug through the texts in search of evidence to prove their views.

In 1904, Littmann launched this scepticism by writing in Latin that 'these flowers could not grow solely from the Ethiopian ground'. He added that the Ethiopian authors must 'in some way have been guided by foreign thought. The language they write, although genuinely Ethiopian, in some places seems to have some flavour of Arabic' (Littmann 1904 as translated in Sumner 1976, 63). Littmann presented no evidence for this claim about Arabic, nor has anyone else; certainly, we saw no evidence of Arabisms. In 1907, Carl Bezold further set the stage by wrongly describing them as 'oases in the desert' of the body of 'strictly religious' and 'grossly superstitious' Geʿez texts (Bezold 1907, 1242, translation mine).

In 1916, the Italian Orientalist Carlo Conti Rossini published an article hinting at his doubts (Conti Rossini 1916). In 1920, he published an article arguing outright that Ethiopians did not write the texts in the 1600s. Conti Rossini alleged that the author was a Capuchin Roman Catholic missionary from the province of Lucca in present-day Italy. His ordination name was Father Giusto da Urbino (1814–1856), but he was born Giovanni Iacopo. (Although it is often said his first name was Jacopo alone and his last name was Curtopassi, neither is correct, as I address in a following section.) Selected to participate in the Sacra Congregatio de Propaganda Fide mission to Ethiopia, Giusto da Urbino arrived in December 1846 at Massawa,

---

[1] Regarding the chain of events, see (Sumner 1976: 63). Getatchew Haile prefers the Turayev edition to the Littmann edition (Getatchew Haile 2017). In general, neither edition is reliable (pace Conti Rossini's praise of the Littmann edition), which is why we used the manuscripts themselves for our translation.

on the Red Sea coast of what was then Ethiopia. Until his expulsion in May 1855 by the head of the EOTC, he lived in the Amhara region, in a town called Beta Lehem, which is near Dabra Tabor and 100 miles southeast of the then-capital Gondar (see Map 1). He dedicated time to learning Ethiopian languages, especially Geʿez. By the time he left the country, he had produced a Latin-Geʿez dictionary, a Geʿez grammar, and a French to Geʿez translation of a missionary tract (Conti Rossini 1916; Mittwoch 1934; Sumner 1976, 204–207).

It was Giusto da Urbino who sent the two *Hatata Inquiries* in Geʿez to the French Orientalist and manuscript collector Antoine d'Abbadie (1810–1897) in 1853 and 1854 (Sumner 1976, 62; Zitelmann 2005). He claimed in the accompanying letters that he had bought them from Ethiopians as rare and unusual texts. Giusto da Urbino died in Khartoum three years later, and the two texts remained, unexamined, in d'Abbadie's private collection until it was bequeathed to the Bibliothèque nationale de France (BNF) in Paris in 1902, after d'Abbadie's death.[1]

In his 1920 article, Conti Rossini scornfully asserted that Ethiopians could not author philosophical texts, arguing that their 'blind faith' and mode of biblical interpretation posed an 'insurmountable barrier' to 'free thinking' (Conti Rossini 1920, 214, 215).[2] Only a European could have written philosophical texts like these, he asserted. These racist views are unsurprising in a man who had served as a colonial officer in Eritrea for four years (1899–1903) (Ricci 2003) and as a member of the Fascist Italian government's administration. Indeed, Conti Rossini's theory about authorship must be considered in the context of the Italian build up to a second attempt to colonize Ethiopia (in the 1930s), as supported by scholar-functionaries

---

[1] Regarding the extant archived works by Giusto da Urbino, they include his letters, manuscripts, and publications. Some of his letters (written between 1846–1855) are in Lucca Convento Cappuccini, Archivio Provinciale (the Provincial Archives of the Capuchin Convent of Monte San Quirico, Lucca) and Archivio Storico di Propaganda Fide (the Historical Archives of the Propaganda Fide) in Rome, in the Congressi collection for 'Ethiopia (Vol. 4 [1841–1847], 5 [1848–1857], and 6 [1858–1860]) and Egypt (Vol. 19 [1854–1861]). His 1856 publications appear in the periodical *Spettatore egiziano*. His works are contained in seven manuscripts: at the Biblioteca della Società geografica italiana in Rome, Italy (MS. 167; a grammar and dictionary); Biblioteca nazionale Vittorio Emanuele (now New Library of Rome) in Rome, Italy (MS. Orientale 134; a grammar, dictionary, and notes); Bibliothèque nationale de France, Paris, France (MSS. D'Abbadie 215 [both Hatata Inquiries]; 216 [a grammar, poems, etc.]; 217 [a dictionary]; 234 [*HZY* Inquiry alone]), and the Vatican Library, Italy (MS. Ethiopian 165; a translation of *Soirées de Carthage*, most of which is in Giusto da Urbino's hand, while some is in his scribe's hand). Other relevant documents not authored by Giusto da Urbino are at the Parrocchia di San Michele Arcangelo in Lucca; Biblioteca nazionale Vittorio Emanuele; Biblioteca dei FF. Minori Cappuccini S. Lorenzo da Brindisi, Gaggiret, Asmara, Eritrea; Archivio Storico di Propaganda Fide, and others.

[2] I am grateful to Lea Cantor for translating (Conti Rossini 1920) into English for the *In Search of Zara Yaqob* conference of 2022 (Conti Rossini 2022).

like Conti Rossini.¹ The existence of an Ethiopian philosophical text was inconvenient, as it disproved the claims of African barbarism used to justify the war against Ethiopia. Conti Rossini's ideology does not in itself rule out his theory, but his later actions bear out the racist rationale for his writing that only a European could have written the texts.

Conti Rossini's views about Africans only grew more extreme over time. Fifteen years after his first article on the *Hatata Inquiries*, two weeks before the Italian invasion of Ethiopia, he published an article with the egregious title 'Ethiopia Is Incapable of Civil Progress'.² In it, he summarized his position on the *Hatata Inquiries*' authorship as follows: 'the only philosophical text that was the gem of Abyssinian [that is, Ethiopian] literature ... was demonstrated by myself to be a falsification by an Italian monk, who through an Ethiopian form vented his feelings, exacerbated by the isolation of his mission and his bitter religious scepticism' (Conti Rossini 1935 as translated by Srivastava 2022).

Within a decade of Conti Rossini's 1920 article, even the texts' original promoters wilted, changing their minds and dismissing the texts (Turayev 1920; Littmann 1930). Prominent Italian Ethiopianists joined the chorus against Ethiopian authorship (Cerulli 1926; Guidi 1932). Their primary motivation in doing so was the same as their predecessors. The Italian Orientalist Ignazio Guidi wrote that the *Hatata Inquiries* could not be the product of 'the Ethiopian psychology' (Guidi 1932).³ Only one Ethiopianist stood against the tide, a Russian scholar who pointed out that all the evidence presented was about the first *Hatata Inquiry*, not the second, and therefore the case should not be considered closed (Krackovskii 1924).

In 1934, the German Orientalist Eugen Mittwoch took up the case, examining the texts on the same racist grounds: that 'the appearance of rationalistic, almost European-looking trains of thought in the otherwise exclusively ecclesiastical-oriented writings of the Abyssinians' was suspicious (Mittwoch 1934).⁴ He uncovered perhaps the most damning piece of evidence, which I will discuss in the next section.

---

1 Regarding the Italian 'scholar-functionary', see (Srivastava 2022; Dore 2003). The Italians lost the First Italo-Ethiopian War (1895–1896), one of the first clear victories for an African nation's military over a modern European power. This loss fed Mussolini's attempt to conquer and colonize Ethiopia in the Second Italo-Ethiopian War (1935–1941), which was also unsuccessful. On the Italian Orientalists, see (Maiocchi 2015; Mallette 2011).
2 Conti Rossini published this in a paper in the Fascist mouthpiece *New Anthology* two weeks before Italy's invasion of Ethiopia (Conti Rossini 1935). On it, see (Maiocchi 2015).
3 'Non ha alcun legame con altre opere ge'ez o arabe, e non concorda punto con le condizioni del tempo e la psicologia abissina' (Guidi 1932, 77).
4 'Das Auftauchen rationalistischer, fast europaisch anmutender Gedankengange in dem sonst ausschlieBlich kirchlich orientierten Schrifttum der Abessinier, obenclrein bereits im 17. Jahrhundert, erregte allenthalben berechtigtcs Anfselten' (Mittwoch 1934). As Luam rightly critiques:

After that, European scholars treated the case as proven and the texts as fraudulent, with scholars adding no new evidence and recycling the arguments previously made (Simon 1936; Ullendorff 1945; Ullendorff 1960; Ricci 1964; 1969).[1]

However, just as the case was being closed in Europe, it was being re-opened in Ethiopia. The first essay arguing for Ethiopian authorship appeared in 1945, in the English-language newspaper based in Addis Ababa, the *Ethiopian Herald* (Kamil 1945). Then, Za-Manfas Qeddus Abreha translated the *Hatata Inquiries* into Amharic in 1955, arguing for their value as Ethiopian-authored texts (Za-Manfas Qeddus Abreha 1955). The English Ethiopianist Sylvia Pankhurst wrote a chapter in 1955 saying the same (Pankhurst 1955).

The next fifteen years saw a growing number of articles published in Ethiopia arguing for Ethiopian authorship—some in Amharic (Amsalu Aklilu 1961) and some in English in the *Ethiopian Herald* (Bahru Zewde 1968; Tesfaye Debesay 1970; Solomon Ghebre Giorghis 1972). These were the first works to ever appear in English about the *Hatata Inquiries*.

Meanwhile, in Europe, in 1965, the Italian scholar Lino Marchiotto translated the texts into Italian from Littmann's Latin translation and took issue with previous Italian Ethiopianists. He insisted that the issue of authorship was unsolvable but also lambasted previous Italian scholars for their overconfidence and their contemptuous views (Marchiotto 1964–1965). Also, Giusto da Urbino's biographer, the Capuchin priest F. Carmelo da Sessan, asserted in his biography that the priest had not written the heretical *Hatata Inquiries*. None of the evidence justified attributing to Giusto da Urbino 'an unqualifiable work of apostasy', he wrote (da Sessano 1951 as cited in Sumner 1976, 82).

This research reached a critical mass in 1968, when Alemayyehu Moges wrote a ground-breaking dissertation on the *Hatata Zara Yaqob* (Alemayyehu Moges 1968). His exegetical argument for Ethiopian authorship was so detailed and persuasive that Claude Sumner, a Canadian Jesuit professor and linguist who lived in Ethiopia and taught at Addis Ababa University for half a century (1953 to 2001), decided to investigate the matter further.

In the late 1970s, Sumner published two volumes in English on the topic (Sumner 1976; 1978). They were part of his four-volume *Ethiopian Philosophy* set, published by Addis Ababa University Press. He provided not only a translation of the two texts into English but also an extraordinary tour de force of scholarship, with hundreds

---

'Diese Aussage ist problematisch, weil überhaupt nicht erklärt wird, inwiefern die inhaltlichen Aussagen der Hatätas "europäisch" anmuten, wie auch immer "europäisch" zu definieren ist' ('This statement is problematic because it is not explained how the content of the Hatatas is "European", however "European" is to be defined') (Luam Tesfalidet 2007, 28–29). On Mittowch, see (Voigt 2007).
[1] For a full summary of these works, see (Sumner 1976, 77, 79).

of pages dedicated to exploring and evaluating the various claims about the authorship of the *Hatata Inquiries* in all the previous scholarship. He concluded that two Ethiopians, Zara Yaqob and Walda Heywat, wrote the *Hatata Inquiries* in the 1600s.

In a service to all future discussions of the texts, not only did Sumner examine and summarize all previous scholarship on the topic, in all languages, but he also translated huge blocks of them, especially work in Amharic. He also supplied translations of an astounding number of primary sources, from an impressive array of European archives, including Giusto da Urbino's letters, breaking them down into their constituent parts for analysis of themes and emphasis. His exegesis of these documents is forensic. His footnotes are exceptional, packed with page-long biographies, detailed information on locations (down to their seasons and crops), illuminating etymologies, extensive descriptions of archival sources, corrections of typos in the sources, and so on and so forth. He left no stone unturned. These volumes represent a magnificent piece of scholarship. One of their most remarkable features is how much he cites Ethiopian scholars, which to this day is rare. It is their research, often in Amharic, that had brought the issue to Sumner's attention and their arguments that had persuaded him of Ethiopian authorship. He rightly credits them throughout. The *Hatata Inquiries* would have sunk into obscurity without the care and dedication of these Ethiopian scholars and Sumner.

Sumner's translation of the *Hatata Inquiries* into English inspired a surge of interest in them. In the 1980s and 1990s, as African philosophy began to grow as a field, the texts became foundational, discussed as examples of African rationalism (Mudimbe 1988; Eze 2008; Bell and Fernback 2015; Serequeberhan 1994). Many scholars also taught the texts in their classrooms. In the twenty-first century, scholarship on the texts surged, with Teodros Kiros publishing a series of works analysing the texts' philosophy (Kiros 2001; 2004; 2005a; b; 2022) and Dawit Worku writing a dissertation on the texts' ethics (Dawit Worku 2012). Others wrote books (Sumner and Samuel Wolde Yohannes 2002) and articles (Chemeda Bokora 2004; Tassew Asfaw 2004).[1] It has even been a popular topic of undergraduate research in Ethiopia (Gobezayehu Baye 2005; Gizaw Belayneh 2005; Yonas Zerfu 2005; Mohammed Seid 2005).

---

1 This is not to mention other works that at least mention or discuss the *Hatata Inquiries*, including (Anonymous 1961; Pankhurst 1969; Cowley 1974; Knibb and Ullendorf 1978b; a; Hopfmann 1992; Krause 2003; 2006; Cohen 2007; Habtemichael Kidane 2010; Meley Mulugeta 2010; Damon-Guillot 2014; Habtemichael Kidane 2014; Asale 2016; Binns 2016; Petros Solomon 2018; Getatchew Haile 2018).

At this point, the debate seemed closed, decided in favour of Ethiopian authorship. As Luam Tesfalidet put it in her 2007 master's thesis on the *Hatata Inquiries*, 'Regarding the question of the authenticity of the Hatatas, it can be stated in closing that this question is no longer in the foreground.... The focus of interest is now on the content of both Hatatas and their distinctive features... [They] are now increasingly considered to be not only a significant part of Ethiopian philosophy, but also of African philosophy'.[1]

However, in 2013, the French Ethiopianist Anaïs Wion revived the debate by returning to the work of Conti Rossini and Mittwoch and insisting that they had been right all along, that Giusto da Urbino had fraudulently authored the *Hatata Inquiries*. She published two rich articles on the topic based on careful analysis of the archive of Giusto da Urbino's work, including his letters and translations. Originally published in French, the essays appeared in English translation in 2021 (Wion and Mbodj-Pouye 2013; Wion 2013b; a; 2021b; a). Her articles were the first in many decades to argue for European authorship.[2]

Wion did not long stand alone. Several Ethiopian scholars argued that the texts were not Ethiopian and had to be European (Fisseha Taddese 2014; Merawi and Kenaw 2019; Daniel Kibret 2019).

In 2022, Jonathan Egid, Lea Cantor, and Fasil Merawi held a conference on the topic at Oxford University, *In Search of Zara Yaqob*, opening the debate to many perspectives. Then, in 2024, we published this volume on the *Hatata Inquiries*, summarizing the debate to date, providing our own evidence, and strongly asserting our confidence in their authorship by Zara Yaqob and Walda Heywat.

The Case for European Authorship

Below, I will present the prosecution's case without any rebuttals, and only then will I turn to rebuttals and the case in favour of Ethiopian authorship. As you will be reading the European authorship case first, keep in mind the wisdom of Proverbs 18:17: 'the first to state his case seems right until someone comes to cross-examine him'.

---

1 'Zu der Frage betreffend der Echtheit der Hatätas, kann abschließend festgestellt werden, dass diese Frage längst nicht mehr im Vordergrund steht.... Im Zentrum des Interesses stehen nun die inhaltlichen Themen beider Hatätas und die Charakterisierung derselben.... betrachtet man nun zunehmend die ḤZY und die ḤWḤ nicht nur als einen bedeutenden Teil der äthiopischen Philosophie, sondern auch der afrikanischen Philosophie' (Luam Tesfalidet 2007, 77–78).
2 Although, as it turned out, the German Ethiopianist Manfred Kropp had an unpublished article on the topic (Kropp 1992).

So, what evidence has been presented in favour of a European author?

Two of the main pieces of evidence assume that Giusto da Urbino wanted to leave some trace of himself in this text, some clue of his deceptive authorship.

First, Conti Rossini argued that the first *Hatata Inquiry*'s named author Zara Yaqob (meaning 'Scion of Jacob') was intended as a version of Giusto da Urbino's supposed baptismal name of 'Jacopo Curtopassi' (meaning 'short steps') (Conti Rossini 1920). For Giusto da Urbino to use a variant of his birth name in combination with a Geʿez word meaning something close to 'son' would be a clever way of hinting that the author Zara Yaqob was his son, his creation. I would add for their case that the name Walda Heywat also includes the word 'son' (although meaning 'Son of the [Christian] Faith', which is not apt).

Second, Mittwoch uncovered that the author Zara Yaqob's birthdate, as announced in the text, is (almost) the same as Giusto da Urbino's birthdate (Mittwoch 1934). This is the strongest piece of evidence for the prosecution's case, seemingly too close to be mere coincidence. The first *Hatata Inquiry* gives the author Zara Yaqob's birthdate as the '25th of Nahase, in the 3rd year of the reign of Yaqob, 1,592 years after the birth of Christ' (61). When this date is converted from the Ethiopian (Julian-based) calendar to the European Gregorian calendar, it corresponds to 28 August 1600. Giusto da Urbino's birthday was 30 August 1814, two days later. So, they are close but not the same. However, because of differences between the Gregorian and Ethiopian calendar over time, the 25th of Nahase in the 1800s *would have been* 30 August 1814, the year of Giusto da Urbino's birth. The day and the month match exactly. This is extremely tough to explain away. For many, the improbability of Giusto da Urbino and Zara Yaqob's birth days and birth months matching is so high that they consider this a closed case.

The third major pillar of the prosecution's case is a rumour that Giusto da Urbino had authored the *Hatata Zara Yaqob*. In 1916, during World War I, Conti Rossini translated into Italian a biography written in Amharic by his friend *Abba* Takla Haymanot, a Catholic convert who had died in 1902 (Takla Haymanot 1914). Conti Rossini also translated a few of the notes that Takla Haymanot had made for this biography (Conti Rossini 1916) and then later published the original Amharic wording (Conti Rossini 1920). In these notes for the book, which only Conti Rossini has ever seen, Takla Haymanot stated that Giusto da Urbino had 'purchased a book containing the evil/false doctrine of the heretics called the freemasons [framassoni]' (Conti Rossini 1916, 77). He gave the title of this book as *Uorché* (the nickname, Warqe, given in *Hatata Zara Yaqob* for its author). In this sentence, Takla Haymanot states, in effect, that Giusto da Urbino was *not* the fraudulent author of this book. He confirms what Giusto da Urbino claimed, that he 'purchased' the book. However, according to Conti Rossini's Italian translation of these Amharic notes, Takla Haymanot privately wrote another sentence, contradicting his previous one. He stated,

'Some of those who saw the book say that it was not by Uorché, but that it had been written by himself and that it had been falsely attributed to Uorché' (Conti Rossini 1916, 78, as translated in Sumner 1976, 65).[1]

Based on the similarity of names and birthdays and the hearsay about authorship, scholars began to ask important questions about Giusto da Urbino's skills, personality, and writing. For a European to produce a fake of this complexity, he would need to have superb skills in Ge'ez and be an unethical heretic. Also, aspects of his writing found elsewhere should peek through in the *Hatata Inquiries*.

In fact, Giusto da Urbino had real skills in Ge'ez (Conti Rossini 1920, 214–216), as demonstrated by his dictionary and grammar.[2] Most European scholars of Ge'ez only translate *from* Ge'ez. An unusual skill he had was translating *into* Ge'ez, meaning that he would be more able to draft an original composition in Ge'ez. He also took notes on Ge'ez poetics, demonstrating a clear interest in literary matters.

Conti Rossini and Wion also argued that he had the personality traits required to commit this forgery. Conti Rossini claimed that Giusto da Urbino had an 'excessive affection' for Ethiopia, boasted about his Ge'ez skills, was 'embittered', and had doubts about his faith (Conti Rossini 1920, 217, 216, 219–220). The article is quite short, as is the evidence. But Wion expanded on his point by using Giusto da Urbino's letters to create a psychological profile of the priest. He was, she wrote, 'a man caught between the desire to hide, to bury himself, to be forgotten by his society and its constraints, and the desire to be recognized, to shine, to contribute something new, something real' (Wion 2013a; 2021a, 17). Specifically, she reported, Giusto da Urbino thought he was 'born to write' (32) and wanted to write an autobiography titled 'History of My Thought' (32); however, he concluded that he was only capable of writing a novel (Wion 2013a, 32, 32, 16). He believed that all his writing was 'worthless' 'nonsense' (12) but asked that, if someone found otherwise, that his writing be published 'anonymously or under some other name . . . This is so that my work doesn't perish with me—I who am very perishable' (27). Wion's portrait of Giusto da Urbino's mental state is a major contribution to the debate.

---

[1] In her draft translation of Conti Rossini 's article, Lea Cantor translates the last words of the sentence as 'fictitiously attributed to Uorché' (Conti Rossini 2022).

[2] Regarding the Ge'ez texts in the five manuscripts that Giusto da Urbino wrote, see the full citations and contents in (Sumner 1976, 216–217, passim). He created a Ge'ez-Latin dictionary (56 folios), which he describes as the 'first . . . product of his first studies' in Ge'ez (Sumner 1976, 219). He later expanded this (102 folios) (Sumner 1976, 221–222). He wrote a short grammar (a study of Ge'ez verbs; 7 folios), and then expanded this (137 folios) (Sumner 1976, 219, 221–222). It is digitized and available online at https://eap.bl.uk/archive-file/EAP286-1-2-13, last accessed on 14 June 2023. He wrote an analysis of Ge'ez poetry (29 folios) (Sumner 1976, 221). He translated from Latin into Amharic (the *Doctrina Christiana*) and from Ge'ez into Latin (the Book of Baptism and the Missal).

Scholars have also sifted through Giusto da Urbino's writing to look for associated topics and wording in the *Hatata Inquiries*. They see correspondences in these two things as additional proof. Some topics that appear in the *Hatata Zara Yaqob* also appear in Giusto da Urbino's Geʻez (and Amharic) translation of a French text called *Soirées de Carthage*—a Catholic tract composed by the priest Francois Bourgade and published in Paris in 1847 (Bourgade 1847). *Soirées de Carthage* discusses Islam and Indian religions; the *Hatata Zara Yaqob* briefly addresses Islam and Indian religions (Conti Rossini 1920; Mittwoch 1934; Wion 2013b). *Soirées de Carthage* mentions 'Sabaeans'; *Hatata Walda Heywat* mentions 'Himyar and Saba' (121) (Mittwoch 1934). In terms of wording, some have argued that the *Hatata Inquiries*' tendency to place the subject before the verb suggested the author was a native speaker of a Romance language (Mittwoch 1934). Wion has argued that the *Hatata Zara Yaqob's* way of announcing the year is rare.

In terms of his writing in general, Wion has examined the manuscripts and made new philological arguments. She argues that the differences between the two manuscript copies of the *Hatata Zara Yaqob* (d'Abbadie 215 [which contains both *Hatata Inquiries*] and d'Abbadie 234 [which contains only the first *Hatata Inquiry*]) suggest a process of revision by Giusto da Urbino (Wion 2021b, 18–20). Wion created a chart of differences she felt were too substantial to be anything other than an author revising his own work. Wion also argues that a short ten-line poem in Geʻez written in Giusto da Urbino's handwriting at the beginning of his Geʻez translation of *Soirées de Carthage* (Vatican Et. MS No. 165) and his grammar (Wion 2021b, 13) is his own composition and that the presence of both names—Yostos and Yaqob—in the poem is evidence of a split self that produced the forgery (Wion 2021b, 11–12).

To sum up, the case for European authorship depends most strongly on three pillars: the similarity of Giusto da Urbino's name and birthdate with the author of the *Hatata Zara Yaqob* and the hearsay about Giusto da Urbino's authorship. Others have added to the case by examining Giusto da Urbino's skills, personality, and writing.

Rebuttal of the Case for European Authorship

No unequivocal evidence exists that a European wrote the *Hatata Inquiries*. First, there is no signed confession from the alleged European author. A signed confession has always been the gold standard of proof. Should one be uncovered, it would have to be indisputably from the period, indisputably in this author's handwriting, and indisputably state that he invented the texts wholesale, on his own, without extensive drafting or editing by Ethiopians. Second, there is no extant autograph (original manuscript) of these texts in the alleged European author's handwriting. Should some be uncovered, the drafts would need to be of both texts, indisputably in his handwriting, and indisputably demonstrate the composition process. Third, there is no self-plagiarism—no sentences in the *Hatata Inquiries* can be traced directly to something Giusto da Urbino is known to have wrote. We have no confession, no drafts, no sentences. As the scholar Marchiotto concluded, 'without proofs external to the works themselves', the case against their Ethiopian authorship can never be proven.[1]

Names and Birthdays

Two of the most significant pieces of evidence for European authorship are similarities in name and birthdate. Rebutting this evidence depends in part on arguing that the similarities are not meaningful but rather statistically possible coincidences, the result of random chance. Fortunately, the defence's case is stronger than that—the similarities are not exact.

Regarding the potential coincidence of names, the premise is wrong. Giusto da Urbino did not consider his first name to be Jacopo (Jacob in English). He told his patron d'Abbadie that his birth first name was Gian-Giacomo (John-James in English) (Sumner 1976, 202).[2] If he were intending to leave a trace of himself with the name Zara Yaqob, he would not have told his patron that his name was something other than Jacob. So, the two names are not similar—John-James and Zara Yaqob. Even if they were, Jacob has long been the most popular name for men in

---

[1] (Marchiotto 1964–1965, 174–175, as cited and translated in Sumner 1976, 80). He also wrote that 'nothing decisive for the question of authenticity can honestly be concluded' if the argument is based 'exclusively on the internal examination of this work, even if this examination is conducted with cool philological and scientific competence' (Marchiotto 1964–1965, 32, 19–20), as cited and translated in (Sumner 1976, 80).

[2] According to his own baptismal record, Giusto da Urbino's name was 'Giovanni Iacopo' (note that there is no *J*) (Sumner 1976, 201). The first work on him mistakenly said that his baptismal name was Jacopo Curtopassi (Tarducci 1899). Scholars followed, with Conti Rossini wrongly giving his name as 'Jacopo Curtopassi di Matraia' (Conti Rossini 1916, 498). But that is not his name. Rather, that is a misspelling of his grandfather's name—'Iacopo Cortopassi di Matraja' (no *J* in the first name and no *u* in the second name)—according to the matrimonial license cited and translated in (Sumner 1976, 200, 202, 203). As Sumner points out, his birth name could have been rendered into Ge'ez quite naturally (Sumner 1976, 202). Meanwhile, he appears in the scholarship under several names. In the French scholarly literature, he is referred to as Juste d'Urbin, Just d'Urbin, Iustus Urbinos, or Abba Iustus (Conti Rossini and BNF 1914, 222; Grébaut and Tisserant 1935, 170–172). He published in Italian under 'G. d'Urbino' (Sumner 1976, 242). In Ge'ez texts, he is called *Abba* Yostos (Grébaut and Tisserant 1935, 613–614). See also (Pietruschka and Bausi 2010; Crummey 2007).

the Christian world, competing only with John in popularity. Indeed, the name is so common that another Catholic priest in Ethiopia at the time, the one about whom Takla Haymanot wrote his book, was called Giustino da Jacob.[1] So, Jacob is one of the few names where coincidence is a reasonable explanation.

Regarding the potential coincidence of birthdates, again, the premise is wrong. The birthdates are not the same. Zara Yaqob's birthday was 25 Nahase 1592 (28 August 1600), and Giusto da Urbino's was 30 August 1814. It is two days off. If Giusto da Urbino had been born in 1600, his 30 August birthday would have fallen on 27 Nahase, not 25 Nahase. However, due to increasing differences between the European Gregorian and Ethiopian calendar, Giusto da Urbino's birthday in 1814 would have fallen on 25 Nahase. Now, if Giusto da Urbino allegedly wanted to put a subtle clue to his authorship, he faced a dilemma. Either he made the month and day match his modern birth date or he made it match the historical period he had painstakingly invented. Why would Giusto da Urbino go to all the trouble of making the stated birth date so extremely precise in the manuscript (25th Nahase, 3rd year of Yaqob's reign, 1,592 years) only to ruin it with his modern birth date? Certainly, the other dates in the *Hatata Inquiries* for the 1600s are remarkably precise (such as the years of kings' reigns, the beginning of Catholic persecution of EOTC members, and the weekday name matching the weekday number for that month in a particular year of the 1600s).[2] If he was a fraud, he was a meticulous one who did not make dating errors.

An alternate explanation would be that Giusto da Urbino himself altered the day in the manuscripts, upon seeing that he shared the same month of birth with the author. Statistically, it is more likely that Giusto da Urbino spent a few minutes tampering with the date than two years faking the texts. In the end, however, this evidence is very tough to explain away. It is the prosecution's best and strongest evidence.

However, even if Zara Yaqob and Giusto da Urbino were born on the same day and month, such a coincidence is not impossible. Statistically, the chance is one in

---

[1] Also called Mgr. de Iacobis or Justin De Jacobis (Takla-Haymanot 1914, 1). Alemayehu adds that most of the foreigners who came to Ethiopia had some variant of this name, including James Bruce. In the *Encyclopaedia Aethiopica* Index, these names appear frequently: Yaʿəqob (122 times) and Zärʾa Yaʿəqob (62 times); Jacob (98 times), James (44 times), and Jacques (12 times).

[2] Even today, using computerized calendars, scholars find matching days, dates, and years in the past tremendously difficult. Sumner documents the numerous computer programs, sources, and people he had to consult to affirm the dates (Sumner 1976, 136). Unfortunately, some conjectures that Getatchew Haile made about dating in the *Hatata Inquiries* (Getatchew Haile 2017), which I would otherwise have mentioned here, turned out to be erroneous because he had access only to the murky black and white images of the texts.

365 rather than, say, one in a million.¹ The chance of being born in the same month is one in 12. Since August is the second most common birth month in both Italy and Ethiopia, the chances of this coincidence are even a bit higher than that.² Birthday coincidences are unlikely, but they are possible. Further, one must compare this one-in-365 chance with the one-in-a-million chance that a pious European priest would learn enough Ge'ez to invent two long, complicated, accurate, and deeply ethical works from another period and unethically pass them off as his own.

Of course, the prosecution could argue that Giusto da Urbino deliberately differentiated the names and dates and the slight difference is what really proves he invented the texts. He wanted to leave a clue but not too obvious a one. But this is a slippery slope. At first, similitude is the proof; then, variation is the proof. At what point is the distance too far to be proof?

In the end, the prosecution's proof depends on a paradox, requiring both a trace and the lack of a trace. Perhaps this is why, tellingly, neither Conti Rossini nor Mittwoch articulate what the observed similarities means. They simply declare the similarities.³ Maybe they realized that articulating the assumption at the heart of their argument would sound silly: A European carved versions of his name and birthday on two magnificent texts of extraordinary depth so that future generations could come to know that they were fraudulent and admire him.

Hearsay

There is only one other strong piece of evidence for European authorship—Takla Haymanot's hearsay about Giusto da Urbino's authorship. As it is hearsay, it would not be admissible in a court of law. Even if it were, this form of it would not be.

For one, Conti Rossini is the only person who has ever seen Takla Haymanot's notes with the relevant sentence. The scholarship has assumed that Conti Rossini accurately represented the notes' contents. But if the Italian priest Giusto da Urbino

---

1 It is interesting to note the probability theory called the 'birthday paradox' (Relf 1999). Counterintuitively, due to compounding, in a random group of twenty-three people, the chance that two people will have the same birthday is 50 percent. In a group of fifty-seven people, the chance is almost 100 percent. (Kostadinov 2013).
2 In Italy today, September and then August are the most common birth months (United Nations Statistics Division 2022). The UN has no statistics on common birth months in highland Ethiopia, but data on neighbouring countries suggests that July and August are the most common birth months (Taei 2018; United Nations Statistics Division 2022). Therefore, an August birthdate for two different people, one born in Italy and one born in Ethiopia, is statistically more likely than a common birthday in ten other months.
3 Conti Rossini wrote only 'Iacopo finds a match in the name of the author' (Conti Rossini 2023, 219).

can be suspected of spending two years falsifying two entire books, then the Italian Fascist Conti Rossini can certainly be suspected of spending a few minutes inventing or tampering with a single sentence. For instance, Conti Rossini recorded that Takla Haymanot's notes use the word 'freemason' to describe the *Hatata Inquiries*. Why would Takla Haymanot use this term? Freemasonry only arrived in the Horn of Africa in 1909, after Takla Haymanot died (in 1902) (Prijac 2014). Perhaps Takla Haymanot had learned the term during his Catholic education as a generic term used to condemn 'free thinkers' of any sort, but the word 'freemason' does not appear anywhere in Takla Haymanot's book. Nor does the term appear anywhere else in the archive as a veiled reference to Giusto da Urbino, who definitively was not a member of the freemasons (which Catholicism had long condemned as bordering on the Satanic).

Now, for the sake of argument, let us assume that Conti Rossini reported accurately on Takla Haymanot's notes. But Takla Haymanot had never himself seen, much less read, either text (Sumner 1976, 250). He knew so little about them that he gave the wrong title for the first *Hatata Inquiry* and accused it of expressing materialism and atheism, which is the direct opposite of its contents (Sumner 1976, 187–188, 197–198). Further, Takla Haymanot hated Giusto da Urbino, in part for bringing to light what Takla Haymanot felt were shameful texts (Sumner 1976, 187–193, 250–252).[1] His actions against Giusto da Urbino were so marked that the Catholic Church conducted a covert investigation of Takla Haymanot.[2]

I suspect that what really happened is this. The good Christian Takla Haymanot had heard about these heretical texts and was upset about their association with Ethiopia. Someone else saw Giusto da Urbino writing out his copy of the *Hatata Zara Yaqob* on paper (Abb 234). This observer, never having seen a European write Ge'ez before, commented on this surprising act to others. Someone else misheard or took the opportunity to insinuate that Giusto da Urbino was no mere copyist but the actual inventor of this offensive text.[3] Takla Haymanot heard about this rumour

---

[1] Among other actions, Takla Haymanot machinated to prevent Giusto da Urbino's return to Ethiopia (Sumner 1976, 193). Also, although present at the events that led to Giusto da Urbino's forced expulsion, Takla Haymanot wrote that Giusto da Urbino was not forced out but left of this own free will (Sumner 1976, 243–245).

[2] In the report, the church accused him of 'calumny' (Sumner 1976, 193). Of course, it is quite possible that an Ethiopian Catholic would have on-the-ground knowledge that the European missionaries did not. But it is clear Takla Haymanot does not, as he wrote secretly to an Ethiopian monk soliciting any negative information about Giusto da Urbino, never mentioning the issue of authorship (Sumner 1976, 192–195).

[3] (Krackovskii 1924, 205–206) makes a similar argument, commenting that 'there is no doubt that Takla Haymanot was a better Catholic than Giusto da Urbino' and that this heretical text 'arose indignation among pious Catholics'—so much so that it was 'only one step' to 'insinuate that the

and documented the face-saving theory that the text was heretical and (therefore,) a (wicked) foreigner wrote it, not any (good) Ethiopian.

One reason I suspect this is what happened is that Takla Haymanot himself clearly doubted the rumour. He did not include it in the actual book. He did not word his report on it strongly, even in his own private notes, where he was free to be direct. He uses passive voice thrice in the Amharic of the sentence: 'Some of those who saw the book say that *it was not by* Uorché, but that *it had been written by* himself and that *it had been* falsely attributed to Uorché' (Conti Rossini 1920, italics added). In court cases, lawyers frequently interpret witnesses using passive voice as due to their 'doubt' about defendants' 'culpability' (Krishnakumar 2011). The purpose of the passive voice is to avoid naming actors. Here, Takla Haymanot absented not just the offender and the accusers but also the attributor.[1] Takla Haymanot's tentative wording demonstrates that he himself did not trust the information he had collected. Despite this, scholars have treated as fact what Takla Haymanot presents as speculation.

To sum up, this hearsay evidence is unreliable. It appeared in a single sentence in a handwritten note, absent any names, written by a person angry with another about a text he had never read, repeating information he had heard third-hand, that he did not trust—and only one (hostile) scholar ever saw it.

Ge'ez Skills

Conti Rossini argued that Giusto da Urbino had the skills in Ge'ez to pull off a forgery of this sophistication. Yet it strains credulity that Giusto da Urbino's Ge'ez became so good in just 3.5 years (from 1849, when he began his studies in Ge'ez, to early 1853, when the first *Hatata Inquiry* is dated) that he could do the following: produce two long, well-written and largely error-free texts—drawing deeply on a huge corpus of Ge'ez proverbs, stories, and literature, as well as specific forms of prosody and rhetoric and before any published Ge'ez dictionary existed—in about eight months.[2]

---

work of a freethinker whose copies Padre Giusto distributed to a friend was written by himself' (as cited and translated in Sumner 1976, 84). (Marchiotto 1964–1965, 183) also dismissed the allegation, saying that perhaps Takla Haymanot was jealous.

1 The wording of 'falsely attributed' suggests that someone other than Giusto da Urbino was trying to pass the text off as authentic. Yet it cannot be that Giusto da Urbino innocently drafted them as his own works and someone else circulated them falsely. Giusto da Urbino always claimed that others had written them.

2 Giusto da Urbino began studying Arabic in 1845 (Pietruschka and Bausi 2010) and Ge'ez in the middle of 1849 (Simon 1936, 96), as cited and translated in (Sumner 1976, 236). Giusto da Urbino first mentions the *Soirées* translation three years later, in a letter from 26 May 1852, as cited and translat-

This would be a superhuman accomplishment. Even Ethiopian scholars with deep lived knowledge of Ethiopian languages take decades to learn the various Geʿez texts and their interpretative traditions. Further, none of Giusto da Urbino's other work in the language of Geʿez was in the genre of the *Hatata Inquiries*. It was all technical and linguistic—producing dictionaries and grammars—not writerly or philosophical. A feat of fakery at this skill level and in this short a time is impossible.

Giusto da Urbino's known work in Geʿez proves that he was no such superhuman expert. Sumner eviscerates its quality, agreeing with Giusto da Urbino's own assessment that it was 'imperfect'.[1] A survey of his copying of qene poems reveals an 'appalling' number of errors, those of someone without an ear for the language (Sumner 1976, 253). For instance, he has miscopied word endings at line ends, thus ruining the rhyme, and made mistakes in the number of syllables, thus ruining the rhythm (Sumner 1976, 226–227). As Sumner wryly notes, a poet making these types of mistakes in front of Ethiopian qene poets would be drummed off the stage (Sumner 1976, 227).[2] In a publication in Italian, he misspells an ethnic term and a geographic term, terms always spelled correctly in the *Hatata Inquiries*.[3] Perhaps most telling, errors occur in Giusto da Urbino's rendering of one of the church's most common prayers, one every Ethiopian knows by heart. Giusto da Urbino had 'a serious ignorance of the language' (Sumner 1976, 219).[4]

Sumner adds that it would be 'useless to record all the mistakes' as it 'would require hundreds of pages'; therefore, Sumner provides examples from just the first nine pages of one work (Sumner 1976, 219–221). In one case, Giusto da Urbino 'makes 48 mistakes out of a total of 118 words: an average of one mistake for every

---

ed in (Sumner 1976, 73). Giusto da Urbino sent the *Hatata Inquiries* to d'Abbadie eight months after that, in February 1853 (Sumner 1976, 67, 82). Thus, Giusto da Urbino would have had a mere eight months for composition. Meanwhile, he could not have been focusing exclusively on them. During this period, he was also composing his dictionary (the first draft of which he completed around April 14, 1853) and his grammar (Sumner 1976, 219).

1 It appears in a note that Giusto da Urbino wrote on 14 April 1853 in his dictionary on folio 2v, describing it as 'imperfect' and warning anyone from treating it as an 'authority... on the subject of the Ethiopic language'; as cited and translated in (Sumner 1976, 219).

2 'At this point, Ethiopian poets stop listening any more to a poem that is twice "broken;" they agitate the sistrum to indicate that the rhythm of the poem is "broken"' (Sumner 1976, 227).

3 In the Italian publication, he spells አምሐራ (Amḥara) as Amara (omitting one of the consonants) and ተከዜ (Täkkäze) as Taccare (replacing the final *z* with an *r* instead) (Sumner 1976, 241–242). In particular, the latter error reveals a person with little ear for the language. In addition, the Takkaze River is very important in the HZY, where it is spelled correctly.

4 Other evidence that he was no language savant is that his written French was full of errors (Wion 2013b; Sumner 1976, 224, passim). Finally, even if one could prove that Giusto da Urbino was *capable* of forging some kind of Geʿez text does not prove he *did* do it. That he had the skills is necessary evidence for the prosecution's case, not sufficient evidence.

2.45 words' (Sumner 1976, 219). This would not be A+ work in a Ge'ez class of today; in fact, it would not earn a passing grade. Indeed, Sumner concludes, 'the number and the magnitude of the errors [in Giusto da Urbino's extant Ge'ez manuscripts] are so great that one wonders how the author of such incorrect Ge'ez could turn out to be, in the short space of three or four years, one of the greatest masters of qene Ge'ez Ethiopia has known' (Sumner 1976, 219, 250). Now, some have privately said to me that Sumner's own work on Giusto da Urbino's errors has errors, with some typos and mistakes. But even if only a quarter of what Sumner lays out is true, Giusto da Urbino was no Ge'ez savant.

Further, the Ge'ez of the two *Hatata Inquiries* is much better than the Ge'ez in Giusto da Urbino's translation of *Soirées de Carthage*, which he ostensibly did in the same year. In the latter appear mistakes in subject-verb agreement, confusions of subject and object, correct letters 'corrected' to wrong letters, and non-existent word forms (Sumner 1976, 237–238, 253). And it cannot have been that the Ethiopian who served as Giusto da Urbino's scribe corrected the *Hatata Inquires* to be better. Sumner and the scholars he consulted did not judge his Ge'ez good enough to do so (Sumner 1976, 235–236, 253). He was an excellent copyist, not a scholar.

An experience that we had in translating the *Hatata Inquiries'* content brought home to me the improbability of European authorship. Ralph Lee, the primary translator, is a gifted European scholar of Ge'ez. He lived in Ethiopia for decades, far longer than Giusto da Urbino's handful of years. Like Giusto da Urbino, Lee studied Ge'ez language and literature exclusively, with EOTC intellectuals. Indeed, he became so knowledgeable that he was invited to teach (in Amharic) at the EOTC seminary for many years, a rare honour. There, he spent years discussing EOTC theology, commentary, and Ge'ez texts. Several Ethiopians have privately told me that his Amharic and Ge'ez are flawless. He has published many scholarly articles and books, especially on the Ge'ez Bible. No matter how good Giusto da Urbino became in a few years, it is impossible that Lee is not better. Now, in completing the first draft of the *Hatata Inquiries*, one thing Lee did was work to identify which passages were quotations, paraphrases, or allusions to other texts. While Sumner and others worked on this already, Lee was able to identify many more. He knows the tradition more deeply. Then, we invited Mehari Worku to join the translation team. Like Lee, Mehari had spent many years studying EOTC theology and Ge'ez literature. But he also grew up in the church, got his first education in the church, and memorized vast swathes of the Bible as a child, unlike Lee or Giusto da Urbino. Something became quite clear to me through the process for Mehari's contributions to the translations, which involved me reading Lee's draft translations aloud while Mehari read along in the original Ge'ez manuscripts (not the Littmann edition), offering his thoughts on how the translations could be refined. He had many great suggestions. But what struck me most was how frequently Mehari would be reading a Geʿez sentence and say, instantaneously, 'That's from Psalm 118 verse 71' or 'That's a proverb in Amharic, which goes like this...' or 'that's from *Sayings of the Philosophers*, Chapter 3...' The language of the Geʿez was so familiar to him, and the array of Geʿez texts so known, that the many allusions were immediately apparent to him. He quickly and easily recognized many allusions that European scholars had missed. For me, this was a profound proof. If Lee, one of the best European scholars of Geʿez, could not do what Mehari Worku could do, how could Giusto da Urbino?

Personality

Conti Rossini's and Wion's proofs about Giusto da Urbino's state of mind are among the strongest proofs we have that he was *not* the author. Their premise is wrong, based on a fundamental misunderstanding of the tenor of the *Hatata Inquiries*. Both texts are quite joyful. They are not in any way bitter screeds but rather are celebratory—whether about creation, marriage, or humanity's intellectual capacity. Yes, both have sober warnings about humanity and religion, but they are not despairing. Yes, the author of the *Hatata Zara Yaqob* had a grim time when he fled human company, and declared that he hated it, but that is only in the opening of the text. Most of his life happened after he found a new family and happily lived in their community for decades. It is during those years that he wrote his text, and it shows. Meanwhile, the always forgotten *Hatata Walda Heywat* has no moments of even momentary loneliness or bitterness. If Giusto da Urbino is the bitter, disturbed, unethical person Conti Rossini and Wion say he was, he did not write these texts.

Meanwhile, the arguments about Giusto da Urbino having unorthodox religious views are ill-supported. Sumner argued that Giusto da Urbino's letters and scholarship do not reveal someone in 'spiritual crisis' (Sumner 1976, 137). A great disparity exists between Giusto da Urbino's traditional views, as revealed by his letters and writing, and the radical views of the *Hatata Inquiries* (Sumner 1976, 175–181, 251, passim). As he summarized, 'on all the substantial points of the Catholic religion [his] agreement [with church doctrine] is complete', and 'he believed in essential tenets of revealed Christianity[, ones] which are in direct opposition to [those of the *Hatata Inquiries*]' (Sumner 1976, 166).

Sumner reviews Giusto da Urbino's attitude toward each of these tenets. Nothing in Giusto da Urbino's letters suggests that he had radical beliefs for a Catholic priest of the 1800s. Yet the *Hatata Inquiries* have sections on women's equality and sensual pleasure. Giusto da Urbino was actively engaged in attacking heresy and forwarding Christian doctrine (Sumner 1976, 256). For instance, he published articles 'in favour of the Catholic truth' and wrote letters that 'said such beautiful things in favour of the

Pope and of Catholicism, that it endeared him' to church leadership (Sumner 1976, 251). By contrast, the *Hatata Inquiries* reject Christianity and its various churches. Giusto da Urbino earnestly explained to the Oromo community why priestly celibacy was important (letter sent on 24 February 1848), as cited and summarized in (Sumner 1976, 217). By contrast, the *Hatata Inquiries* both lambasted priestly celibacy. Giusto da Urbino was very Christ-centric (Sumner 1976, 166–173) and very devoted to the Virgin Mary (Sumner 1976, 141, 216). By contrast, the *Hatata Inquiries* never mention her and Jesus Christ only rarely. While Giusto da Urbino did admire the Ethiopian language, he repeatedly celebrated his civilizing mission to 'savages' and lambasted the beliefs of Orthodox Christians as 'heretical' in a multiplicity of ways.[1] No such contempt is found in the *Hatata Inquiries*.

Manuscript Philology

Some scholars have argued that the syntax or diction of the *Hatata Inquiries* reveals a European author. As mentioned before, Mittwoch wrote that the *Hatata Inquiries*' tendency to place the subject before the verb meant the author was a native speaker of a Romance language (Mittwoch 1934). But Amsalu Aklilu provided proof that this is a common pattern of Geʿez texts, giving dozens of examples from the Geʿez Bible, dozens and dozens of examples from Geʿez poetry, and many from original prose compositions in Geʿez (Amsalu Aklilu 1984). He also cites no less an authority than August Dillmann, who commented on the loose sentence construction of Geʿez, in which 'sometimes the verb comes before the subject, while at other times the subject is found written before the object' (Dillmann 1899 as cited and translated in Sumner 1976, 87). Indeed, this openness, Amsalu argued, constitutes the greatness of the Geʿez language.

As mentioned, Wion has argued that *Hatata Zara Yaqob's* way of announcing the year is telling. It uses the phrase አም ልደተ ክርስቶስ (əm-lədätä Krəstos) (after the birth of Christ) (61) rather than the more common ዓመተ ምሕረት (ʿamätä məḥrät) (year of mercy) or ዓመተ ሥጋዌ (ʿamätä śəggawe) (year of incarnation). All of Giusto da

---

1 In letters to his sister, he regularly referred to some Ethiopians as 'savages' and bemoaned his 'arid study of a savage language', as cited and translated in (Sumner 1976, 138, 141, 143). For instance, he wrote her that he was proud 'to propagate the principles of European civilization amongst savage peoples, ... to educate, to civilize, ... to milden barbaric customs', as cited and translated in (Sumner 1976, 215). In one of his Italian publications, Giusto da Urbino wrote regarding 'Abyssinian Christianity' that 'the baptism conferred by [these] heretics is not valid, and so many other heretical or superstitious beliefs I do not remember' (*Spettatore egiziano* No. 19, page 2, as cited and translated in Sumner 1976, 248–249).

Urbino's colophons, including that of the translation of the *Soirées de Carthage*, use the first phrase. However, this wording is not at all rare. In a single hour, we found many examples in Geʿez manuscripts across the centuries.[1]

As mentioned, Wion believed that a ten-line poem in Geʿez was Giusto da Urbino's own composition, with traces of the split self that produced the forgery (Wion 2021b, 13). But, Mehari Worku explains, the poem being in Giusto da Urbino's handwriting is easily explained: Ethiopian poets never write down their qene—considering them ephemeral, occasional. The poem exists in Giusto da Urbino's handwriting because he copied it down during a performance in his honour. Instantly composing and performing a poem for a visitor is a long-time tradition in Ethiopia; a foreigner can have the experience even today by visiting an establishment with Ethiopian bards, called Azmaris, who compose double-meaning, pun-filled songs on the spot. We know that this is the case, that the poem was composed *for* him, not *by* him, because of the opening line: 'Abba Yostos says'. Authors do not begin poems in the third person. Rather, the Ethiopian author is setting up his teasing commentary, ventriloquizing Giusto da Urbino. Further, Mehari Worku points out that Giusto da Urbino would not be allowed to study formally in *qene bet* after just a few years of studying Geʿez. Finally, Giusto da Urbino is not known to have written any fiction or poetry, whether in European languages or Geʿez, despite scholars mistakenly asserting that Giusto da Urbino composed 'poems' in the language, due to carelessly repeating I. I. Krackovskii's and Enrico Cerulli's misunderstanding of a sentence in Conti Rossini (Sumner 1976, 225; Conti Rossini and BNF 1914).[2]

As mentioned, Wion has argued that the differences between the two manuscript copies of the *Hatata Zara Yaqob* are too substantial to be anything other than an author revising his own work (Wion 2021b, 18–20). Yet Wion acknowledges that

---

[1] In an hour, Mehari Worku found this phrase in multiple manuscripts, including a 1300s Library of Congress manuscript (Ethiopic 6, f. 199v) that has አም ልደተ ክርስቶስ እስከ ዲዮቅልጥያኖስ (after the birth of Christ to Diocletian...); a 1400s HMML manuscript (EMML 2063, f. 47v) that has አም ልደተ እግዚእነ ክርስቶስ (after the birth of Our Lord Christ); and a late 1600s HMML manuscript (EMML 50, f. 138v and f. 152v) that has እምልደተ ክርስቶስ እመንግሥተ ባዜን እስከ አብርሃ ወአጽብሐ (after the birth of Christ, from the reign of Bazen to Abräha and Aṣbaḥa) and እምልደተ ክርስቶስ እስከ እምነተ ኢትዮጵያ (after the birth of Christ to Ethiopia's conversion). One sees the phrase today in print manuscripts, as in the 1996 *Taʾammera Maryam*, which has ወበሠርቱ ወሰመንቱ ምዕት ስማንያ ወክልኤቱ ዓመት እምልደተ ለእግዚእነ ኢየሱስ ክርስቶስ (In the 1882nd year after the birth of Our Lord Jesus Christ) (Tasfa Gabra Selasse 1996, 1000). It also appears in the 1500s in Confessio Fidei of King Claudius of Ethiopia 'written in the year 1555 from the birth of our Lord Jesus Christ' (Ullendorff 1987).

[2] Regarding the error of mistaking copied poems for composed poems, see (Sumner 1976, 225, 235). Regarding the poems he copied, see (Grébaut and Tisserant 1935; Grébaut 1935; 1926). Takla Haymanot's notes, according to (Conti Rossini 1920, 218), also state that Giusto da Urbino composed poems but Takla Haymanot's knowledge and motivations are suspect.

the changes are rarely to the ideas, only to the wording: 'Most of the modifications consist in slight adjustments to the syntax which serve to clarify, specify, embellish or nuance the first version of the text' (Wion 2021b, 21). For her, however, this very slightness is still telling: 'One senses an author anxious to deliver a beautiful text but unwilling to modify the content' (Wion 2021b, 21). Our interpretation, following Getatchew Haile, is quite different, as we lay out in full in our Manuscripts of the Text section and the Appendices. Such changes, both minor and major, are common in the Ethiopian copying process. As one scholar puts it, 'It is hardly exaggerated to say that every Ethiopian scribe in his own way is an "Editor"' (Zuurmond 1989, 39). In the end, the minor changes in Abb 215 (the later manuscript) make it more closely resemble Abb 234 (the earlier manuscript). This is the opposite of writerly revision, returning it to the original. Then, the few substantive changes in Abb 215 likely arise for two reasons. One, from being copied from a different manuscript than Abb 234. Two, from Walda Heywat editing his teacher's work, intensifying Zara Yaqob's points, especially regarding Islam (see Appendix 2).

Wion's articles would have been strengthened if she had consulted the research about authorship published after the 1930s. Her articles proceed without awareness of the rebuttals of Conti Rossini and Eugen Mittwoch's work. For instance, she takes as given Conti Rossini's overvaluation of Giusto da Urbino's skills, while Sumner has dozens of pages of proof showing that they were weak. She cites only one Ethiopian article on the authorship debate, and then only to say that it 'ignored the Western academic debate' (Wion 2021b, 21). Wion does cite Sumner, but only his helpful primary source translations—she does not discuss his arguments or evidence.

Topics and Wording

A final type of evidence is the similarities between the *Hatata Inquiries* and Giusto da Urbino's life, letters, and other known writings. I find this evidence the least persuasive and so have left it for last. Too much of it is a kind of astrology, manufacturing signs of deep meaning out of the perfectly ordinary. Not one of the similarities are the type of similarity that would constitute real proof: whole paragraphs or sentences repeated verbatim.

In terms of Giusto da Urbino's life, we get such banal observations as the following: Zara Yaqob had an ugly wife, while Giusto da Urbino had an ugly maid; Zara Yaqob lived in Aksum, Tigré, and Enferaz, Amhara, while Giusto da Urbino lived in Gwala, Tigré, and Beta Lehem, Amhara; Zara Yaqob mentions the labour of the poor, and Giusto da Urbino too mentions the labour of the poor. Certainly, any two religious and scholarly men living in the same country will have similar lives.

In terms of content, as mentioned earlier, some have made much of *Soirées de Carthage* (a French text that Giusto da Urbino translated into Geʻez) and the *Hatata Inquiries* having three topics in common. Are these topics peculiar, rare ones, about which one could make a compelling argument? No, quite the opposite.

First, both texts address the perennially popular topic of Islam. The assumption that Islam is a uniquely European topic is odd to say the least. The differences between Muslims and Christians are a frequent topic of conversation in Ethiopia, especially in church schools.[1] The *Hatata Zara Yaqob*'s critique of Islam for its practices of polygamy and the slave trade are nothing unusual for Ethiopia, needing no dependence on *Soirées de Carthage*'s critique of the same. As early as the 1300s, Ethiopian intellectuals were criticizing slavery (Anonymous 1906, 19). Further, the tenor of the remarks about Islam are quite different. Giusto da Urbino and the author of *Soirées de Carthage* made some positive statements about Muslims, and were great admirers of the Quran, while the *Hatata Zara Yaqob* describes Islam only negatively (Sumner 1976, 208–209).

Second, both texts address Indian religion. Yet India has been Ethiopia's major trade partner for over a thousand years. The Geʻez *Synaxarium* depicts preaching the Gospel in India (Alemayyehu Moges 1968, 24) and the Geʻez *Taʼammera Maryam* (Book of the Miracles of Saint Mary) depicts apostles living in India. The Indian contributions to the design of the castles built in Ethiopia in the 1600s are well documented (Windmuller-Luna 2016). The ancient Saint Thomas Christian Church of India was even non-Chalcedonian like the EOTC. A man like Zara Yaqob, known by the king, would easily meet people of different religions in Aksum, a cosmopolitan centre through which merchants and pilgrims from all over the Red Sea and the Indian Ocean travelled.

Third, both texts mention Sabaeans and Homerites. Yet these are common terms in Ethiopia (Alemayyehu Moges 1968) as cited in Sumner (Sumner 1976, 107). Sumner supports this point with their presence in the various Geʻez dictionaries (Sumner 1976, 107). Further, the wording in the *Hatata Zara Yaqob* about the Sabaeans is different. Unlike *Soirées de Carthage*, it uses the local compound term 'the people of Himyar and Saba' (121), which is what the people of Yemen have used to refer to themselves since antiquity. Further, Himyar has long been famous in Ethiopia as the site of its most famous international victory, in the 500s CE. An Ethiopian text does not need a European text to discuss Ethiopia's nearest neighbour to the east.

Finally, as Wion points out, Conti Rossini's and Mittwoch's linguistic arguments about *Soirées de Carthage* are undermined because they did not have access to the

---

[1] Regarding polygamy and Islam, 'so common in Ethiopia', he said: 'everyone was gossiping about them' (Alemayyehu Moges 1968, 31, as cited and translated in Sumner 1976, 209).

Geʽez translation but only the Amharic translation of the Geʽez translation (Wion 2013b, 13, 16).[1] Conti Rossini 'had no knowledge of the Geʽez text, nor of the Amharic versions that derive from it.... Hence C. Conti Rossini's arguments are solely based on similarities in content' (Wion 2013b, 13). Further, 'he mentions at the outset that the two texts are very different in terms of the opinions they express' (Wion 2013b, 13). Likewise, Mittwoch's linguistic arguments about the similarities are vitiated because they are based only on the Amharic translation (Wion 2013b, 16). That both *Hatata Inquiries* use common words (like 'why', 'light of reason', and 'to demonstrate') a lot (Mittwoch 1934, 7; Wion 2013b, 15) is not a convincing proof of both being authored by the same person.

Meanwhile, in terms of content, other nineteenth-century texts invented by Europeans about the other, ethnic forgeries, are always a farrago of stereotypes. One would expect a European inventing such a text to mention Solomon and the Ethiopian Queen of Sheba at least once. Aksum is named without mentioning the stelae; Gondar is named without mentioning the palaces—European authors never resisted the opportunity to add travelogue detail.[2] We see nothing of the sort.

In terms of wording, some have pointed out that Giusto da Urbino's compositions and the *Hatata Inquiries* share some quotations. For instance, both use the same biblical verse: 'the fruit of your/his/their labour' (Wion 2021b, 6). Yet this verse is one of the Bible's most famous phrases, so famous it appears constantly in Christian literature, including Geʽez literature. Further, no trace of Latin, French, or Italian appears in the *Hatata Inquiries* (Sumner 1976, 258).

Another scholar argued that a word is used once in the *Hatata Zara Yaqob* and several times in *Soirée de Carthage* with its minority meaning—ባሕር, *bäḥər*, with the meaning of 'section', 'paragraph', of a text.[3] But the use of this word with this meaning is not at all rare; it is the primary way to refer to sections of the Bible.

Most bizarre of all is when Giusto da Urbino's quoting of Amharic and Geʽez literature is used as proof that a European wrote the texts. When Giusto da Urbino quotes famous Amharic proverbs in his letters, and those same proverbs appear in the *Hatata Inquiries* (Wion 2021b, 4–6), this is not evidence that he forged the *Hatata*

---

1 Although they did not have access to the Geʽez version of the *Soirées de Carthage,* it does exist, according to Sumner: 'The manuscript of the Ethiopic translation of *Les soirees de Carthage* was bought from an Ethiopian and not without difficulties, in the neighbourhood of Addis Ababa in March 1926 by Sylvain Grébaut. It was catalogued as MS. Ethiopian 165 in the 1935 Catalogue of the Vatican Library' (Sumner 1976, 233). See (Grébaut 1935, 613–14).
2 Hundreds of Europeans wrote travelogues about Ethiopia in the 1800s; for example, (Annesley 1809; Portenger, De May, and Phillips 1819; Parkyns 1853; Stern 1862). Regarding their common fixations, see (Belcher 2000).
3 (Getatchew Haile 2017, 59).

Inquiries. It is evidence that he was learning the Ethiopian wisdom tradition. It would be most peculiar if such proverbs did not appear in both. How can a scholar write that a European's 'own words' are found in an Ethiopian's 'mouth' (Wion 2021b, 6) when those words are most common in Ethiopians' mouths? This is a Eurocentric inversion, using what's Ethiopian about the text to prove it is European.

Meanwhile, a fundamental problem attends arguing that Giusto da Urbino's own compositions have commonalities with the *Hatata Inquiries* and therefore he must have invented them. Why assume this direction of influence? It is a certain fact that his deep engagement with Geʿez literature as well as the *Hatata Inquiries*, including laboriously copying them and likely discussing them with others, must have influenced his own thinking and writing. Incapable of imagining this fact, some scholars have published nonsense. To claim that Geʿez texts about 'hypotheses', 'examinations', and 'independent thinking' must have been composed by a European merely because he also thought about 'hypotheses', 'examinations', and 'independent thinking' is shocking (Wion 2021b, 8). The opposite is likely true—that Giusto da Urbino met some radical Ethiopian thinkers, and they challenged him to reconsider his conventional thinking, perhaps before he ever came across the *Hatata Inquiries*.

Worst of all is the underlying assumption that if any 'European' wording or ideas can be found in the texts, this proves that only one man, the nineteenth-century Italian priest Giusto da Urbino, could have written them. Getatchew Haile commented that some might argue that the untraditional perspective on stars in the *Hatata Zara Yaqob* (that they are small due to their distance) is evidence that a foreigner, a European wrote it.[1] Yet it is more likely, Getatchew Haile writes, that the Ethiopian author learned this idea from the Europeans with whom he trained.[2] Unfortunately, this nuanced concept of hybridity is inconceivable to those arguing for European authorship. Proving that something is 'European' does not prove that

---

[1] The *HZY* has 'but who knows the stars' number, or distance, or size, which seem small to us because of their remoteness' (97). While the point about distance may be unusual, making cosmological remarks is not. Several texts in Geʿez do so. First, the Didascalia and the Ethiopic Liturgy of the Hours; for instance, they say ወኖሎቌሙ ለኮከብት በምልዖሙ፤ ወሰመይኮሙ ለኩሎሙ በበአስማቲሆሙ (you have counted all the stars and named each of them). Second, the Book of Enoch; for instance, ወርኢኩ መዛግብተ ፀሐይ ወዘወርኅ እምአይቴ ይወፅኡ ወአይቴ ይገብኡ ወግብአቶሙ ስቡሕ፤ ወአፅ ይከብር አሐዱ ሰካልኡ ወምሕዋሮሙ ብሩል ወኢየኃልፉ ምሕዋረ ወኢያዴዉስኑ ወኢየጽጽኡ እምሕዋረ ዚአሆሙ ወያይማኖተ የዕቅቡ ጀምሰለ ካልኡ በመሐላ ዘደሩ (I saw the sun and moon's dwelling place, from where they come out and return, and their glorious return, and how one is more honoured than the other, their stately orbit, and how they do not stray from them. Indeed, they never add or subtract from their orbit. They keep faithfully the pact which they have with one another [to keep to different paths]) (1 Enoch 41:5).

[2] 'It makes more sense to suspect the influence of Catholic teaching on the thinking of Zara Yaqob than to ascribe his Ḥatäta to da Urbino' (Getatchew Haile 2017).

Giusto da Urbino wrote it but only that the author who wrote it did so in a context informed by European discourse. We must accept that Ethiopians writing in the 1600s, ones who frequently talked with Coptic and Catholic Christians during a time of tremendous political and religious turmoil, might write sentences like these. Human beings are more than their nations.

Arguments about similarities are so weak that this game can be played both ways—by focusing on their lack. For instance, Giusto da Urbino wrote about the Oromo regularly in his correspondence, as he served among them. Nowhere do the *Hatata Inquiries* mention the Oromo people. Why not use that hard-earned knowledge to make the text more believable?

The similarity in names and birth dates has inspired many scholars to rush down the wrong path, as if similarities were some kind of real proof. Human beings are pattern seeking animals and tend to see meaningful connections where there are none. Despite a hundred years of work on Giusto da Urbino's work and the *Hatata Inquiries*, no substantial matches in sentences have been found.

Conclusion

To sum up, the main pillars of the case for European authorship are a rumour about authorship and some similarities in name, birthdate, wording, and topic. The birthday similarity is their most compelling evidence, and even that could be mere coincidence. No court would rule in favour of the prosecution based on this evidence.

It bears mentioning here, at the end of this section, that even if it were definitively proven that Giusto da Urbino composed the *Hatata Inquiries,* they are still African texts. They were composed in Africa. They were composed in an ancient African language and script, Geʻez. They were composed deploying a wealth of Ethiopian proverbs, folktales, and folk wisdom. They were composed with numerous quotations from the exact wording of the Geʻez Psalter and liturgy. They were composed with a reliance on Ethiopian history as written by Ethiopians, and on Ethiopian religion as innovated by Ethiopians. They were composed by someone(s) trained in the elaborate EOTC educational system. They were composed by someone(s) who regularly consulted that system's scholars.[1] They were composed by

---

[1] Giusto da Urbino praised his Ethiopian instructors, writing in his dictionary that 'As for me, I have learned the pronunciation and the whole Ethiopic language not by the means of grammars and dictionaries nor under European masters in Europe, but l have learned all that in Ethiopia through the *live voice of Ethiopian masters* with whom I have remained for many years' (MS. 216, f. 4, as cited and translated in (Sumner 1976, 224) (italics mine). In his grammar, he wrote that 'nearly every day' he spoke 'with *my master of Ethiopic language* and with the other learned men who

someone(s) steeped in Geʽez literature, which informed everything about the texts' formulas, themes, and structures. No matter what, the *Hatata Inquiries* were deeply formed by millennia of Ethiopian thought and are deeply Ethiopian.[1]

In the end, Giusto da Urbino is either the hero or the villain of this tale. If he faked the manuscripts, he is a villain. But if he was part of preserving these remarkable manuscripts and introducing them into global history, then he is a hero, and we owe him a debt of gratitude. I like to think that this man who devoted his time to admiring the rich Ethiopian intellectual tradition was the latter. And that we slander him by saying otherwise.

The Case for Ethiopian Authorship

The case for Ethiopian authorship of the *Hatata Inquiries* rests on the rebuttals in the previous sections but also on principles of logic, philology, theology, similar Geʽez texts, and motive.

Law of Simplicity

The argument for non-Ethiopian authorship of the *Hatata Inquiries* does not pass the Occam's Razor test. The simplest explanation for any text is that those who say they authored it actually authored it. Ethiopian authorship is the explanation that depends on the fewest variables. That is, as the American expression goes, the texts are 'innocent until proven guilty', and the burden of proof lies on those who argue against Ethiopian authorship. Unfortunately, those arguing for European authorship too often assume that it is the other way around, that their opponents have the burden of proof. That stance must be rejected. As scholars, we must rigorously require of ourselves the scientific stance that the texts are what they say they are

---

were around me', as cited and translated in (Sumner 1976, 235). He also worked with an Ethiopian scribe, with whom he did his translation of *Soirées de Carthage* into Amharic (Mittwoch 1934, ix) (Sumner 1976, 236). However, see (Wion 2021b, 15).
1 As Luam Tesfalidet put it, 'Die Frage nach der Echtheit entscheidet nicht mehr, ob die Hatätas zur äthiopischen Literatur gehören. Entscheidend ist in dieser Hinsicht die Sprache der Hatätas, welche eben eine äthiopische ist. Entscheidend ist auch, dass der Inhalt sich nicht als unvereinbar mit der äthiopischen Tradition darstellt' (The question of [author] authenticity no longer decides whether the Hatatas belong to Ethiopian literature. The language of the Hatatas, which is an Ethiopian one, is decisive in this respect. It is also crucial that the content is compatible with the Ethiopian Tradition) (Luam Tesfalidet 2007, 77).

until proof 'beyond a reasonable doubt' has been laid out. So long as the defence can provide reasonable explanations against the evidence produced by the prosecution, the texts must be 'presumed innocent'.

Differences between the *Hatata Inquiries*

The two *Hatata Inquiries'* form and content suggest that two people authored them. They are quite different from each other, as over a dozen of scholars have argued.[1]

In the 1970s, Claude Sumner performed perhaps the first computational analysis of African literature using a new form of textual data analysis.[2] In comparing the two texts with each other, Sumner found differences too great for them to be by one author, especially one new to Geʿez writing (and composing the two texts within a year or two of each other). Sumner presented this evidence regarding syntax, diction, form, tone, concerns, and substance in a series of detailed charts (Sumner 1976, 111–120). For instance, the two texts differ in their sentence and chapter length: the author of the first uses long chapters and short sentences; the author of the second uses short chapters and long sentences. Further, the first is personal in tone, the second is impersonal; the first tells no stories with a moral, the second tells many stories with a moral. Also, in ratio of words, the first refers much more to 'God' and 'wise' while the second refers much more to 'human' and 'good', reflecting their differing concerns—the first with the spiritual (human beings' relation with the divine) and the second with the moral (human beings' relation with each other). Their metaphors and similes differ as well; with the second using more metaphors and more diverse ones (Sumner 1976, 262). The first is concerned with individual ethics; the second with social ethics, our obligations to others (Sumner 1976, 267–269). The first depends heavily on Psalms (mentioning them around 70 times); the second mentions them less (around 30 times) (Sumner 1976, 259). The first Hatata distinguishes between two types of foreigners—Europeans and Coptic Egyptians—and in three separate chapters makes theological points based on their differences. Coptic Egyptians are not mentioned once in the second Hatata. They

---

[1] Sumner (Sumner 1976, 110) lists fourteen scholars who published this opinion: (Abbadie 1859; Turayev 1903; 1905; Bonus 1905; Nöldeke 1905; Wey 1906; Bezold 1907; Baumstark 1911; Littmann 1904; Nöldeke 1925; 1909; Krackovskii 1924; Harden 1926; Budge 1928; da Sessano 1951; Contri 1957; Marchiotto 1964–1965).

[2] The first computation analysis of any body of literature was likely in 1946 and the field was large enough to establish journals in the 1960s (such as *Computers and the Humanities*, established in 1966) (Sula and Hill 2019).

reflect different views of teleology, the divine, society, human psychology, etc.[1] Overall, the numerous differences suggest two authors. These differences have not been much noticed because the *Hatata Walda Heywat* is consistently ignored in discussions of authorship. Only the first *Hatata Inquiry* has been scoured for evidence.

They are so different that it is surprising that the pro-European authorship side has not argued that the second text was Giusto da Urbino's attempt to mimic the *Hatata Zara Yaqob*, a real text from the 1600s. I suspect they have not done so for a problematic reason: because scholars perceive the *Hatata Zara Yaqob* as more philosophical than *Hatata Walda Heywat* and thus it *must be* European.

Theology

The two *Hatata Inquiries'* theology and cultural knowledge strongly suggest an Ethiopian author. As many have noted, no historical or cultural material in the *Hatata Inquires* is factually incorrect.[2] As Turayev put it, these *Hatata Inquiries* cannot have been written by 'foreigners' as they 'only understand half of what is going on around them' and so it must have been written by 'educated indigenous thinker[s]' (Turayev 1903, 475–476 as translated in Sumner 1976, 134).

The theology of the texts is particularly striking. Take, for instance, the authors' stance on the existence of God. Zara Yaqob writes 'Why do all human beings agree in saying that there is a God, the Creator of all?' (82) Walda Heywat makes a similar statement about God's existence: 'All of humanity's teachers and every nation's books agree on this truth' (116). He adds about angels and demons that 'all human beings believe in their existence'. A European author would not write such sentences, being perfectly aware of the long history of atheism. Indeed, Giusto da Urbino himself is on record as wondering about whether it was possible that God did not exist.[3] Such agnosticism is not the position of either of *The Hatata Inquiries*, which assert God's existence and praise God in prose and poem.

---

[1] Describing the many, many differences takes up dozens of pages in Sumner's work, with the summary alone taking fifteen pages (Sumner 1976, 260–275).

[2] (Krackovskii 1924; Alemayyehu Moges 1968; Solomon Ghebre Ghiorgis 1972; Bahru Zewde 1968; Tesfaye Debesay 1970; about which, see Sumner 1976, 135). In the French essays of 2013, Wion announced that she would write two further articles on the topic—one on whether the texts have any anachronisms regarding the 1600s and another on 'the second life of the Ḥatatā in the context of African philosophy' (Wion 2021b, 22; 2013b). We found no evidence of anachronisms, so perhaps that explains why, ten years later, neither has been published or is forthcoming.

[3] 'It is also almost impossible for me to imagine an immense being'; cited and translated in (Wion 2013a).

Also, only a seventeenth-century Ethiopian author could have produced two texts so ignorant of the history of Christian theology and the genealogy of its thinkers, Mehari Worku points out. Giusto da Urbino's was too highly trained to do so. A Capuchin priest, one who had spent decades reading theological texts in Latin and steeped in the Christian theology of his day, could not produce texts with no trace of that complicated understanding of what Christianity is. Yet the *Hatata Zara Yaqob* proffers no knowledge of Christian theology. Even its objections to Islam are cultural, not theological. At one point, the *Hatata Zara Yaqob* states that all religions have messengers, a statement no highly trained Catholic theologian would make. Theologically, Christ is not a messenger; Christ is the message. Likewise, Catholic theologians were obsessed with the virtues and had highly elaborate theories about them. Yet the *Hatata Zara Yaqob*'s author discusses them only in an elementary way. Ignorance of the history of Christian theology would be typical of an Ethiopian in the 1600s, having little access to histories of such. Relatedly, the author of *Hatata Zara Yaqob* articulates a particularly non-Chalcedonian and Ethiopian perspective that human beings can and should 'become perfect' (89). It is difficult to imagine a disillusioned Catholic priest stating that perfection was the purpose of life.

The use of the Bible in the *Hatata Zara Yaqob* also suggests an Ethiopian author, says Alemayyehu Moges, in one of the most important and detailed works in support of Ethiopian authorship, a work that Sumner quoted at length (Sumner 1976, 89–97). In two chapters of Alemayyehu Moges' thesis, he argues that, for instance, the passages quoted in Psalms are those that most often appear in the liturgy and its hymns (such as those in the Divine Office *Me'eraf*). This reflects daily practices, the oral tradition, not a laborious study. Also, memorized biblical passages (such as Psalms) were quoted more exactly than non-memorized passages (such as the Gospels) (Sumner 1976, 259). This reflects the learning pattern of an Ethiopian, not a European, he said. He also believed that Zara Yaqob saying he took only one book with him into exile, a Psalter, instead of the whole Bible, reflected the practice of an Ethiopian, not a European. He also notes that the author of the first *Hatata Inquiry* criticizes scripture but never the Psalter. Again, he saw this devotion as Ethiopian, not European.

Getatchew Haile agreed, adding that the author must have been a '*Dawit dägami däbtära*' (Psalter-reciting cleric) (Getatchew Haile 2017, 66). Only Ethiopians had the Psalms as their daily prayer book; Giusto da Urbino would have had his Catholic prayer book, which overlapped with the Ethiopian Psalter almost not at all. 'It is impossible to think of any reason for anyone to be obsessed with so many psalm verses, unless the Psalter is his daily prayer book', Getatchew Haile concluded (Getatchew Haile 2017, 66). This cannot be the case of a European author learning a few Psalms and sprinkling them throughout for veracity. The authors of the *Hatata Inquiries* quote not just dozens of passages from Psalms, but over 150 of them.

We noticed similar things about the use of the Bible. The two texts' heavy dependence on the Geʿez Bible's wording, especially that of the Psalter, reflects a memorization of that book, not simply having it at hand in manuscript form. That is, the specific wording of the Geʿez Bible often prompted points in the *Hatata Inquiries*. The authors did not simply have ideas and then provide biblical quotations as proof texts, woven in as afterthoughts or to prove learnedness. Rather, the idea arose from specific words in the Geʿez Bible. One example is the author's use, in *Hatata Walda Heywat*, of the Geʿez version of Psalm 140:5, which has 'stumbling block', as opposed to the Septuagint and Vulgate's 'trap'. An Ethiopian would use this from memory; a scholar would have had to have studied the differences, something we know that Giusto da Urbino did not do, based on his surviving scholarship. The author's rhetorical point depends on blocking someone's path, not trapping someone. Most Christians work from the wording of the Bible of their youth, and without exception the Bible quotations in the *Hatata Inquiries* reflect the Geʿez Bible. By contrast, when Giusto da Urbino quoted from the Bible in his correspondence, he always quoted from the Latin Vulgate (Sumner 1976, 132–133, 255).

Finally, separate schools of theology are often forming in and around the EOTC educational system. Schools with radical, excommunicable views have always existed and continue to exist in Ethiopia. No less a figure than Conti Rossini speculated that Zara Yaqob started such a school and Walda Heywat was his first disciple.[1] *Hatata Zara Yaqob* and *Hatata Walda Heywat* would seem to be its foundational texts. The principles of Zara Yaqob's school were anti-Christological, explaining why Jesus Christ is mentioned only twice and the Holy Spirit, God the Father, and the Virgin Mary are not mentioned at all, which is highly unusual in Geʿez literature. A school of thought that rejected Christ would have to be extremely secretive. Its texts would be passed down, hand to hand, by a few teachers to trustworthy students as hidden wisdom. They would continue to be distributed in this intimate way, even over several generations. Getatchew Haile's work on the extant *Hatata Zara Yaqob* manuscripts, arguing that their differences arise from different base texts, supports the conclusion that these foundational texts have been transmitted through copying over time (Getatchew Haile 2017). We provide a manuscript stemma in our Manuscripts of the Text section (Figure 4).

---

[1] Conti Rossini wrote that 'the text of a disciple of his attested to the fact that that he had founded a real school in the Emfrāz [district] and in neighbouring districts of Bēgamder—a school which lasted for a time. But regarding such a school and its founder no further information could be found' (Conti Rossini 2023, 214).

Some evidence for this radical school is a unique de-Christianized Psalter that Giusto da Urbino copied.[1] Considered alongside the two *Hatata Inquiries*, it suggests that Giusto da Urbino was intentionally collecting texts from an anti-Christological school. Most Geʿez Psalters include Christ's name in the titles of those Psalms that Christians consider prophetic. This Psalter omits Christ's name from these titles.[2] It also has another telling title change: the title for Psalm 23 has been changed from በእንተ ትሩፋን (Bäʾəntä Tərufan; About the Virtuous) to include the word *Hatata*, having ሐተታ ፍጥረት (Ḥatäta Fəṭrät; The Inquiries of Creation) (on f. 45v). Stephen Delamarter, a scholar who has examined over 1,600 Geʿez Psalters, confirms that this Psalter is 'quite different from the norm' (Delamarter 2022). For instance, it contains only Psalms and Canticles, omitting the Song of Songs and the prayers to Mary. The Psalter also does not include the modern longer version of Psalm 150 but rather the earlier, shorter version common in the 1600s. The absence of Marian texts might suggest it was a Beta Israel Psalter made by Ethiopian Jews. However, one expert on such, Sophia Dege-Müller, took a quick look at this manuscript and thought that unlikely.[3] In other words, Giusto da Urbino preserved not just two rare anti-Christological texts but three.

Similar Ethiopian Texts

Thousands of original texts written by Africans for Africans in African languages about Africans before the twentieth century exist and have been documented. East and West Africans have been composing literature for millennia and written literature since at least the 1300s and sometimes long before that. While texts of philosophy are rare among them (as they are in the Western canon), they do exist. Numerous early African texts have elegantly argued rhetoric, be they works of theology, biography, history, or poetry. Yet much of the debate about the authorship of the *Hatata Inquiries* has arisen from the view that the philosophical *Hatata Inquiries*

---

1 Vatican Ethiopic Manuscript, in the Borgia collection, shelf mark: Borg.et.8, viewable at https://digi.vatlib.it/view/MSS_Borg.et.8 (last accessed on 14 June 2013); catalogued in (Grébaut and Tisserant 1935, 798).
2 For instance, Psalms 2, 8, 44, and 109 are typically titled ትንቢት በእንተ ክርስቶስ (tənbit baʾəntä Krəstos; Prophecy about Christ). On 21v in this Psalter, the title for Psalm 2 is instead ጥበብ ፈጣሪ ወማዕለቶሙ ለዕቡያን (ṭəbäbä fäṭari wä-maʿəletomu lä-ʿəbuyan; The wisdom of the Creator and the rebellion of the arrogant). On 27r, the title for Psalm 8 is instead ስብሐተ ፈጣሪ በስነ ፍጥረት (səbḥatä fäṭari bä-sənnä fəṭrät; The Creator's praise through creation's beauty). On 73r, the title for Psalm 44 is instead ክብሩ ለንጉሥ ሠናይ (kəbru lä-nəguś śännay; A good king's glory). The Giusto da Urbino Psalter has no mention of Christ at these locations.
3 Regarding Betä Ǝsraʾel Psalters, see (Dege-Müller 2020).

are peculiar and unrepresentative of Geʿez literature. But assuming the absence of similar texts is wrong.

Early Geʿez texts with radical analyses of religion are part of what the scholar Maimire Mennasemay calls a long 'trail of emancipatory critique in Ethiopia' (Mennasemay 2010, 5).[1] For instance, the fifteenth-century Geʿez text of the *Life and Struggles of Estifanos*, authored by a monk named Tewalda Madhen, details the thought of the dissident monk and thinker *Abba* Estifanos (c. 1380–1450), who rebelled against the monarchy (Tewalda Madhen 2006). He inspired a reformation movement named after him, the Stephanites (1406–1478), which Mennasemay describes as attracting the 'oppressed' and having 'a Utopian, rational and political critique of Ethiopian society mediated through a religious discourse' (Mennasemay 2010, 6). Their texts express the ideal of 'following one's mind' (Getatchew Haile 2004, 23, 44, 70, 79, 94), as cited in (Mennasemay 2010, 14–16).[2] In some respects, the *Hatata Inquiries* are less controversial than these texts.

Geʿez texts with brief autobiographical openings were written as early as the 1500s. One was by the monk Pawlos (regarding the war with Ahmad ibn Ibrahim al-Ghazi), while another was by the noble Ras Semeʾon (in his *Book of Gratitude* and *Taʾammera Maryam* stories).[3] The hagiographies of the Ethiopian tradition are similar in format and tenor. Some have the exact format of the *Hatata Inquiries*, opening with biography and then engaging in extensive theological discussions. For instance, one of the most famous, the fifteenth-century *Gadla Kristos Samra* begins with a brief biography of the saint followed by a first-person account of the saint's opinions on various theological issues and her visions. First-person accounts in the *Taʾammera Maryam* (Miracles of Mary) are so common that Mehari Worku created with a term for them: miracle memoirs. So, a *Hatata Inquiry* having an autobiographical component does not make it unique in Geʿez literature.

Of course, heretical texts are rare because the Ethiopian libraries of the day—the churches and monasteries—were not going to preserve them, as Amsalu Aklilu has also argued (Amsalu Aklilu 1961) as cited in (Sumner 1976, 85). But we know that such texts existed because other texts refute them. For instance, in the 1400s,

---

[1] See also (Mennasemay 2009). He does not discuss another, the influential Ethiopian abbot from Yemen, Enbaqom Qala Wald (c. 1470–1560), who was a convert from Islam and authored a polemical book of exegesis አንቀጸ አሚን (*Anqäṣä Amin*) with arguments against his former faith, including disputations regarding passages in the Quran.
[2] Getatchew Haile translated these texts together into Amharic (Getatchew Haile 2004), including *Gädlä Abäw wä-Aḫaw, Gädlä Abäkaräzun*, and *Gädlä Abuna Ǝzra*. On the movement, see also (Taddesse Tamrat 1966; Getatchew Haile 1983).
[3] For discussions of these, see (Sokolinskaia 2010; Martínez d'Alòs-Moner 2010; Getatchew Haile 2005; Wion 2013b; Conti Rossini 1918).

King Zara Yaqob wrote a rebuttal to those Ethiopian scholars who disputed the biblical canon. According to his report, the Ethiopian scholars heretically stated that the various books of the bible conflicted so much with each other that 'if the books had sticks, they would fight each other' (Zara Yaqob 1992, 64, 107). Yet that text critiquing the canon has not survived.

The *Hatata Inquiries* also took advantage of the styles and forms of philosophical texts from elsewhere, some of which mentioned the ideas of such thinkers as Plato and Aristotle. Three are worth mentioning here: a text from Egypt cataloguing and interpreting the natural world titled *Physiologus* (which was translated from Greek into Geʻez in the Aksumite period, likely by 600); a text of Greek philosophy that opens with an autobiography and is titled *The Life and Maxims of Secundus the Philosopher* (which was translated into Geʻez in the 1300s); and a Persian collection of proverbial philosophy titled *The Book of the Wise Philosophers* (which was translated from Arabic into Geʻez in the 1510s).[1] Indeed, *Hatata Walda Heywat* borrows a bit from the last (Sumner 1976, 121–124). Nothing in the *Hatata Inquiries* can be traced directly to a source outside of the Ethiopian tradition.

Motivation

Giusto da Urbino's motivation in allegedly composing these texts set in the 1600s *and* unethically and dishonestly claiming that Ethiopians composed them has never been reasonably explained. I treat this topic here rather than in my rebuttal section because it is rare to see *any* explanation of his motives, much less convincing ones.

The challenge for the prosecution is providing a motivation that explains four of Giusto da Urbino's actions at once. That is, one cannot simply give a motive for Giusto da Urbino authoring the texts; one must also give a motive for him denying that he authored the texts *and* a motive for his perpetrating a fraud with them. One most also explain his motivation for setting the *Hatata Inquiries* so far in the past, deliberately making errors so as to be discovered, and inventing named authors with extensive biographies, faking not just a text but human beings.

Now, Giusto da Urbino's motives for *composing* in Geʻez are easily imagined—for the fun of it, the opportunity to learn the language more deeply, and/or the chance to impress others with his learning. Scholars have argued that Giusto da Urbino was proud of his knowledge of Geʻez language and literature, regularly boasting about it

---

1 These titles are, respectively, ፊሳልጎስ (Fisalgos); ዜና ስክንድስ ጠቢብ ለእንደርያኖስ ንጉሥ፡ ወጠቢቡ ወተሰአሎታቲሁ (Zena Səkəndəs ṭäbib lä-ꓱndəryanos nəguś wä-ṭəbäbu wä-täsäʾəlotatihu); and መጽሐፈ ፈላስፋ ጠቢባን (Mäṣḥafä fälasfa ṭäbiban) (Weninger 2005; 2010; Pietruschka 2005).

(Conti Rossini 1920, 216). But the next pair of acts—denying his skills *plus* unscrupulously perpetrating a fraud—have no motivation that fits the first action.

Let us consider his possible motivations for fraud. The most common motivation is financial gain. But Giusto da Urbino did not make money off this alleged forgery and had no reason to expect that he would do so. He did not seek to get paid extra for offering these particular texts to d'Abbadie nor ask him to attempt to resell them or publish them and pass along the earnings. Finally, the motive of financial gain is not a reasonable conjecture about a priest who had moved to Ethiopia to serve and lived simply. We have no evidence of any sort that he was motivated by money in any aspect of his life.

Perhaps the next most common motivation is a desire for fame. But this must be excluded by definition: Giusto da Urbino denied authorship and so cannot have gained fame from the texts. Now, it might be argued that an author can desire for a text to become famous, and thus satisfy this narcissistic desire by proxy. When we look at the motivations for ancient forgeries, they seem to have this motivation and were generally an attempt to get the text more widely circulated, more known, more trusted. The ethnic impersonator autobiographies that arose in the complicated racial terrain of United States were motivated mostly by financial gain but also to forward a political cause or, more rarely, to gain fame by proxy.[1] Again, by definition, these motivations must be excluded. For Giusto da Urbino did nothing to bring attention to these texts. He did not circulate them to anyone beyond a few Ethiopian friends and his patron, nor did he ask his patron or family members to circulate them or publish them. He did so little that the books remained entirely unread by anyone for decades. This was characteristic of him—he desired anonymity (Wion 2013b, 27). A desire for fame is not a reasonable explanation of motive for someone who did nothing to seek fame for himself or the books.

Resentment and revenge are possible motives for Giusto da Urbino *composing* the texts, but they make no sense as motives for *denying* his authorship. That is, if he composed them because he resented Ethiopians' dismissal of his skills and wanted the revenge of proving them wrong, this is quite believable as a motivation for authorship. But again, by definition, this cannot be the motive for denying authorship as that utterly undercuts the aim of proving others wrong by writing them. If his resentment were aimed elsewhere, at his patron d'Abbadie, he could not reasonably expect that his fraud would harm him. Indeed, no one has ever faulted d'Abbadie for this alleged fraud.

---

[1] Regarding the motivations for ethnic forgeries, see (Matthewson 2021; Browder 2000). For other scholarship on this form of passing, on those pretending to be their ethnic others, see (Ruthven 2001; Ryan and Thomas 2003).

Mental illness also cannot be seen as the cause of Giusto da Urbino's actions. For instance, we have no evidence that he was so delusional that he composed these texts and presented them as others' work because he forgot that he wrote them or could no longer distinguish between the reality of his own authorship and his invention of others' authorship. We have no evidence that he had dementia or delusions; quite the contrary. Now, Wion argues that Giusto da Urbino's mental state was relevant; that he was isolated, disaffected, bitter, depressed, and suicidal (Wion 2013a; 2021a). But depression is precisely the mental state of inaction, the lack of motivation to do anything. A person this depressed could not write two, long, complicated treatises (to say nothing of hundreds of pages of a dictionary and grammar).

Getatchew Haile also raised questions about Giusto da Urbino's possible motivations. As the texts directly address an Ethiopian audience throughout, his failure to circulate the texts in Ethiopia does not make sense. The purpose cannot have been, Getatchew Haile points out, 'to teach Ethiopians, because he shipped both copies out of Ethiopia' (Getatchew Haile 2017, 65). If he wrote them to encourage Ethiopians to be better, kinder, more thoughtful, he did nothing to distribute them. Nor could a possible motivation be teaching Europeans, for the ideas in the *Hatata Inquiries*, while unusual for the 1600s, were more commonplace by the 1800s.

Most implausible of all, we are asked to imagine that Giusto da Urbino authored two deeply ethical texts and then deliberately perpetrated a fraud with them. One cannot argue that Giusto da Urbino got a little mixed up, that it was an innocent exercise for his own satisfaction that others later misconstrued. If he did compose them, he clearly intended to perpetuate a fraud, creating not one but two hybrid autobiographical philosophical texts, with named authors of detailed and complicated backgrounds from two centuries previously, authors he depicted as in a sustained dialogue with each other. If he did compose them, he twice created an elaborate backstory, with many complicated elements, about how he came to find them. If he did compose them, he did so not to express his own beliefs, which were traditional, but as bizarre inventions of utter others with whom he utterly disagreed. Writing a polemic as an exercise and then later trying to pass it off is one thing. But the autobiographical element, writing in authors with backstories, would mean the fraud was intended from the beginning, as a clear attempt to make the fraud more convincing.

If he did compose them, he simultaneously engaged in the dishonesty of regularly sending letters to many praising all aspects of Catholicism, regarding which, see (Sumner 1976, 196). If he did compose them, he forced a copyist to participate in the fraud knowingly (the scribe had to have copied something in Giusto da Urbino's handwriting). If he did compose them, he unnecessarily and falsely inserted a note in d'Abbadie MS 234 of the *Hatata Zara Yaqob* stating that he 'found' it and saying the same in two letters (Sumner 1976, 257). These series of acts over several years would have been part of a long-term, cunning, and compunctionless deception.

A fundamental contradiction exists between the texts' repeated insistence on truth and Giusto da Urbino's alleged act of dishonest trickery. Let us go through just a few examples. The *Hatata Inquiries* condemn lying and deceitfulness. The author of *Hatata Walda Heywat* thanks God for 'guiding me to write the truth and keeping me away from all deceptiveness in my writing' (122). He says, 'Listen, my friend who reads this book of mine, know that I wrote it with great [and reverent] fear of God, which totally prevents me from lying' (114). He says, 'we should strictly abstain from all lies' (not just some) because they violate 'the creator's established order' and 'extinguish the love and harmony needed for human beings to live together' (136). Meanwhile, the author of the *Hatata Zara Yaqob* states that eternal punishment awaits those who do lie: 'if human beings choose to be evil and liars', they will 'receive the judgement that their evil deserves' (73). The author of *Hatata Walda Heywat* makes a similar statement about judgement. Most of all, the *Hatata Inquiries* praise goodness and assert that becoming good is the purpose of human life. The author of *Hatata Zara Yaqob* writes, 'He put us amidst this world's trials so that we could become perfect, and worthy of our Creator's reward after our death' (89). Yes, people who value truth can be dishonest, but they usually do so accidentally, briefly. A sustained pattern of authorial deception over many years is the behaviour of a con artist who does not value truth in any form. It beggars belief that such a person wrote these ethical texts.[1]

Further, as others have shown, Giusto da Urbino was not a person known for his ability to be discrete, hide his thoughts, or remain silent (Wion 2013b). His letters were 'unprofessional' in their level of self-disclosure. Giusto da Urbino seems incapable of hiding anything from d'Abbadie, treating him as his confessor. Yet we are to imagine that a person incapable of reticence would be secretive enough to sustain this deception.

In short, no convincing motive has been given for Giusto da Urbino perpetrating this fraud.

---

[1] Wion argues that in a particular sentence the *HZY* promotes deceit (Wion 2021b, 1–2). But she does not provide the narrow context, which is the author being deceitful to avoid hideous torture and a brutal death. We also translate quite differently. Our translation is: 'And I thought and said [to myself], "Is it a sin before God for me to appear to be a believer when I am not, and in this way deceive human beings?" I said [to myself], "[No,] people are willing to deceive others and if I reveal the truth to them they won't listen to me, rather they will insult and persecute me"' (109).

Conclusion

In the West, math and science reign supreme. For Westerners, the fact that Zara Yaqob was born on 25 Nahase in 1600 and Giusto da Urbino was born on 25 Nahase in 1814 is the type of fact that erases every other fact. In conversation, I have seen the effect of mentioning this fact. Faces close, and the person exits the conversation quickly, pitying me. It will never matter to that person that this fact stands alone, that the prosecution has not a single other fact, despite a century of digging. It will never matter that there is no confession and no motive. It will never matter that if this were a court case, the judge would dismiss it before it ever entered the court room.

And that is a tragedy. Because, for any person who is deeply familiar with Ethiopian culture and Ge'ez literature, the experience of reading these texts is profound. The longer you read, the more an inescapable feeling grows—Ethiopians wrote these texts. The evidence in wording, sentiment, outlook, theology, rhetoric, style, technique, and a thousand other things is too overwhelming. Every sentence has something deeply Ethiopian. Almost everyone who has argued against their Ethiopian authorship has not read them in Ge'ez. The scholars who have—like Mehari Worku, Getatchew Haile, Ralph Lee, Jeremy Brown, and countless others—stand almost united in believing them authored by Ethiopians. Two who did not and read them in Ge'ez—Conti Rossini and Mittwoch—had racist axes to grind. They simply could not accept that Ethiopians had authored two texts this rhetorically and argumentatively sophisticated.

A European with superb Ge'ez could fake a sentence, a paragraph, maybe even a few pages. But a European who spent only five years in Ethiopia without mastering Ge'ez and who had just a few months to write could not fake the whole of these two extraordinary texts from two centuries earlier without a single ahistoricism. If the chance of the former, the birthday coincidence, is 1 in 365, the chance of the latter, a European getting these thousands of details right, is 1 in a million.

So, this is what we ask you to do before you make up your mind. Really read the two *Hatata Inquiries*. And think deeply about what they are saying and how. We hope that our new translation, based on modern translation principles and made with a full apparatus, substantive notes, contextualizing introduction, and a comprehensive bibliography of all scholarship on the topic will make that easier.

Based on our rebuttals of the prosecution's evidence and our compelling evidence for the defence, we take Ethiopian authorship as proven in the rest of the book and proceed accordingly. We hope that this allows the *Hatata Inquiries* to take their proper place in the global history of philosophy

Wendy Laura Belcher and Ralph Lee
Translation Principles

We created this new translation of the *Hatata Inquiries* of Zara Yaqob and Walda Heywat in response to the increase in contemporary interest in the works. Few know the ancient African language in which they were composed, Geʿez, sometimes called classical Ethiopic. Therefore, to increase access, a translation was essential.

Our translation differs from previous translations in the following ways. It uses contemporary English accessible to those outside the field of Ethiopian studies. It significantly revises many important passages, clarifying meanings left opaque in previous translations or even misunderstood. It identifies far more intertexts, noting many more biblical quotations and allusions in the works as well as the many Ethiopian texts deployed, such as proverbs, folktales, and church liturgy. It provides many more substantive and philological footnotes, which richly describe the cultural, religious, and linguistic context and provide information on the works' people, places, events, practices, and so on. Also, our translation is based on both extant manuscripts of the first work. Previous translations tended to follow the one prioritized in the print critical edition by Enno Littmann (Littmann 1904). Given the significant differences between the two manuscripts of *Hatata Zara Yaqob*, our two-manuscript basis is a substantial contribution. Finally, errors in previous editions have been corrected. Mistaken dates were given—the date of Zara Yaqob's birth is not 1599 but 1600. References to foreigners were untangled, revealing that both Coptic Christians and European Christians were under discussion, not just European Christians. The place where Zara Yaqob lived after fleeing has been clarified; it is not on the Takkaze River. In these ways, we have sought to support the teaching of and scholarship on the works more effectively.

To aid scholars in comparing the works across editions, translations, and manuscripts, we have provided cross-references in the margins of our translation. 'Abb215' indicates the matching folio in d'Abbadie manuscript no. 215; 'Abb234' indicates the matching folio in d'Abbadie manuscript no. 234; 'Litt Ed' indicates the matching page in the Littman Geʿez critical edition; 'Sum' indicates the matching page in the Sumner translation; and 'Chap' indicates the original chapter numbers in the Geʿez manuscripts.

In the following, we provide information about our translation priorities, process, and choices.

Translation Process

Our collaborative process for this translation was as follows. Ralph Lee drafted a full translation of each *Hatata Inquiry*. He also composed philological, biblical, and interpretative footnotes. Previous translations and scholarship (for instance, Littmann and Sumner provided many sources for biblical intertexts) informed some of these footnotes. Then, he and Wendy Laura Belcher went over every word together, in video meetings while sharing screens, discussing where the meaning could be made clearer or the language more natural, and changing it as they went along. Lee then went through that edited draft, making final decisions on wording. Then, Belcher and Mehari Worku went over every word of that final draft, likewise in video meetings while sharing screens, with Belcher reading the English translation aloud while Mehari Worku followed along in the original Geʿez manuscripts. He suggested changes or corrections to the translations and added philological, biblical, and interpretative notes. Mehari Worku's church education gave him much insight, beyond the reach of western scholars, into metaphors, idioms, and terms, especially those borrowed from Amharic or used in the EOTC. Ralph Lee then went over the whole again, making final decisions on wording.

Our process for the appendices was similar. Ralph Lee created a first draft of Appendix 1: Chart of Differences between Abb 215 and Abb 234 of *Hatata Zara Yaqob*. Mehari Worku then edited it, paying particular attention to spelling. Jeremy R. Brown then completed it, adding the scribal emendations and correcting the whole against the newly available colour scans of both manuscripts. Jeremy R. Brown then created a summary of those emendations, in Appendix 2.

Language and Spelling

The Geʿez language is part of the Afro-Asiatic language family, which extends across the Middle East and Africa, including languages from Hebrew and Arabic to Amazigh and Hausa. Evidence for the Geʿez language dates back to the early first millennium BCE.

Ethiopians adapted their own script for this language, beginning to use it in the 200s CE. Called fidal, it has over 200 characters that form a syllabary (each character represents both a consonant and a vowel). Representing the sounds of these characters with Latin characters is difficult (e.g., the 26-character alphabet cannot represent Afro-Asiatic ejective consonants), so scholars use Latin characters with additional marks called diacritics. So, for instance, following the *Encyclopaedia Aethiopica* system (as of 2014), the fidal character መ represents the consonant sound *w* and the short vowel sound *a*, and is transliterated into Latin script as *wä*. Likewise, ተ is transliterated as *tä* and ሠ as *śə*, and so on.

Where smoothness of reading is key, we use simplified spellings without any diacritics. In the footnotes and appendices, however, we mostly use the Geʿez script, sometimes with a transliteration into Latin script using diacritical marks.

Finally, for English words, we have used British spelling conventions, not US ones.

Footnotes

Our footnotes provide four types of information.

The first type is intertextual. Wherever the authors quote from another text, or allude to one, we provide that source in the footnote (e.g., Matthew 7:7; Luke 11:9).

The second type is contextual. We give information on cultural and religious practices, places, famous historical figures, and so on. For instance, the footnotes give the dates of the Ethiopian kings Susenyos and Fasiladas and the historical circumstances that caused Zara Yaqob to flee.

The third type is literal translations or definitions. If our footnote begins with Geʿez script, those words are exactly what appear in the manuscript at that point. When we translated more freely (because we felt that a literal English translation would be unclear or even unhelpful to readers), we left a record of the literal meaning. For instance, in *Hatata Zara Yaqob*, we translated the Geʿez phrase እግዚአብሔር አውጽአኒ እምዓይነ ሞት (Ǝgziʾabḥer awṣaʾani əm-ʿayna mot) as 'death stared me in the face' when the literal translation of the Geʿez would be 'God brought me out from the eye of death' (63). We put the former into the translations and the latter into the footnote. We did the same when there were two possible translations of the meaning. We put the most likely in the translations and the other in the footnote. For instance, the word መቅሠፍት (mäqśäft) can be translated as a physical 'whipping' but also as a spiritual 'punishment' and we used the latter in the translation (104). We also provided the meanings of Ethiopian names; for example, ወለተ ጴጥሮስ (Wälättä Peṭros [Daughter of (Saint) Peter]). Due to this transparency, readers can see which words represent our interpretations and make their own decisions about whether they accurately reflect the original authors' intention.

The fourth type is manuscript variation, differences in wording between the two manuscripts of the *Hatata Zara Yaqob*. That is, we have noted where the Abb 215 manuscript includes words that do not appear in Abb 234 or alters them. For example, one footnote mentions that Abb 215 has a whole phrase that Abb 234 does not have: 'Abb 234 omits: and from where did I come?' (68)

Chapter Titles, Paragraphs, Punctuation, and Pronouns

In composing the translations, we have attempted to be as faithful to the Geʿez as possible while communicating the meaning in clear English. Where the two came into conflict, we made the following choices. Some of the following is reproduced, in an only slightly adapted form, from Belcher's previous Geʿez translation work since many of the processes and choices were the same (Gälawdewos 2015).

As is typical of early modern Geʿez manuscripts, *Hatata Zara Yaqob* has only a few chapter breaks, and those are marked with numbers only, not chapter titles. We added explanatory chapter titles, as well as more chapter breaks, to aid contemporary readers. *Hatata Walda Heywat* had many chapter breaks, so we did not insert any, but we did provide explanatory chapter titles.

Geʿez manuscripts rarely break prose into paragraphs, instead running sentences continuously without indents, line spaces, or paragraph breaks. For readability, we have inserted them, especially for dialogue.

To improve clarity or provide information omitted in the texts, we sometimes have added words or short phrases into the English translation that do not appear in the Geʿez original. We have marked those added words with brackets. Like the footnotes documenting the literal translation, these brackets make it easy for readers to evaluate whether the words accurately reflect the original authors' intention. For instance, in a sentence in *Hatata Zara Yaqob*, we made clear that the author was speaking to himself, not another human being: 'I thought and said [to myself], "If I am a rational being, what do I understand?"' (72). The literal translation of the Geʿez would be 'I thought and said if I am a rational being, what do I understand?' The bracketed material is our addition, intended to promote clarity or smoothness. In another case, we added a date that did not appear in the *Hatata Zara Yaqob*: 'a year later, [in 1645,] Lord Habtu died' (107). Although the author did not provide the year here, the other dates provided in the *Hatata Zara Yaqob* suggested that Lord Habtu died in 1645.

We also added many punctuation marks, as Geʿez lacks marks now available in Latin scripts, or uses them differently. Therefore, all quotation marks, exclamation marks, colons, hyphens, and dashes are our additions. While Geʿez does not have a question mark, it uses interrogative pronouns or particles to indicate questions, and we have signalled that with question marks. Geʿez does have periods but uses them more frequently than written English, and so we have sometimes omitted them.

Finally, we often have replaced pronouns with their full referent to help readers keep track of actors and who is doing what. Because Geʿez uses focus particles, as well as endings distinguishing gender and number, readers of Geʻez can easily follow authors who regularly omit full names. But English does not have these features, so translating Geʻez into English with strings of pronouns is confusing. So, for instance, a literal translation of a Geʻez phrase might be 'he did not give her the capacity' but we would translate this as 'God did not give the soul the capacity' (86). We did not provide brackets for such replacements, treating them as within the semantic range of the pronoun. In cases where we were in doubt as to whom the pronoun referred, we translated only the pronoun or put a discussion of the issue in the note.

Philosophical Terms

We were faced with several decisions regarding conceptual vocabulary in Geʻez. Previous translators have tended to overuse Western philosophical terms in their translations. We did not feel that this accurately reflected the Geʻez language nor the texts' meaning. Also, we often wanted to retain the poetry of an expression. At the same time, we did not want to prevent readers from seeing where such philosophical terms were possible. So, we have used notes to signal terms.

The main term we translated differently had to do with the root ልብ (ləbb, heart). Such Geʻez words as ልቡና (ləbbunna, intelligence) and läbbawi ለባዊ (rational, intelligent, one who reasons) are used throughout the Hatata, all based on 'heart'. As Teodros Kiros has argued in his book *Zara Yacob: Rationality of the Human Heart*, this is not an accident (Kiros 2005b). That is, in Geʻez and other Semitic languages, the seat of both thought and emotion is the heart. In modern Western thought, by contrast, the two are divorced, with the seat of thought in the head and the seat of emotion in the heart. As a result, in Geʻez, rationality is wisely understood as exercising emotions alongside thought. So, we have translated ለባዊ (läbbawi), an adjective which also serves as a noun, differently according to context, with such variations as 'rational', 'faculty of reason', 'rational being(s)', 'understanding being(s)', 'intelligent', or 'wise'. Through this consistent language, Teodros Kiros has argued, Zara Yacob has conquered the fatal Western binary, the Cartesian 'dichotomy between the body and mind' by focusing on the 'rationality of the human heart' (Kiros 2022, 109).

Biblical Quotations

The authors of the *Hatata Inquiries* often allude to Psalms. Instead of quoting the entirety of a Psalm the authors have in mind, they often reference the whole with a quotation from its beginning. That is, they are anticipating that the reader will know the whole Psalm and that they only have to say the first line to prompt the entirety to come to mind. Readers are advised to read the entire Psalm to fully understand the author's meaning.

Previous translators have followed extant English translations of the biblical passages too closely, despite the authors not always quoting the Bible exactly. For instance, the authors often personalised biblical passages by changing pronouns and verbs to the first person. So, we have been careful to translate what is there while consulting the New English Translation of the Septuagint for the Old Testament (since the Septuagint is the source of the Ge'ez Bible) and the New Revised Standard Version for the New Testament. Where needed, we have consulted English translations of so-called apocryphal or extra-biblical texts.

Ralph Lee with Mehari Worku and Wendy Laura Belcher
Translation of the *Hatata Zara Yaqob*

Part I: My Life (1600–1632)

Introduction[1]

In the Name of God, who alone is righteous, I, *Walda Heywat*,[2] shall write down[3] the life story,[4] wisdom, and philosophical inquiry of *Zara Yaqob*,[5] which he himself composed.

    Zara Yaqob said the following:

Litt Ed 3
Abb215 1r
Sum 3
Abb234 2r

Chapter 1: My Birth

Come and hear me![6] Let me tell all you who stand in awe of God about what he has done for me![7] Now, I begin![8]

---

[1] The extant manuscripts of HZY (Abb 215 and Abb 234) do not have chapter titles, only chapter numbers. Thus, the wording and placement of all chapter titles in our translation are our inventions, to aid the reader. We have floated the page or folio number of the relevant HZY manuscripts, editions, and translations in the margins: 'Abb215' indicates the matching folio in d'Abbadie manuscript no. 215; 'Lit Ed' indicates the matching page in the Littman Geʿez critical edition; 'Sum' indicates the matching page in the Sumner translation; and 'Chap' indicates the original chapter numbers in the Geʿez manuscripts. If a footnote begins with Geʿez script, those words are from Abb 215, our base source.
[2] This name 'Walda Heywat' does not appear here, but the postscript identifies the writer as such, so we have inserted his name here for clarity.
[3] እጽሕፍ (I shall write). See Manuscripts of the Texts on what this means in this context.
[4] ገድል (striving, combat, struggle) but often translated as 'life' or 'life story' because the word appears in the titles of Ethiopian hagiographies (e.g., *Gädlä Paṭros*).
[5] ወሐተታሁ (and his inquiry). ሐተታ is one of the most important words in this text and has the meaning of 'inquiry' or 'investigation', so we translate it here as 'philosophical inquiry'.
[6] Abb 234 omits the introductory sentences and starts with 'Come and hear me!'
[7] ለነፍስየ (for me *or* for my soul *or* for my inner self). We have translated it contextually throughout. Psalm 66:16 (65:16 LXX).
[8] Abb 234 omits: Now, I begin!

In the name of God, the creator¹ of all things, the first and the last, the almighty,² the fountain of all life and all wisdom, I will³ write about just a few of the many things that have happened to me during the long years of my life.

May my soul be glorified by God, may the humble listen and delight, for [as it says in Psalms,] 'I have sought God, and he answered me'. 'You should all come close to him now, and he will enlighten you, and you will not be ashamed'. 'Glorify God with me, and together we will exalt his name'.⁴

Originally, my lineage is from the priests of Aksum.⁵ But I was born from a poor farmer in the region of Aksum,⁶ on 28 August⁷ in the third year of the reign of Yaqob I,⁸ 1,600⁹ years after the birth of Christ. By Christian baptism, I was named Zara Yaqob, but people call me Warqe.

Abb215 1v
Sum 4

---

1 ፈጣሪ (creator), from the root ፈጠረ (create, fashion, produce). This term also appears in the Ge'ez Bible, to refer to God.
2 አኀዜ ኩሉ (the holder of everything, but also: all-embracing, omnipotent, almighty). In Ge'ez, the term አኀዜ ኩሉ has often come to reference how God holds up everything rather than how God has power over everything.
3 Abb 234 adds: begin to.
4 Psalm 34:5, 4, 3 (33:5, 4, 3 LXX). The author often slightly alters his quotations from Psalms for a rhetorical purpose. Here, he has flipped the order of three verses to build a story of seeking God, learning from God, and then exalting God.
5 Aksum is an ancient city in the northern Ethiopian highland region of Tigré, the capital of the Aksumite Empire into the 700s CE. Aksum remains the most holy city of Ethiopian Christianity, as it is where the Ark of the Covenant is said to be kept.
6 Priests are of a higher class than those who are just farmers, especially priests for the prestigious and wealthy city of Aksum. Getatchew Haile argues that the author has 'violated local tradition' by not naming his birth village, likely due to fear of his family being persecuted for his views (Getatchew Haile 2017, 68.)
7 ጽዋዕሊኁስ, (the 25th [day in the month of] Nahase in the Ethiopian calendar). The Ethiopian calendar marks hours, days, months, and years differently; 25 Nahase corresponds to Monday, 28 August, in the Western/Gregorian calendar for that year.
8 ያዕቆብ (Yaqob [Jacob]); that is the Ethiopian King Yaqob I (1597–1603 CE, 1605–1607 CE).
9 በ፲፻፭፻፺፪ዐመ፳ (In 1592) in the Ethiopian calendar, which corresponds to 1600 in the Western/Gregorian calendar, which is indeed the third year of Yaqob I's reign.

Chapter 2: My Schooling

When I was old enough, my father sent me to school to study,[1] and after I had learned to recite the Psalms of David,[2] my teacher told my father, 'This child, your son, is brilliantly intelligent,[3] and is diligent in studying, and if you send him for further schooling, he will become a great scholar and teacher'.

When my father heard this, he sent me to study the sacred music of *Zema*.[4] Unfortunately, my voice was no good, and my throat was coarse, so I became a laughingstock to my friends, my fellow students. I stayed there[, at the school for Zema, only] three months, and then left with a grieving heart.

Then, I went to another teacher, one who taught *Qene*[5] poetry and Ge'ez grammar.[6] God granted me the wisdom to learn more quickly than my friends, my fellow students, and this gave me joy instead of my previous grief, so I stayed there for four years[, spending one year on grammar and three years on *Qene*].

During that time, death stared me in the face, but God saved me.[7] While I was playing with my friends, the fellow students, I fell over a cliff. I don't know exactly how I was saved, only that God saved me by a miracle. After I was rescued, I measured the [height of the] cliff with a long rope, and it was

---

1 Abb 234 omits: sent me to school to study. The EOTC traditional educational system is one of the longest running educational systems in the world. See the Introduction regarding its complexity, content, and stages.
2 መዝሙረ ዳዊት (Psalms of David), a shorthand title for the Psalms and accompanying prayers in the Ge'ez Psalter. In the EOTC, a child might learn to read Ge'ez letters around the age of four and then, starting around the age of seven, spend the next three years complete the tasks of learning memorizing Psalms.
3 ብሩህ ልቡና (brilliantly intelligent). Such Ge'ez words as ልቡና (intelligence) and ለባዊ (rational, intelligent, one who reasons) are used throughout the Hatata, all based on the root ልብ (heart). In Ge'ez and other Semitic languages, the seat of both thought and emotion is the heart. On this topic, see (Kiros 2005b).
4 The EOTC traditional education system has five areas of study; the second is *zema bet* (the house of music), in which you learn chanting and memorize hymns. See our Introduction to the Hatata Inquiries.
5 The third EOTC educational stage is *qene bet* (the house of poetry), perhaps the most difficult stage, in which one studies grammar, style, and history; analyses the canon of poetry going back centuries; and composes original poetry. The text of the HZY bears witness to the author's intensive study of poetry, as it plays with words and meaning.
6 ሰዋስው (ladder, but also grammar), which is the name for Ethiopian grammar treatises and which more broadly became the term for 'grammar'.
7 በእማንቱ መዋዕል እግዚአብሔር አውጽአኒ አምዓይነ ሞት (in those days God brought me out from the eye of death).

Abb234 3r   more than ten meters.¹ I got up alive and went to my teacher's house, glorifying God who had saved me.

After that, I left and went to study scripture interpretation.² I continued with this stage of learning for ten years. I studied [sacred] books, [both] how the foreigners,³ [the European Catholics,] interpreted them and how our [Ethiopian] country's teachers interpreted them. Often, both of their interpretations were not in harmony with my reason, so I just kept silent and hid⁴ all the thoughts in my heart. Then I returned to my region, of Aksum, and taught for four years.

Chapter 3: My Days of Persecution

Those days were evil ones, because in the nineteenth year of the reign of *Susǝnyos*,⁵ Bishop *Efons*[, that is, Afonso Mendez,]⁶ came from the land of
Abb234 3v   the foreigners[, the Europeans]. Two years later, a terrible persecution arose
Abb215 2v   across the whole land of Ethiopia, because the king embraced the faith of the foreigners[, the European Catholics], and so the king began to persecute everyone who did not accept it.

---

1 ጛወጽበእመት ወጽስዝር (25 cubits and 1 hand span). The cliff was 10 to 15 meters (34 to 50 feet) deep.
2 The third EOTC educational stage is *matsehaf bet* (the school of exegesis), in which you learn to interpret scripture and texts.
3 ፍራንጅ (färanǧ, also spelled färänǧ, probably derived from 'Frank'), which in Ge'ez texts usually refers to foreigners of European origin but in this text usually appears to mean Catholics. For instance, later in the text, the ፍራንጅ are connected to 'the Throne of Peter', that is, the See of Rome and the Bishop of Rome. We translate it as 'foreigners' and add '[European Catholics]' to clarify the specific group.
4 ኃባእኩ (I hid). This seems to be an allusion to Luke 2:19: 'But Mary treasured all these words and pondered them in her heart'.
5 ሱስንዮስ (Susǝnyos) was king of Ethiopia from 1606 to 7 September 1632. Persuaded by European Jesuit missionaries, he converted from Ethiopian orthodoxy to Roman Catholicism in 1621. His edict that all Christians had to become Roman Catholics triggered a religious civil war. It ended in 1632 when Susǝnyos rescinded that edict and soon afterward died.
6 አፎንስ. As is consistent with other Ge'ez texts of the period, this text gives only *Ǝfons* the name to the European Catholic Jesuit Afonso Mendes. Mendes was appointed, by the Bishop of Rome, as the third Catholic Patriarch of the EOTC, in 1622 CE. The author refers to him throughout with the lesser title: አቡነ (our father), the title of a bishop. Mendes is remembered for his harsh Latinising reforms of the clergy, the church, and the calendar.

While I was in my hometown and teaching the sacred texts, many of my friends began to hate me. This was because in those days [the principle of] loving one's neighbour[1] had vanished, and jealousy took hold of my friends, since I was better at learning and loving my neighbour than they were.

However, I was on friendly[2] terms with everyone, with the foreigners[, the European Catholics,] and with the Copts[,[3] the Egyptian Orthodox Christians]. So, while teaching and expounding the books [for my students], I said, 'the foreigners[, the European Catholics,] say these things, and the Copts[, the Egyptian Orthodox Christians,] say these other things'. I did not say, 'this interpretation is good' or 'that interpretation is bad'. Rather, I said, 'all of these interpretations are good if we ourselves are good'.

They all hated me for this, since to the Copts[, the Egyptian Orthodox Christians,] I seemed like a foreigner[, a European Catholic,] and to the foreigners, I seemed like a Copt. Frequently, they made false charges against me to the king. But God kept me safe.[4]

Then, *Walda Yohannes*,[5] one of my enemies, a priest from Aksum, became a friend of the king—because kings' friendship can be gained through deceitful words. This deceiver went to the king [Susenyos], and said of me, 'Look, this man misleads the people,[6] telling them that we should rise up because of our faith, kill the king, and expel the foreigners[, the European Catholics]'. He made many other similar false accusations against me.[7]

---

1 Leviticus 19:18, Matthew 25:39, Mark 12:31
2 Abb 215: I was on friendly terms; Abb 234: because I was on friendly terms.
3 The patriarch of the EOTC was always Egyptian, appointed in Alexandria for life. Therefore, a large community of Egyptian Coptic Christians lived in Ethiopia, near the mother church in Aksum. Interacting with Coptic Christians would have been typical of someone who lived in Aksum.
4 Abb 215: and God kept me safe; Abb 234: but God kept me safe.
5 ወልደ ዮሐንስ (Son of [Saint] John).
6 Luke 23:2; this phrase is similar to the charge made against Christ.
7 Abb 215: 'and kill the king' is added in the margin by a secondary hand; in Abb 234 the phrase is in the body.

Chapter 4: My Fleeing into the Wilderness

As soon as I found this out,[1] I became afraid. I had three ounces of gold,[2] so I took that with me, [along with] a book and a psalter[3] for my personal prayers, and I fled during the night. I did not tell anyone, nor did anyone ask me, where I was going, and I arrived at an isolated place[4] by the *Takkaze* River.[5]

By the next day, I was starving, so I fearfully went out to beg for some bread from the wealthy in a nearby town. They gave me some, and I ate. Then I fled [to my next hiding place]. I did the same thing [,begging and walking,] for many days.

Abb234 4v

While heading towards the region of Shewa,[6] I found another isolated place.[7] At the bottom of a high cliff, there was a beautiful cave, and I thought, 'I can stay here without anyone knowing'. I lived there for two years, until Susenyos died.

Abb215 3v

Sometimes I went out, heading to the market[8] or to one of the Amhara towns.[9] The Amhara people thought that I was a hermit monk begging for alms, and they gave me food.

---

1 Abb 215: as soon as I found this out; Abb 234: as soon as I heard this.
2 ያእወቃያት ወርቅ (three *awqayat* of gold) One ወቀት (*waqet*) is approximately equivalent to 1 ounce, or 28 grams.
3 Abb 234: a book of the Psalms of David. *Psalms of David* is the title of an Ethiopian book that actually includes more than Psalms. This daily prayer book, the Psalter, also includes other biblical songs, the *Song of Songs* and Ethiopian hymns and prayers to Mary.
4 ገዳም (wilderness or monastery), here and several sentences later, and by implication a place where someone goes to be a hermit monk, isolated from all others, hence its second meaning.
5 ተከዚ (*Täkkäzi*) is a river marks the southern boundary of the northernmost Ethiopian region of Tigré. This is an alternate spelling of the term, common in older manuscripts.
6 ሸዋ (*Šäwa*), the southernmost Ethiopian region. The modern city of Addis Ababa is at its centre, about 570 kilometres (350 miles) south of Aksum. Abb 234: ሰዋ (*Sewa*).
7 Previous translations did not make clear that the place where he stayed was not on the Takkaze River.
8 In highland Ethiopia, markets are not found in towns (which are only for homes) but are held on two or three days a week between different towns on main roads. Only a place outside of town has enough space for all the people, animals, crops, crafts, and so on.
9 The Amhara are a people of highland Ethiopia, who live in Shewa, but also in the historical region directly west of the historical region of Shewa and south of the historical region of Tigré, which is the author's home region. The centre of the Amhara people is Lake Tana, with Begemder to the north of it and Gojjam to the south.

People didn't know where I lived or returned to, and when I was alone[1] in my cave, I felt like I was living in the Kingdom of Heaven, because I hated to be with human beings,[2] knowing their limitless evil.

I improved my cave with a fence of stones and thorny branches to prevent wild animals from eating me during the night. Also, I made a way to escape in case anyone came searching for me.

I lived there in peace, and I prayed the Psalms of David with all my heart, and I trusted in God who hears me.[3]

Part II: My Inquiries

Chapter 5: My Inquiry regarding Wickedness

[Every day,] I had nothing to do after making my prayers, so I meditated all day on humanity's quarrels and wickedness, and also on the wisdom of the Lord their creator, who keeps silent[4] when they act wickedly in his name, persecute their neighbours, and kill their own brothers and sisters, due to the power of the foreigners[, the European Catholics,] in those days.

It was not just the foreigners[, the European Catholics, who acted wickedly], but as for the nation's people[, the Ethiopian Orthodox,][5] they were even more evil than the foreigners. Those [of my country] who accepted the foreign [Catholic] faith said, 'the Copts[, the Egyptian Orthodox Church,] have denied the true faith[6] of the Throne of Peter,[7] and they are the Lord's enemies'. So, the [Ethiopian] Catholics persecuted the Coptic [leaders, and

Chap 3
Abb234 5r

Abb215 4r

Sum 6

---

1 Abb 234: when I was a hermit (or solitary).
2 ሰብእ (human). The author uses this word frequently and we have translated it variously according to context, including 'human', 'human being', 'all human beings', 'humanity', 'people', 'all people'.
3 Abb 234: and I trusted that God hears me.
4 That is, he is pondering why God would keep silent when people rebel in his name. What wisdom would make God silent?
5 Abb 234: for our nation's own people. However, the more impersonal wording in Abb 215 (as opposed to the more personal wording in Abb 234) could be put down to scribal error of miscopying the pronominal suffix -ነ (our) with the particle -ኒ (also).
6 ሃይማኖተ ርትዕት (Orthodox faith).
7 Abb 234 omits: of the Throne of Peter. This refers to the seat of the Bishop of Rome, also known as the Pope, the head of the Roman Catholic Church.

their Ethiopian followers,] and the Copts did the same on account of their own faith.¹

I turned over in my mind, 'If God is the guardian of humanity, how has their human nature been ruined in this way?'

I wondered, [as it says in Psalms,] 'How can God know [about human depravity]? Is there knowledge in the Most High?'²

And if there is such knowledge, why does God keep silent on human depravity, when they defile his name or act wickedly in his holy name?

I turned this over in my mind many times, but I did not understand it at all.

I prayed [with Psalms]:³

'O my lord and creator—who created me intelligent—make me understand'⁴

'Tell me your hidden wisdom!'⁵

'Give light to my eyes, so that I don't sleep the sleep of death'.⁶

'Your hands made me and formed me, make me understand and I will learn your commandments'.⁷

'Because, as for me, my feet almost stumbled, and my steps almost slipped'.⁸

[When I tried to understand wickedness,] 'this was wearisome for me'.⁹

As I prayed, this and similar [thoughts] continued [to turn over in my mind].

---

1 Abb 234 omits: on account of their own faith.

2 Psalm 73:11 (72:11 LXX). We have added the subject of God's knowledge, 'human depravity', based on an earlier verse in this Psalm. The author often alludes to the meaning of a whole Psalm by giving just one line from it, assuming that his Ethiopian audience, who knew all the Psalms by heart, will understand the overall themes, subject, and context to which the quotation alludes.

3 The author is creating his own Psalm, on a particular theme, by yoking disparate passages in various Psalms together.

4 Psalms 119:34 (118:34 LXX). ዘፈጠርኒ ለባዊ አለቡኒ (you who created me intelligent, make me understand).

5 Psalm 51:6 (50:8 LXX).

6 Psalm 13:3 (12:4 LXX).

7 Psalm 119:73 (118:73 LXX). In the Psalms and other biblical passages, 'commandments' include the Ten Commandments but are not limited to them.

8 Psalm 73:2 (72:2 LXX).

9 Psalm 73:16 (72:16 LXX).

Chapter 6: My Inquiry regarding the Existence of a Creator

One day, though, I pondered, 'Whom do I myself pray to? Is there a Lord who hears me?'

I was deeply troubled, and I said to myself, just as David said [in Psalms], 'Surely in vain I have kept my heart pure?!'[1]

Later, I pondered [something else] that David had said, 'Does he who planted the ear not hear?'[2]

I thought, 'In reality, who is it who gave me ears to hear, and who created me as intelligent? How did I myself come into this world? Where did I come from?'[3]

For, I didn't exist prior to the world,[4] I don't know [the time] when my life and my intellect began. But who created me? Did I create myself with my own hands? But I didn't exist when[5] I was created [so how could I create myself?].   Abb234 6r

If I say that my father and my mother created me, then my parents' creator and their parents' creator must still be searched for, until arriving at the first ones who were not conceived like us, but who came into this world in another way, without parents.   Abb215 5r

For, if they were conceived, I don't know where their genealogy begins unless I say, 'There is one being who created them out of nothing,[6] one who was not created, but rather already existed and will exist forever,[7] Lord of all, the Almighty, who has no beginning or end, immutable, whose years are innumerable'.

---

1 Psalm 73:13 (72:13 LXX). That is, if there is no creator, one need not behave correctly to satisfy him.
2 Psalm 94:9 (93:9 LXX).
3 Abb 234 omits: and from where did I come?
4 He seems to have in mind the opening from the divine liturgy of the Anaphora of Dioscorus: አምቅድም ዓለም ወእስከ ለዓለም ሀሎ እግዚአብሔር በመንግሥቱ እግዚአብሔር በትሥልስቱ እግዚአብሔር በመለኮቱ (From before the world [began,] and for eternity God exists in His kingdom; God exists in His trinity; God exists in His divinity).
5 Abb 234: when.
6 እምነበ አልቦ (from that which is not), a phrase expressed in Latin as *ex nihilo* (from nothing).
7 ዘሀሎ ወይሄሉ (the one who is and will be), from Exodus 3:14, which is included in the hymn *Wəddase Maryam*, the part recited every Monday in the liturgy. This whole sentence has set expressions from the EOTC liturgy and many of them rhyme, as with the example given here.

I said, 'Therefore, there is a creator', because if[1] there were no creator, then the creation would not have existed. Because we exist and are not creators but rather are created, we have to say that there is a creator who fashioned us.

Further, this creator who fashioned *us* with the faculties of reason and speech[2] cannot himself be without these faculties of reason and speech, because from the abundance of his reason he created us with the faculty of reason. 'He understands all things, because he created all things, and he sustains all things'.[3]

I thought, 'My creator will listen to me when I pray to him', and I was very happy with this thought.

So I prayed with great expectation, loving my creator[4] with all my heart, I prayed [aloud with the Psalms], 'You, O Lord, know all the thoughts of my heart from far away. For look, you yourself knew all things, in the first and the last, and you knew all my ways in advance'.[5]

So, I thought, because of this [truth], it said [in the Psalms],[6] 'You know from far away'; [that is,] because the Lord knew my thoughts before I was created.

I prayed aloud, 'O my creator, give me understanding!'

Chapter 7: My Inquiry regarding the Truth of Different Religions

And later, I thought, 'Is all that is written in the sacred books[7] true?' I thought a lot, but [in spite of this thinking,] I didn't understand anything.

---

1 Abb 234 omits: if. This appears to be a scribal error of omission.
2 ለባውያን ወነባብያን, (as ones with intelligence and beings with speech). That is, they can understand the world and they have the linguistic capacity to articulate that understanding. The same two words appear in the next two phrases as well.
3 These phrases are repeated many times during the EOTC liturgy of hours and the divine liturgy (for instance, during the concluding part of the Anaphora of Dioscorus).
4 Abb 234: our creator.
5 Psalm 139: 2, 5, 3 (138: 2, 5, 3 LXX).
6 ይቤ (it *or* he said). The opening phrase of this sentence is the standard formula for opening commentary on a biblical text in the Ethiopian tradition.
7 መጻሕፍት ቅዳሳት (holy books), but in the Ethiopian tradition, few churches or monasteries would have manuscripts with every book of the Bible (an extended canon of 81 books), and many other texts are regarded as sacred, so these words are not referencing a defined set of biblical books.

So, I said [to myself], 'I will go, and I will ask learned people and those who question deeply, and they will tell me the truth'.[1]

And after this, I thought, 'What answer will people give me except that which is already present in their hearts?'

In fact, everyone says, 'My religion[2] is correct, and those who believe in another religion believe in something false, and they are enemies of God'.

Abb234 7r

Now, the foreigners[, the European Catholics,] say to us, 'Our creed is good, and your creed is evil'.

But we [Ethiopians] answer them, 'It is not evil; rather your creed is evil and our creed is good'.

Now, suppose we asked Muslims and Jews [about their belief]? They would say the same thing to us.

Abb215 6r

Also, if they argued the case in this debate, who would be the judge?

No human being[3] [could judge] because all human beings have become judgemental, and they condemn each other.

First, I asked a foreign[, European Catholic] scholar about many things concerning our [Ethiopian] creed[4] and he decided everything [was right or wrong] according to his own creed.

Afterwards, I asked a great Ethiopian teacher, and he [likewise] decided everything according to his creed.

If we asked Muslims and Jews about the same things, they would also decide according to their own religion.

Where will I find someone who will decide [on the religions and creeds] truthfully? Because [just as] my religion seems true to me, so does another's religion seem true to them. But, there is only one truth.

---

1 Abb 234 omits: and they will tell me the truth.
2 ሃይማኖት (belief, creed, faith, or religion).
3 እጓለ እመሕያው (children of the mother of the living [Eve]). In Ethiopia, this is a typical formulation for expressing the idea of humanity, emphasizing that we all come from one mother. For instance, in the English Bible, Christ is called 'the Son of Man' while in the Ethiopic Bible he is called ወልደ እጓለ እመሕያው (the Son of the Children of the Mother of the Living) (John 3:13–14).
4 Abb 234 omits: about many things concerning our creed.

As I turned these things over in my mind, I thought, 'O wisest[1] and most righteous Creator, who created me with the faculty of reason, give me understanding'.[2]

For wisdom and truth are not found among human beings, but as David said [in Psalms], "indeed, everyone is a liar'.[3]

I thought and said [to myself], 'Why do human beings lie about these vital matters [of religion], such that they destroy[4] themselves?'

It seemed to me that they lie because they know nothing at all, although they think they are knowledgeable. Therefore, because they think they are knowledgeable, they don't search to find out the truth.

David said [in Psalms], 'their hearts are curdled like milk',[5] Indeed their hearts are 'curdled' by what they have heard from their ancestors. Furthermore, they never investigated whether what they heard is true or false.

As for me, I say [with Psalms],

'It was good for me, O Lord, that you inflicted suffering on me so that I may learn your judgement.'[6]

'Rebuke me with truth and reproach me with mercy. Don't let my head be anointed[7] with the oil of sinners'[8] and false teachers.[9]

[I add,] 'Give me understanding for you have created me as a rational being'.[10]

I thought and said [to myself], 'If I am a rational being, what do I understand?'

I thought, 'I understand that there is a creator who is greater than all the creation'. For, out of the richness of his greatness he created great things. Also, he is a rational being, understanding all things, for out of the richness of his

---

1 ጠቢብ ጠቢባን (wisest of the wise), the normal way to express a superlative in Ge'ez, but perhaps also an allusion to the Ge'ez hymn of the same name, ጠቢብ ጠቢባን, a short narration of the history of salvation.

2 A frequent request of the Psalmist in Psalm 119, for instance verses 34, 73, 125, 144, 169 (118: 34, 73, 125, 144, 169 LXX).

3 Psalm 116:11 (115:2 LXX).

4 Abb 234: to ruin themselves.

5 Psalm 119:70 (118:70 LXX).

6 Psalm 119:71 (118:71 LXX).

7 ኢይትቀባዕ ርእስየ (Don't let my head be anointed).

8 Psalm 141:5 (140:5 LXX).

9 Abb 234: liars.

10 ለባዊ, (rational, intelligent, one who reasons), an adjective which also serves as a noun, which we have translated differently according to context; sometimes as 'rational', 'faculty of reason', 'rational being(s)', 'understanding being(s)', 'intelligent' (as describing Hirut), or 'wise' (again as describing a person as 'wise and inquisitive').

understanding he created us as rational beings. So, we should worship him, because he is the Lord of all, and when we pray to him, he hears us,[1] because he is the almighty.

And I thought and I said [to myself], 'When God created me as a rational being, it was not purposeless that he created me so'. Rather, [he did it] so that I would seek him, and understand him and his wisdom, creating me in the way he did.[2] I will glorify him for as long as I live.

Chapter 8: My Inquiry regarding Falsehood

I thought, and I said [to myself], 'Why don't all human beings understand the truth instead of [believing] lies?'

It seemed to me that it is because the nature of human beings is weak and lazy. Human beings do delight in the truth, and they love her[3] greatly, and they desire to know[4] creation's mysteries, but doing so is difficult. The truth won't be found without great toil and patience.[5]

As Solomon said [in the Bible], 'I gave my heart to seek out and examine, with wisdom, everything that happens under the sun, because God gave human beings a vile burden for them to be exhausted by'.[6]

Because of the vileness of this burden, human beings don't want to ask questions,[7] and they rush to believe what they have heard from their ancestors, without questioning.

Also, God created human beings to be the owners of their own actions, to be what they want to be, whether good or evil.

If human beings choose to be evil and liars, they can be, until they receive the judgement that their evil deserves.[8]

---

1 Abb 234: when *I* pray to him he hears *me*.
2 Abb 234: Rather, so that I would seek him, and his wisdom with which he created me.
3 the soul, the mind, human nature, wisdom, truth, and many other abstract qualities are feminine. This text here treats 'truth' as feminine.
4 Abb 234: and they greatly love to know.
5 Abb 234: But this is difficult, and will not be found without toil and great patience.
6 Ecclesiastes 1:13.
7 ኢይፈቅዱ ይሕትቱ (they don't want to inquire).
8 Abb 234: they can be.

Also, human beings choose fleshly pleasure, because they are fleshly beings.¹ They seek to satisfy the desires of their flesh in every way that they can be found, whether good or evil.

It is not God who created human beings as evil, rather it is God who gave them the choice to become whatever they want. Because God gave them this choice, any human being will be worthy of a reward if they are good or judgement if they are evil.

If a liar who seeks wealth or prestige among human beings wants to obtain these through lying, he will speak lies, representing them as true. To human beings who don't want to question, his lies will seem to be true, and they will believe in them with unshakable faith.

Look, how many lies our people believe with unshakable faith! They believe² in astrology³ and other prediction practices, in [the power of] repeating secret names, in omens, in demon summoning, and all charms, and in everything fortune tellers pronounce. They don't believe in all these because they investigated them and found them to be true, rather they believe in them because they heard about them from their ancestors.⁴ Why did these people lie, except to gain wealth and prestige?

Likewise, those who want to rule the people⁵ say, 'God has sent us to announce the truth to you'.

As a result, the people believe. Those who came later didn't question the belief of their fathers, rather they accepted it⁶ without question. They even strengthened it,⁷ by adding stories of signs and miracles to prove the truth of their belief.⁸ And they declared, 'God did these signs and miracles!' Thus, they made God an attesting witness of lies and a collaborator with liars.⁹

---

1 Romans 8:5, but also expressed in the Anaphora of Dioscorus: ንሕነሰ ሥጋውያን ንሕሊ ሕገ ሥጋ ወንገብር ግብረ ሥጋ ወካሁውር በፍኖተ ሥጋ (We, however, are fleshly. We think according to the law of the flesh; we do the work of the flesh; and we proceed in the path of the flesh).
2 Abb 234 adds: why do they believe?
3 For an example of Ethiopian astrology, see the fifteenth-century Ge'ez text ዑደ ነገሥት ወሐሳብ ከዋክብት (The Divine Cycle of Kings and the Computation of the Stars).
4 Abb 234: but because they heard it from their ancestors.
5 Abb 234: those who wanted to rule human beings.
6 Abb 234: They did not inquire, rather they accepted the faith of their fathers.
7 Abb 234 makes the pronoun 'it' explicit with ሓሰት (the lies), making the object of the verb clear.
8 Abb 234: In order to strengthen their religion.
9 Abb 234 omits: and a collaborator with liars.

But to the one who searches, truth will quickly[1] be revealed. For, because the one who inquires with the pure reason which the Creator has put into the human heart, to perceive the creation's established order and laws,[2] will find the truth.

Chap 5

Chapter 9: My Inquiry regarding Jewish, Islamic, and Christian Laws about Sexuality and Bodies

[Regarding the Jews,] Moses said, 'I was sent from God to announce to you all His will and His law'.[3]

Abb234 9v

But those who came after him, they added stories of miracles which they allege were done in the land of Egypt and on Mount Sinai.[4] They made their additions appear like the truth of what Moses had [originally] said.

Abb215 8v

But, to the one who investigates [these stories], they don't seem like the truth. For, in the books of Moses, [that is, Genesis, Exodus, Leviticus, Numbers, and Deuteronomy,] detestable wisdom is found,[5] that is not in harmony with the Creator's wisdom, nor creation's established order and laws.[6]

For, under the authority of the Creator's will and the creation's established order, men and women should[7] have the bodily communion of intercourse,[8] joining together in their flesh. [In this way,] they [conceive and] give birth to children so that humanity will not disappear. This union, which God has estab-

---

1 Abb 234 omits: quickly.
2 Abb 234: And into the ordering of creation, which is clear to our intelligence.
3 Moses does not say this sentence in the main Biblical books about him, Exodus and Deuteronomy; rather, the author here creatively summarizes various things Moses said about his relationship with God and his people. See Exodus 3:13.
4 In EOTC theology, a distinction is often made between Christian folklore (like hagiographies or miracle collections) and canonical texts, with theologians cautioning against taking miracle stories at face value. HZY is taking that general caution further and using it to question the Bible itself and some of its miracles associated with Moses. On this caution, see the book መጻጌ ሰቤ by Heruy Walda Selassie.
5 Abb 234: For this is found in the books of Moses.
6 Abb 234 omits: and laws.
7 Abb 234: So, the creation's established order commands men and women.
8 ተካቤ, which is derived from ረከበ (to find something or someone). Therefore, it is not a reference to sex alone but to the connection and intimacy that sex provides.

lished as part of human nature, the law of his creation for humanity,[1] cannot be impure, because God will not defile the work of his own hands.[2]

[But,] as for Moses, he said, 'all intercourse is impure'.[3]

It is only our intelligence that makes us sure[4] that anyone who says this is a liar and regards the creator himself as a liar.

Meanwhile, Christians claim that their law is from God, and miracles have been found that assert this.

But, only our intelligence tells us and assures us that marriage is part of the creator's established order.[5] The ascetic monastic life rejects the creator's wisdom, because it prevents conceiving children [and giving birth to them,] and thus destroys the human race.

Also, when[6] the Christians' law says, 'the ascetic monastic life is better than marriage',[7] it's telling a lie and it's not from God.[8] For, how can the Christian law that violates the Creator's law be better than his wisdom? Can human deliberation improve on the work of God?[9]

In the same way,[10] Mohammed said, 'I received[11] from God what I command you to do'.

There were plenty of miracle writers who affirm [the claim] that Mohammed was sent by God and so they believed in him.

As for you and me, we know that Mohammed's teaching [about multiple wives] cannot be from God.[12]

For, human beings, born male and female, are equal in number, and if we count men and women who live in one country, there is one woman for

---

1 Abb 234: This union is the law of the creator.
2 Abb 234: his precepts.
3 Moses does not say this sentence in the main Biblical books about him, Exodus and Deuteronomy; rather he is creatively summarizing the ritual purity laws that appear in the Hebrew Bible, many in Leviticus (e.g., even married people who have intercourse cannot approach the temple or tabernacle for twenty-four hours, which law both Ethiopian Orthodox Christians and Muslims also follow).
4 Abb 234: makes certain.
5 Abb 234: It us that marriage is part of the creator's law.
6 Abb 234 omits: when.
7 It is unclear where this quotation comes from; writing on monasticism and asceticism has regularly affirmed celibacy as spiritually preferable to marriage.
8 Abb 234: and this is a lie.
9 Abb 234 omits: Can human deliberation improve on the work of God?.
10 Abb 234: also.
11 Abb 215: 'I received' added in the upper margin by a secondary hand.
12 Abb 234 omits: Mohammed's teaching cannot be from God.

every man. There aren't eight or ten women for each man, because creation's established order prescribes that one man and one woman will marry. So, if one man marries ten women, nine men will have no wife. This violates the creator's established order and the creation's laws,[1] and it annuls the benefits of marriage.[2] Mohammed, who taught in God's name that it is proper for one man to marry many women, is a liar and was not sent from God.

I investigated a few such things concerning the established order of marriage.

Similarly, even if I were to investigate the rest of the Mosaic Law,[3] Christian law, and Islamic law, I would find many things that are not in harmony with our creator's 'truth and justice',[4] which our intelligence reveals to us.

Because the creator put the light of intelligence in the human heart, that human beings may perceive good and evil; recognise what is and is not proper; and distinguish the truth from a lie, and how 'By your Light, O Lord, we see light'![5]

If we were to see by this light of our intelligence what is our duty, it cannot deceive us, because our Creator[6] gave us this light that we may be saved by it, and not destroyed.[7] And all[8] that the light of our intelligence reveals to us is from the fountain of truth.[9]

By contrast, what human beings say to us arises from the fountain of lies. Our intelligence affirms[10] to us that everything the Creator has established is right.

---

1 Abb 234: and opposes his wisdom.
2 While many critiques of Islam exist in EOTC theology, the focus on polygamy here would seem to be unique to this author. Perhaps this was because polygamy was not so rare among Ethiopian Christians, especially among the nobility.
3 ሕገ ኦሪት, which is a little ambiguous, as the term *orit* may refer to 'the Law', 'the Ten Commandments', or 'the Octateuch' (that is, the first eight books of the Bible, Genesis to Ruth, which are commonly bound together in manuscripts). In this context, it clearly refers to Old Testament Law, but something wider than just the Ten Commandments.
4 Psalm 111:7 (110:7 LXX).
5 Psalm 36:9 (35:9 LXX)
6 Abb 234: the creator.
7 An allusion to John 1:9 and John 3:16.
8 Abb 234 omits: and all.
9 Alternately, ወኵሉ ዘያርእየነ ብርሃነ ልቡናነ እምነቅዓ ጽድቅ ውእቱ might be translated 'our intelligence's light arises from the fountain of truth'.
10 Abb 234: tells us.

Abb234 11r
Abb215 10r

Litt Ed 11

With virtuous[1] wisdom, the creator ordained that each month blood should flow from a woman's womb; and that this flow of blood is essential to a woman's life and the bearing of children.[2] A woman who does not have this flow is barren and cannot bear children, because her womanhood is damaged.[3]

But Moses[4] and Christians have declared that this [particular] wisdom of the Creator is [something] impure. Moses even declares that anything touched by a [bleeding] woman is impure.[5] This 'law of Moses' makes marriage and a woman's entire life difficult because it annuls [the principle of] mutual help, impedes child rearing,[6] and destroys love. Therefore, this 'law of Moses' cannot be[7] from the Creator of women.

[On another issue], our intelligence tells us, 'We should bury[8] our dead relatives'.[9]

Their corpses are not unclean, except in accordance with 'Moses' wisdom'. [That's] not [the case] according to our Creator's wisdom, who made us from earth so that we might return to earth.[10]

On the contrary, God will not defile the order which he himself established with great wisdom as befits all creation. Human beings, however, want to defile this established order so that they might honour the falsehood [of human laws].[11]

Abb234 11v
Abb215 10v

In addition, the Gospel says, 'He who does not leave his father and mother, his wife and children will not be worthy of God'.[12]

---

1 Abb 234: with great.
2 Abb 234: and for childbearing.
3 እስመ ማስነ ፍጥረታ (because her nature is spoiled).
4 The author is precisely focused on what Moses did, not on Jews as a race or Jewish law more generally.
5 Leviticus 15:19–30.
6 Abb 234: Because <and> it annuls the law of mutual help < and . . . of children> and the raising of children.
7 Abb 234: cannot come.
8 Abb 234: our intelligence tells us to bury.
9 አኃዊነ (our brothers), but this word can also mean 'kindred' or 'relatives'.
10 An allusion to Genesis 3:19, but flipping what is a curse, 'By the sweat of your face you will eat your bread . . ., for you are earth and to earth you will depart', into something positive, treating death and burial as part of the natural order.
11 ቃለ ሐሰት (the word of falsehood).
12 Abb 234: The Gospel says that he who leaves his father and his mother, his wife and his children is worthy of God. Paraphrase of Matthew 10:37, Luke 14:26, which is direct speech from Jesus.

This abandonment [of family] undermines the nature of all humanity,[1] and God does not delight in destroying his creation.

Further, our intelligence shows[2] us that abandoning fathers and mothers in their old age, so that they die through neglect, is a terrible transgression. And 'God is not a God who loves violence'.[3]

Also, those who abandon children are more wicked than the wild beasts of the wilderness, for animals don't abandon their offspring.

Also, he who abandons his wife sets her up to commit adultery. He destroys the Creator's established order and the creation's laws.[4]

Sum 11

Consequently, what the Gospel says in this section of the text[5] [about leaving your family] cannot be from God.

Also, Muslims say that it is proper to sell and trade human beings like animals. But only through our intelligence do we realise that this Muslim law cannot come from the Creator of human beings, the one who created us equal, as brothers and sisters, meaning that we call the Creator 'our father' [as members of his family]. But Mohammed regarded weak human beings as the property of strong human beings and equated rational creation[6] with irrational beasts. Can it be that this violence comes from God?

Abb234 12r

Abb215 11r

Chapter 10: My Inquiry regarding Jewish, Islamic, and Christian Laws about Food

Likewise, God will not command pointless things.[7]

He will not say, as those among the Christians who keep fasting laws say, 'Eat this but don't eat that; eat today but don't eat tomorrow; don't eat meat today but eat it tomorrow'.

---

1 ያማስን ኩሎ ፍጥረተ ሰብእ (it ruins the entire nature of humanity).
2 Abb 234: tells us.
3 An allusion to Psalm 5:4 (5:5 LXX); Ethiopic versions of this psalm have አስመ ኢኮንከ አምላከ ዘዓመፃ ያፈቅር (You are not a God who loves violence), and the author has adapted the quotation into reported speech to fit the rhetorical context.
4 Abb 234: the creation's established order.
5 በዝንቱ ብሔር (in this section/region), a formulaic expression used in the Ethiopian *andemta* schools for speaking about sections of text.
6 ለፍጥረት ለባዊት (the understanding *or* intelligent creation [fem.]). In the Ethiopian tradition, the creation is referred to in the feminine, which the author uses here to communicate its uniqueness, beauty, delicacy, and sacred nature.
7 Abb 234 omits: he [God] will not command pointless things.

Also, to the Muslims, God does not say, 'eat during the night[1] but don't eat during the day', nor other similar things.

For our intelligence teaches us that we are permitted to eat anything that does not harm our health or constitution,[2] and also to eat every day enough to sustain our lives. Eating one day and fasting another destroys [our] health. The fasting laws lie outside the established order of the creator, who created food for good health. He desired for us to eat food, and to give thanks to him. It isn't right that we should abstain from this blessing of his.[3]

If there are those who tell me that the fasting law was established to kill the lust of the flesh, I say to them, 'The craving of the flesh, in which a man is attracted to a woman and a woman is attracted to a man, is the creator's wisdom'.

Contradicting this [wisdom, by restraining this attraction,] is not right, it's ignoring the creator's established order of lawful intercourse[4] [through marriage].[5] Indeed, our creator did not put this craving into all human and animal flesh for no reason. Rather, he planted this craving in human flesh as the foundation of life in this world,[6] and he sets all creation on the path established for it.[7]

Also, so that this craving does not exceed its natural limits, we should [only] eat as much as we need[8] because gluttony and drunkenness destroy our health and our work. But as a person does not sin who eats[9] as much as they need on Sunday, or during Pentecost, similarly a person who eats

---

1 Abb 234: Don't eat today but on another day eat. Don't eat meat today but eat it on another day. Eat during the night.
2 Abb 234: for our intelligence with which the creator bestowed us tells us to eat everything that does not harm our constitution.
3 Abb 234: The fasting law and other abstinences, except the abstinence from that which corrupts human nature, cannot be from God. Because God does not command useless things and after he created food for human life, he wants us to eat them and worship him and not to reject his blessing.
4 Abb 234: the creator's established order, which is lawful marriage and intercourse.
5 ወአብጥሎሙክስ ኢይደሉ እንበለ በሥርዓት አምር ዘሥርዓ ውአቱ ፈጣሪ በፍካቤ ሕጋዊ (violating it is not right, only [its fulfilment] in the well-known established order of the creator, lawful sexual communion). This sentence is an example of how the author regularly expresses complex ideas in complex and elegant language.
6 Abb 234: But so that this craving would be for the life of this world.
7 Abb 234: And he sets human nature in the wisdom of the creator and in all of creation's established order.
8 Abb 234: with measure.
9 Abb 234 adds: and drinks.

on Friday[1] or on the days before Easter does not sin,[2] because God created human beings with the desire to eat the same amount of food every day and every month.

The Jews, the Christians, and the Muslims did not comprehend God's work when they established the fasting laws. Rather, they lied saying,[3] 'God established fasting for us and forbids us eating'.

Yet God our creator gave food for our nourishment, for us to eat from it and not to abstain from it.[4]

Abb215 12r

Abb234 13r
Sum 12

Chapter 11: My Inquiry regarding Religious Agreement

Also, there is another great matter for inquiry: because, all human beings are equal in God's presence, and they are all his understanding creation.

Chap 6

He did not create one group of human beings for life and another for death, one for mercy and another for judgement.[5] Our intelligence teaches us that this [sort of] favouritism does not exist in God, who is 'righteous in all his deeds'.[6]

But Moses was sent to teach the Jews alone, and David himself said [in Psalms], 'God did not act like this towards other nations, and he did not tell them his judgement'.[7]

[The matter for inquiry is:] why did God tell his judgements to one nation and not to another? Nowadays, Christians say, 'God's teaching is not to be found except with us', but, the Jews, Muslims, Indians,[8] and others say the same thing.

Litt Ed 13

---

1 In EOTC tradition, Wednesday and Friday are fasting days for most of the year.
2 Abb 234: how does he sin who likewise eats on Friday?.
3 Abb 234: The Jews, Christians and Muslims lie when they say.
4 Abb 234: Because the creator himself gave people their nourishment to eat and not to abstain from it.
5 Abb 234: omits: one for mercy and another for judgement.
6 Psalm 145:17 (144:17 LXX).
7 Psalm 147:20 (147:9 LXX). The primary meaning of the Ge'ez verb is 'telling', while the primary meaning of the verb used in the Septuagint and the Vulgate is 'showing'. Perhaps the wording of this verse focused on the act of speaking, brought it to mind in a section on Moses' teaching. Note that the Ge'ez ፍትሕ translates the Greek τὰ κρίματα αὐτοῦ, understood here as thoughtful and wise deliberations; a legal decision by a judge; or a proper recognition of someone's rights.
8 Ethiopia has had trade connections with Southeast Asia since antiquity, and the author seems to have in mind Indian religions.

Abb215 12v

Furthermore, the Christians don't agree among themselves. The foreigners[, the European Catholics,] tell us, 'you don't have God's teaching, rather we have it'. We too say the same thing [to them].

Abb234 13v

But, if we would only listen to human beings, we would know that God's teaching has only reached a tiny few. Moreover, we don't know to which [few] of all these human beings it reached. Is it impossible for God to establish his word among human beings if he wants to?

Yet, the wisdom of God, with good counsel did not abandon human beings to agree with lies,[1] so that it would appear to them as truth. Because when all human beings agree with each other on something, that thing seems like the truth. [That's why God made it so that] all human beings cannot agree with lies, just as none of them can ever agree in their religious beliefs [which all have elements of falsehood introduced].[2]

If only we would think [about this]: why do all human beings agree in saying that there is a God, the Creator of all?[3]

Abb215 13r

Because the intelligence of every human being knows that everything that we see is created, that no creature may be thought of as created without a Creator, and that if there is a Creator, he is truthful. Because of this, all human beings agree on this point.

Yet when we inquire into the religious beliefs that human beings have taught, we cannot agree with them [all] because lies are mingled together with truth in them.[4]

Human beings quarrel with each other. One person says that something is true, while another says that it is not, it is a lie. All of them lie by regarding the word of human beings as the word of God.

Abb234 14r

I thought and said [to myself], '[However,] even if human religion is not from God, it is desirable because it gets good things done, for it terrifies the wicked into not doing evil things and it consoles the good for their patient endurance'.[5]

For me, religion of this kind is like a man's wife who conceived a child through adultery, without her husband knowing. The husband delights in

---

1 Abb 234: acted so that people would not agree with lies.
2 Abb 234: So now, they agree with lies, because none of the people agree on their religion.
3 The author appears to be unaware of the long tradition of atheism, unlikely in a European author.
4 Abb 234: because it is a lie.
5 Abb 234: people's religion is not from God, and it only becomes good because they produce good things, but it terrifies the wicked into not doing evil, and it comforts good people with their patience.

the child whom he supposes to be his son, and he loves the child's mother. Should he find out she conceived the child through adultery, he would be despondent and would reject and drive out his wife with the child.¹

Likewise, when I realised that my religion² was an adulteress and a liar, I became despondent because of her and of the children of her adultery [with lies]: they are hatred, persecution, physical abuse, imprisonment, and death, which have banished me into this cave.

Yet, for me, it's the truth to say that this Christian religion, established during the time of the Gospel, was not evil. For it instructs human beings to love one another and do every work of mercy.

But today, our country's³ people have banished the love that derives from the Gospel [in exchange] for hatred, dominance, and snakes' venom.⁴ They have torn their religion away from its foundations, and teach hollow things, do violent things,⁵ and are falsely called Christians.

Chapter 12: My Inquiry regarding False Doctrine and God's Established Order

I thought and said [to myself], 'Why does God allow deceivers to deceive his people?'⁶

God has given intelligence to each and every human being, so that they might recognise truth and lies. He has graciously given them the ability to discern, with which they may choose truth or lies, whichever they wish.

If we want truth, let us seek it with our God⁷-given intelligence, to see with it what is best for us⁸ from among creation's desirable things. We don't find the truth in human doctrines because 'Every person is a liar'.⁹

---

1 This type of extended analogy is one of the major rhetorical features of *qene*.
2 Abb 234: religion.
3 Abb 234 omits: our country's.
4 Psalm 140:3 (139:3 LXX). Quoting this phrase from a Psalm about the harm of evil men is likely an allusion to the bitterness among religious groups of the 1600s.
5 Psalm 119:3 (118:3 LXX).
6 Abb 234 adds: in his name.
7 Abb 234: creator.
8 Abb 234: with it to see his wisdom.
9 Psalm 116:11 (115:2 LXX).

If we prefer lies over truth,[1] it won't be the Creator's established order that will be destroyed because of this, nor the enduring law that he established for all creation.[2] Rather, it is we ourselves who will perish through our errors.

God protects the world with the rules that he established, which human beings cannot subvert because God's order and rules are stronger than human order and rules.[3]

For instance, those who believe that monastic celibacy is better than marriage are drawn toward marriage by the strength of the order and rules of the creator.[4]

Also, those who believe that fasting makes the soul righteous, eat when hunger seizes them.

Also, those who believe that giving up their possessions makes them perfect are drawn toward seeking possessions because of their usefulness. After they give up their possessions, they seek them out again, just as many monks have done in our country.

All liars who want to destroy creation's established order are like this. Yet, they cannot do anything but reveal their feeble lies. The Creator 'laughs at them', and the Lord of creation[5] 'mocks them',[6] because 'God knows the working of justice, but the sinner is ensnared by the work of their hands'.[7]

Therefore, the monk who disparages the institution of marriage will be ensnared by adultery, other sins of the flesh which are not natural,[8] or evil suffering.

Those who discard their possessions will become flatterers of kings and wealthy people in order to acquire possessions [again].

---

1 Abb 234: do not seek the truth.
2 Abb 234: of creation.
3 Abb 234 omits: God's order and rules are stronger than human order and rules. The human order includes the religious rules and regulations created by human beings, such as considering women impure during menstruation as well as fasting, monastic life, slavery, and so on.
4 Abb 234: by the power of creation.
5 Abb 234: and God.
6 Psalm 2:4 (2:4 LXX).
7 Psalm 9:16 (9:17 LXX). Note that here and elsewhere in our translation, when a singular masculine pronoun in the Ge'ez does not refer only to men, we sometimes have translated it with the singular 'they' or 'their'.
8 Abb 234 omits: flesh which is not according to his nature. The unnatural sin(s) would primarily be homosexual activity but might include sins like incest and bestiality.

Those who abandon their relatives, saying that it's for God's sake, will lack help when times are difficult for them and they are senile, and they will come to blame and curse God and human beings.

Those who violate the Creator's established order will likewise 'be ensnared by the work of their own hands'.[1]   Litt Ed 15 / Sum 14

In addition, God leaves error and evil among human beings because our souls live in this world, as if in a land of temptation through which God's chosen ones are put to the test.   Abb215 15r / Abb234 15v

As the wise Solomon said, 'For God put the righteous to the test and found them worthy of himself, and he tested them like gold is tested in a furnace, and he accepted them like a pleasing burnt offering'.[2]

Chapter 13: My Inquiry regarding Death

After our death, when we return to our creator, we will see how God established everything truthfully and with great wisdom and how all his ways are right and just.[3]

It is clear that our soul lives after the death of our flesh.[4] For, in this world our desires are not completely satisfied: those who don't have, seek, and those who have, desire more. Further, for those who have [possessions], even if a person possessed everything that exists in the world, they are not satisfied, and they long for [more].

This natural disposition of ours shows[5] that we were not created merely for life in this world alone, but also for the life that is to come.   Abb215 15v

There, souls who have fulfilled the will of their creator will be completely satisfied, and they will not desire anything else.[6] Without this [life after death], human nature would be left wanting and would not get everything intended for it.   Abb234 16r

---

1 Psalm 9:16 (9:17 LXX).
2 Wisdom of Solomon 3:5–6. This Second Temple text is canonical in the Ethiopian and other traditions.
3 Abb 234: as all God's ways are merciful and right.
4 Abb 234: our death.
5 Abb 234: recognizes.
6 Abb 234 adds: because.

Also, our soul[1] is able to imagine God[2] and to see him in her mind. Still more, she is able to imagine eternal life! God did not give our soul the capacity to imagine this for no reason; on the contrary, just as he gave her that capacity, he also gave her the possibility of finding [what she imagined].

Also, all righteousness is not fulfilled in this world.[3]

For, evil human beings achieve satisfaction from the good things of this world, while the gentle starve. There are evil human beings who are happy, and there are good human beings who are sad; there are vicious human beings who live lives of pleasure, while there are virtuous human beings who mourn.[4]

Therefore, after our death, another life and the perfection of justice is needed, in which all human beings will be rewarded according to their actions.[5] He will reward those who did the Creator's will as revealed to them by the light of their intelligence, and also those who followed their human constitution's nature.[6]

Abb215 16r Their constitution's nature is [known and] certain, because our intelligence tells us plainly if we study the matter. But human beings don't like to investigate things, they prefer to believe in human words, rather than truthfully seeking their Creator's[7] will.

---

1 Abb 234: my soul.

2 Abb 234: Lord.

3 The author writes that 'all righteousness is not fulfilled in this world', which phrasing likely arises from Matthew 3:15, in which Jesus says that ወይደልወነ ከመ ንፈጽም ኩሎ ጽድቀ (all righteousness should be fulfilled by us). The author is creatively adapting the famous biblical line, converting it into the negative for his rhetorical purpose.

4 Abb 234 omits: there are vicious human beings who live lives of pleasure, while there are virtuous human beings who mourn.

5 Psalm 62:12 (61:12 LXX); Psalm 28:4 (27:4 LXX).

6 Abb 234: by their intelligence and by the law of creation.

7 Abb 234: the creator.

Chapter 14: My Inquiry regarding Intelligence and the Truth of the Bible

The Creator's will is known[1] through this aphorism [2] that our intelligence tells us, 'Worship God your Creator,[3] love all human beings as yourself'.[4]

Moreover, our intelligence says, 'Don't do to human beings what you don't want them to do to you, but rather do to others what you want them to do to you'.[5]

Furthermore, the Ten Commandments of the Pentateuch[6] are also the Creator's will. The only exception is [the third commandment, about] honouring the sabbath because our intelligence does not confirm or deny it.[7]

But things like: let's not murder, let's not steal, let's not lie, and let's not have sex with another man's wife—our intelligence teaches us[8] that those things aren't right to do.

Similarly, the Gospel's Six Commandments[9] are the Creator's[10] will. For we want other human beings to perform these acts of mercy for us, and we should do for others what we are able to.

---

1 Abb 234: is discovered.
2 ሐጺር (short [saying]).
3 Abb 234 omits: your creator.
4 Allusion to Matthew 22:37–39, Mark 12:29–31, and Luke 10:27, but with the command in the first part of the verse, that we 'love' God, changed to 'worship' God.
5 Matthew 7:12.
6 ፲ ቃላተ ኦሪት (the ten words of Orit). the Ten Commandments are often referred to as the 'Ten Words', a way of emphasizing that they are not merely laws but also words to live by.
7 አእምሮ በእንተ አክብሮተ ሰንበት ያረምም ልቡና, (since our understanding is silent about the honouring of the sabbath). The author is uncertain whether the ritualistic observations of the Sabbath are a good idea because thinking about it has not yielded an answer, only silence.
8 Abb 234: tells us.
9 ፮ ቃላተ ወንጌል, (the six words/commandments of the Gospel). This is an important Ethiopian theological concept. The Six 'Words' of Jesus Christ have primacy over the Ten Commandments as rules for daily living in Ethiopia; the latter are rarely mentioned without the former. Jesus Christ named six works of mercy in Matthew 25:35–36: feed the hungry, quench the thirsty, accept and help strangers, clothe the naked, visit the sick, and visit those in prison. Note that these are not the six of the Ten Commandments that Jesus Christ repeats in the Gospels (Matthew 19:18), about murder, adultery, theft, lying in court, and honouring your parents and loving your neighbour.
10 Abb 234: God.

Furthermore, it's the Creator's will for us to take care of our lives and way of living in this world. Due to the Creator's will, we came into this life and live it, so we should not relinquish it except due to his sacred will.[1]

This same Creator of ours wants us to improve our lives with our knowledge[2] and work, because he gave us the intelligence and skills to do so. For instance, doing manual labour is the Creator's will,[3] because without this we won't get life's necessities. Likewise, [due to the Creator's will,] a man marries a woman and raises children.

Moreover, there are many other actions[4] that are in harmony with our intelligence, and beneficial for our life[5] and all human lives. We should persevere with these[6] actions because such is our Creator's will. We should understand[7] that God did not create us as perfect,[8] but rather as understanding beings with the potential for perfection.[9] That way, we may be perfected while we live in this world,[10] and after, be worthy of the reward that our Creator in his wisdom has prepared for us.

God could have created us as perfect and made us live in a blessed[11] state on earth.[12]

But he did not want to create us as such. Rather, he created us prepared for perfection.

He put us amidst this world's trials so that we could become perfect, and worthy of our Creator's reward after our death. So long as we live in this world, we should glorify our Creator, fulfil his will, and patiently endure until he takes us to himself.

---

1 Abb 234: by the creator's will.
2 Abb 234: knowledge.
3 ገብረ ግብረ እድ (working the work of the hand). The author seems to be challenging negative Ethiopian cultural attitudes toward craftsman, such as blacksmiths and potters, by linking them with more respected forms of manual labour, like that of farmers.
4 Abb 234: things.
5 Abb 234: our nature.
6 Abb 234: we should accomplish them [these things].
7 Abb 234: we should consider.
8 Abb 234 adds: but he put us in this world.
9 In Protestant theology, human beings can never be perfect as the fall is understood to result in total depravity; in EOTC theology (and Orthodox theology more generally), some can and do become perfect. That is the purpose of the human journey, to be perfected through suffering.
10 Abb 234: life.
11 ብፁዓን (blessed, happy [people]), the same word used for such in Psalm 1:1 and the Beatitudes, for instance, Matthew 5:3–12.
12 Abb 234: in this world.

Let us appeal to his goodness to ease the time of our testing and to forgive us our sins and [all] the stupid things we did due to ignorance.¹ Let him give us intelligence] so that we can know and keep the [beneficial] laws of our created nature.

Concerning prayer, we should always pray, because that's what's natural for a rational creature. The rational² soul understands that there is a God³ who knows everything, protects everything, and rules everything.⁴

The soul is drawn to God to pray, and she asks him for good things and to be saved from evil.

The soul takes refuge in the hands of the one who can do all things⁵ and for whom nothing is impossible.⁶ [I praise God:]

The Lord is great and high—
He sees those who are beneath him,⁷
and he sustains everything, and he understands everything, and he teaches everyone,
and he guides everyone.
Our Father, our Creator, our Protector, who is the reward for our souls,
who is merciful,
who is good, who knows all of our suffering,
and who delights in our patient endurance, who created us for life and not for destruction.⁸

As the Wisdom of Solomon says, 'You, O Lord, have mercy on all, because you can do all things, and you overlook human beings' sins while you await their

---

1 Abb 234: in our youth.
2 Abb 234 omits: rational.
3 ወነፍስ ነባቢት ዘትሌቡ ከመቦ እግዚአብሔር (the speaking [or rational] soul that understands that God exists).
4 ወኵሎ ይመልክ (he rules everything). A stock phrase from Revelation (1:8, 4:55, 15:3, 21:23), which has እግዚአብሔር ዘኵሎ ይመልክ (God who is the ruler of all [i.e., Almighty]).
5 Abb 234 omits: and to be saved from evil. She takes refuge in the hands of the one who can do all things.
6 Allusion to the Liturgy of Hours, Luke 1:37.
7 Psalm 138:6 (137:6 LXX). The Ethiopic bible, in line with the LXX, has አስመ ልዑል እግዚአብሔር ወይሬኢ ዘታሕቱ (For the Lord is high and he sees those who are beneath him). The author adds ዓቢይ (great). The addition may be deliberate or arise from textual variations appearing in the Ge'ez Bible the author memorized.
8 The anaphoras composed in Ge'ez often wax lyrical about God as in this paragraph—they include poetry of ecstatic praise layered with multiple rhythmic phrases of repeated diction and syntax (see, for instance, The Anaphora of St. John the Son of Thunder, the Anaphora of St. Dioscorus, and the Anaphora of Mary).

repentance. You love all things that exist, and detest none of the things that you have made'.[1]

You are compassionate and merciful to all creation.

God created us as understanding beings so that we may meditate on his greatness, worship him, and pray to him for our body and soul's necessities. Our intelligence, which our creator put into human hearts, teaches us[2] all these things.

How can the teaching of our intelligence be meaningless and false?

Chapter 15: My Inquiry regarding the Efficacy of Prayer Against Sin and Enemies

I came to know in another way that God hears our prayers when we pray to him with our whole heart, with love, faith, and patient endurance.

For I was a sinner in my youth for many years, not thinking at all about the work of God,[3] nor praying to him, and I was guilty of many[4] things inappropriate for a creature of intelligence. Because of my sin I fell into a trap from which a human being cannot escape safely, and I came close to utter torment, and the terror of death overtook me.

At that time, I turned to God, and I started to pray to him to[5] save me, because he knows all the ways of salvation.

I said to God, 'I will repent of my sins, seek your will, O Lord, and I will do your will! But, right now, forgive me my sin, and save me'.

I prayed with all my heart, for many days, and God heard me, and saved me completely. I worshipped him, and I turned to him with my whole heart.

I recited Psalm 114, [which begins] 'I loved, because the Lord heard the voice of my petition'.[6] It seemed to me that this psalm was written about me.

---

1 Wisdom of Solomon 11:23–24.
2 Abb 234: tells us.
3 An allusion to Psalm 25:7 (24:7 LXX). Abb. 234: I am a sinner. I lived beforehand for a long time not thinking about the work of God. In Ethiopia, the age of accountability is often considered to begin at the age of seven.
4 Abb 234: I did...
5 Abb 234: I started to ask God.
6 Psalm 116:1 (114:1 LXX). While the author rarely gives the number of a Psalm, he does so in a few places in this text (always numbered as in the Ethiopic and LXX). Giving the number as a shorthand for a Psalm is common in such Ethiopian liturgical texts as the Liturgy of Hours and the Book of the Divine Liturgy.

I also said [the Psalm], 'I shall not die, but I shall live, and I will tell of the Lord's work'.¹

For instance, there were those who constantly made false accusations against me to the king. They said to him, 'This man is your enemy, and an enemy of the foreigners[, the European Catholics]'.

I knew that the king's rage burned against me.

One day, king [Susenyos]'s messenger came and said to me, 'The king says, 'Come quickly to me'.²

I was terrified, but I couldn't escape because the king's men were watching for me. I prayed all night, with a mournful heart, and in the morning, I got up, and went to be in the king's presence.

But God had softened the king's heart, and he received me lovingly and didn't say anything about the things that I was afraid [he would accuse me of.] Rather, he asked about many matters of doctrine and scripture.³

He said to me, 'because you are a learned man, you should love the foreigners[, the European Catholics,] because they are very learned'.

I said to him, 'Yes indeed!' because I was afraid, but also because the foreigners[, the European Catholics,] were truly learned.

After this the king gave me five ounces of gold and sent me away in peace. After leaving the king, I was amazed, and I praised God who had made things turn out well for me.⁴

Then, when Walda Yohannes made false accusations against me, I fled, and I didn't pray for God to save me, as I did earlier [with the king], because now I was able to escape [on my own].⁵ Human beings should do everything that they can without asking God to help them for no reason.⁶

Now I worship him. Through my escape and living in a cave, I found the occasion to make a perfect return to my creator, to think what I had never thought before, and to know the truth, which makes my soul rejoice with great joy.

---

1 Psalm 118:17 (117:17 LXX).
2 ነዓእ ፍጡነ ኀቤየ, adding -ሀ at the end of words, as done here, signals the exact words of being quoted and is typical of a royal, official message in Geʿez texts. This is a very archaic practice for marking direct discourse. The author is very learned in a variety of Geʿez discursive practices.
3 Abb 234 omits: and scripture.
4 Possibly an allusion to Psalm 116:12 (115: 3 LXX), as it has the same phrase ዘገብረ ሊተ (what he did for me).
5 He does not explain why he can now escape, but likely it is due to his improved relationship with the king.
6 Abb 234: We should do what we can without asking God to help us for no reason.

Truly, I say to God [with Psalms], 'I deserved what you caused me to suffer so that I could know your statutes'.[1]

For how much more have I understood while living alone in a cave than I understood when I lived with scholars?[2] What I have written here is just a few of the many things that I meditated on while I lived in the cave.

I glorify God who gave me wisdom and who made me understand creation's mysteries.[3] My soul is drawn to him and rejects everything but meditating on the work and wisdom of God.[4]

I prayed all day[5] with the Psalms of David, with my heart outstretched,[6] because [such] prayer benefits me greatly and raises my thoughts to God.

Even if I find something in the Psalms of David which is not in harmony with my thought, I interpret it and harmonise it with my intellect and everything will become well with me.[7] And when I pray like this, it increases my trust in God.

[Following the Psalms,] I always say,[8]

'Give ear, O Lord, to my prayer, don't disdain my petition'. [9]
'Redeem me from the extortion of human beings'.[10]
'But as for you, O Lord, don't take your compassion from me;
     may your mercy and your truth always find me'.[11]

---

1 Psalm 119:71 (118:71 LXX).
2 Abb 234 omits: Truly, I say to God, 'I deserved what you caused me to suffer so that I could know your statutes'. For how much more have I understood while living alone in a cave than I understood when I lived with scholars?.
3 Abb 234: so that I might understand all this.
4 Abb 234: but meditating on God and on his wisdom.
5 Abb 234 omits: all day.
6 Abb 234: with all my heart.
7 Such harmonizing is a strategy taught in the EOTC commentary tradition when dealing with challenging passages in Scripture.
8 The author is creating his own Psalm on a particular theme by yoking disparate passages in various Psalms together. With two exceptions, he has selected only those verses where the speaker is speaking directly to God (in the singular first person) and asking God for mercy, help, and guidance. Then, he has altered the pronouns from third or plural first person to the singular first person. Such play and adaptation is typical of someone who has studied in qene school. For another instance, see ገድለ ፊልጶስ (Gädlä Filəppos)
9 Psalm 55:2 (54:2 LXX).
10 Psalm 119:134 (118:134 LXX).
11 Psalm 40:11 (39:11 LXX).

'Let me not be put to shame, O Lord, for I have called on you'.[1] Abb234 20r
'So, I will sing [Psalms] to your name forever, that you might give me what I long for all day long'.[2]
'Look upon me and have mercy on me; give your strength to your servant and save the son of your serving girl. Make with me a sign for good'.[3]
'For your name's sake, lead me and nourish me'.[4]
'Don't drag my soul away with sinners'.[5]
'Let your mercy be with me, as I trust in you'.[6]
'Make me one who hears of your mercy in the morning'.[7]
'Protect me, and make me happy in the land, don't deliver me into my enemy's hands'.[8]
'Cause me to hear joy and gladness'.[9]
'And don't put me to shame because of my expectation'.[10]
'They will curse, but you will bless'.[11]
'And let them know that [all] this is your hand'.[12]

Sum 18

This [prayer] and ones like it, I was praying day and night with all my heart.

Morning and evening, the prayer I was praying went like this:[13] Chap 10

'I worship you, O my creator and guardian, and Abb215 20v
'I love you with my whole heart, and
'I praise you because of the good things that you have done for me this night'. Abb234 20v

---

1 Psalm 31:18 (30: 18 LXX).
2 Psalm 61:8 (60:8 LXX).
3 Psalm 86:16–17 (85:16–17 LXX).
4 Psalm 31:3 (30:4 LXX).
5 Psalm 28:3 (27:3 LXX). Abb 234 adds: Your mercy will follow me for all the days of my life; quoting Psalm 23:6 (22:6 LXX).
6 Psalm 33:22 (32:22 LXX). Again, the author has changed the pronouns to personalise the Psalm.
7 Psalm 143:8 (142:8 LXX).
8 Psalm 41:2 (40:3 LXX). Again, the author has changed the pronouns to personalise the Psalm.
9 Psalm 51:8 (50:10 LXX, but sometimes 50:8 in Ethiopic bibles).
10 Psalm 119:116 (118:116 LXX).
11 Psalm 109:28 (108:28 LXX). This particular Psalm is full of curses. Since the author emphasizes love instead throughout, he may be demonstrating his point about harmonizing the Psalms with his thinking by omitting the verses that call for condemnation and instead selecting ones opposing human curses with divine blessing.
12 Psalm 109:27 (108:27 LXX).
13 Abb 234: Morning and evening the prayers I was praying, and which I prayed all day with great hope went like this. In what follows, the author has personalized a rhyming prayer sung thrice at the end of the EOTC Liturgy of Hours held at night.

(If it is evening, I say [instead, 'what you have done for me] this day'.)
'Protect me this day also.
(If it is evening, I say [instead, 'protect me] this night'].)[1]
'Give me understanding in this day
'and in all the days of my life,
'that I may know your will for me
'and fulfil it all the days of my life.
'Forgive me my sins.
'Give me every day enough for life's necessities.
'Strengthen me always with trust in you, O my Lord,
'because of your kindness, your power, and your greatness.
'Save me from poverty, from human hands and tongues, and
'from the body's illness and the soul's sorrow'.

After this, I would pray with Psalm 30, [which begins] 'In you I have trusted'.[2]

Chapter 16: My Inquiry regarding Work and Happiness

I meditated, and said [to myself], 'I should work and toil with all my skills to obtain all of life's necessities, for it is not enough for me to pray only. Nevertheless,[3] because I don't have any practical skills,[4] I shall proceed with God's power'.
[I prayed:]

Litt Ed 20
Abb215 21r

'Without your blessing, O Lord, my work won't benefit me at all.[5]
'As for you, [God,][6] bless my thoughts, and my work and my living,[7] give me possessions and happiness on the path according to your knowledge and will.

---

1 በዘቲ መዓልት/ ዕቀበኒ ዓዲ በዛቲ መዓልት/መሥርከስ ዕብል/ በዛቲ ሌሊት/ አለብወኒ በዛቲ ዕለት. The liturgy has ወበከሙ ዐቀብከነ/ እምነግህ እስከ ሰርክ/ ዕቀበነ አግዚአ/ እምሰርክ እስከ ነግህ (As you have protected us from morning to evening, protect us from evening to morning).
2 Psalm 31:1 (30:1 LXX).
3 Abb 234: I, for my part, should work as I can to obtain everything that is necessary for me. Because.
4 ኢየአምር ተግባረ (I do not know [manual] work). The author is a highly educated scholar, who spent years in school and left his home on the farm at an early age to live as a hermit, so he has no skills in physical labour.
5 Abb 234: I shall proceed with God's power, because my ability without your blessing will not benefit me.
6 Abb 234 adds: my dear creator.
7 Abb 234 omits: and my living.

'Turn the hearts of those who live with me to do well by me, because everything happens according to your blessed will,[1] and be gracious to me when I am old and senile'.

I know that our hearts are always in God's hands, and that God is able to make us happy and cheerful, even if we are in the midst of hardship, poverty, or suffering. But, God is also able to make us miserable in the midst of prosperity and all the world's pleasures. Abb234 21r

Because of this, every day we see the poor and the suffering taking pleasure in life with joyful hearts, while the wealthy and the kings are despondent and miserable amid their wealth due to their many cravings.

Although we don't desire sadness, it rises in our hearts without us knowing the reason for its rising. We should pray to God to let us 'hear gladness and joy'[2] and make us happy on earth.

For God makes light rise on the righteous and happiness on the upright in heart.[3] Abb215 21v

God knows and rules over all the ways of our hearts and is able to make us happy despite our anguish and sad despite our good works. Joy and sadness don't come to us in the way that human beings think they do, rather [they come] because God makes us hear them.[4]

So, I said, 'You, O my Lord and my Creator, let me hear gladness and joy, and make me happy as long as I live on earth. After my death, send me to you and satiate me'. Abb234 21v

I was praying like this day and night.

Chapter 17: My Inquiry regarding Nature and the Feebleness of the Human

I was marvelling at the beauty of God's creatures, each in its established order, the animals that eat plants and the animals that eat meat. They are drawn by their nature to preserve their life and to continue their kind.[5] Sum 19

---

1 Abb 234: to do good to me.
2 Psalm 51:8 (50:10 LXX).
3 Psalm 97:11 (96:12 LXX).
4 The author, in the elegant EOTC commentary style, interprets and expands on Psalm 51:8 (50:10 LXX), which he just cited.
5 ዘርአሙ (their seed).

Moreover, the forest's trees and plants, which were created with great wisdom—grow shoots, [then] bud, bloom, and produce fruit of their seed's kind without any mistakes.

It's almost like they have a soul.[1]

Moreover, the mountains and valleys, the rivers and springs, all your works,[2] glorify your name, O Lord. 'Your name is made glorious in all the earth'.[3] In heaven as well, how great are the works of your hands![4]

This sun is the spring of light and the spring of the life of the world.[5]

The moon and the stars, which you yourself established, don't stray from their ordained paths. But who knows the stars' number, or distance, or size, which seem small to us because of their remoteness?[6]

And who understands the clouds, which pour out water, making lush vegetation sprout? Everything is majestic and wonderful, and everything was created with wisdom.

I stayed like this for two years, marvelling [at creation] and glorifying the creator. I thought and said [to myself], 'the work of God is excellent, and his thoughts are deep, and his wisdom cannot be described'.

How can human beings, who are puny and needy, lie and say, 'I was sent from God to reveal his wisdom and righteousness to humanity'?[7]

They reveal nothing[8] to us but their own empty and worthless ideas. Their human nature is so puny.

Yet, with the intelligence our creator graciously bestowed on us, we can know his greatness. [For instance,] I said,

'"I am poor and needy"[9] in your presence, O Lord!

'Give me understanding of what I should know about you,[10]

---

1 Abb 234 omits: grow shoots, bud, bloom, and produce fruit of their seed's kind without any mistakes. It's almost like they have a soul.
2 Abb 234: everything glorifies your name.
3 Psalm 8:1, 9 (8: 1, 9 LXX).
4 Abb 234: How great is your name, O Lord!.
5 Abb 234: spring of life.
6 See the Introduction's Authorship of the *Hatata Inquiries* regarding these remarks on stars.
7 Abb 234: He comes to us and says to us, 'I came to you to reveal the wisdom of God to you'.
8 Abb 234: But they reveal nothing.
9 Psalm 40:17 (39:23 LXX).
10 Abb 234: what a rational creation like me should understand.

'so that I may marvel at your greatness, and
'glorify you all day with new praise!'[1]

Part III: My Life (1632–1693)

Chapter 18: My Becoming a Scribe after the Return of the Orthodox Faith

In 1632 CE,[2] King *Susenyos* died, and his son *Fasiladas* ruled in his place.   Chap 11

    At first, he loved the foreigners[, the European Catholics,] as his father did; however, he did not persecute the Copts, [the Egyptian Orthodox Church,] and there was peace in all of Ethiopia's provinces.

    At that time, I left my cave and went first to the Amhara districts, and then trekked to the Begemder district. To all the enemies of the foreigners[, the European Catholics,] I seemed like one of those monks who had fled in the days of *Susenyos*, so they liked me and gave me food and clothing.   Abb234 22v

    While I was going along from one town to another, I didn't want to return to Aksum, because I knew the wickedness of its priests.

    I was reminded [of the Psalm] that 'a person's path is made sure by God',[3] and I said, '"Show me, O Lord, the path that I should travel",[4] and to the region in which I should live'.

    I thought I would trek to and live in the province of Gojjam but God guided me to a place I had not considered.   Abb215 23r / Sum 20

    One day, I reached the Enfraz district [of the Amhara province], and came across a wealthy man, whose name was Habtu, which means 'the wealth of God' [in Amharic].[5]

---

1 Regarding a 'new song', see Psalm 33:3 (32:3 LXX), 40:3 (39:3 LXX), 96:1 (95:1 LXX), 98:1 (97:1 LXX), 149:1 (149:1 LXX).
2 ወበ፲፻ወ፮፻ወ፳፭ ዓመት እምልደተ ክርስቶስ (In the year 1625 after the birth of Christ). The year is in the Ethiopian calendar; in the Western calendar, this is 1632.
3 Psalm 37:23 (36:23 LXX).
4 Psalm 143:8 (142:8 LXX).
5 The author gives the Amharic meaning of the name 'Habtu', indirectly reminding the reader that in Ge'ez, it means something equally important, 'the gift of God'.

I stayed there for a day. The next day, I asked him for ink and parchment [to write on] so that I could send a letter to my relatives in Aksum.[1]

Lord Habtu[2] asked me, 'Are you a scribe?'

I replied, 'Yes, I am a scribe'.

And he said, 'Stay with me for a while, and write down the Psalms of David for me, and I will pay you a wage'.

I said to him, 'Certainly!'

Abb234 23r — I praised God in my heart, who had revealed to me a way to eat the fruit of my labour.[3] I was loathe to return to my previous profession as I didn't want to teach lies.

Litt Ed 22 — If I were to teach the truth, others would not listen to me without hating me,[4] accusing me, and persecuting me.

I want to live in peace and love with all human beings. I prefer to earn a living from the fruit of my labour.[5] I would rather be forgotten by human

Abb215 23v — beings and live in hiding with my God-given wisdom, 'than to live honoured in the house of sinners'.[6]

In a few days, I prepared the ink and parchment for a manuscript.[7] I wrote down in one book the Psalms of David.

Lord Habtu and all who saw my writing were astonished at its beauty. Lord Habtu gave me my wages: one fine set of clothing.

Later, Habtu's son, whose name was Walda Michael,[8] said to me, 'write down [a book] for me, just as you did for my father'. So I wrote one and he gave me a cow and two goats.

---

1 Although sending written messages would have been rare in those days, it was not unknown. For instance, kings had a specific method of sending written messages to their officials by way of messengers carrying the letters in a cleft stick.

2 Throughout this section, the wealthy nobleman Habtu is addressed as እግዚእ ሁቡቱ (Lord Habtu). እግዚእ (Lord) is an honorific title for a master, patron, or noble and also was used to address God, especially the Lord Jesus Christ.

3 ዘአርአየኒ ፍና በዘአሰሰይ ፍሬ ግብሬ (who has shown me the way I will eat the fruit of my labour), here and in several sentences. This is an allusion to Psalm 128:2 (127:2 LXX) ፍሬ ግብከ ተሰይ (may you eat the fruit of your labour).

4 Abb 234 omits: hating me.

5 Abb 234: from the work of my hands.

6 Psalm 84:10 (83:10 LXX).

7 It can take many months to prepare the ink and parchment for a manuscript, so it is likely that he 'prepared' by purchasing them.

8 ወልደ ሚካኤል (son of [Saint] Michael), an Ethiopian Christian name often given to a son born or baptized on St. Michael's day, the twelfth day of every Ethiopian month.

After this, many people came to me, to create copies of the Psalter, and other books and letters, because this place had no scribe other than me. They gave me clothes, goats, salt, grain,[1] and other similar things.

Lord Habtu also had two younger sons, one called Walda Gabriel,[2] known as Tesemma,[3] and the other called [Walda] Heywat, known as Metekku.[4]

Their father Habtu said to me, 'Teach them how to read the Psalter, and I will give you a wage: enough food to feed yourself.[5] What extra you earn as a scribe will be yours'.

I replied, 'Certainly, my father! I'll do everything that you've commanded me to do. Only, stand in the stead of my father and my mother and my relatives, because without you I have no family'.

Chapter 19: My Getting Married and Starting a Family

I knew that it wasn't good for a man to live alone, without a wife, because this path draws one into sin. Human beings shouldn't live in a way that isn't true to their nature,[6] to stop them from being entangled by false accusations about what they have done. As the ancestors said, 'It is not good for a man to live alone', for a man needs a wife.[7]

I said to Lord Habtu, 'I'm not a monk, I just seemed like one because of the hard times'.

There was a servant of Lord [Habtu] called Hirut.[8] She wasn't extraordinarily beautiful, but she was a good person, intelligent, and patient.

So I asked Lord Habtu, 'Give me this servant to be my wife'.

---

1 Abb 234 omits: grain.
2 ወልደ ገብርኤል (son of [Saint] Gabriel), an Ethiopian Christian name often given to a son born or baptized on St. Gabriel's day, the nineteenth day of every Ethiopian month.
3 ተሰማ (He Was Heard [in Amharic]), a very common Ethiopian boy's name.
4 ምትኩ (His Replacement [in Amharic]), a common Ethiopian boy's name, given to a son who came after the loss of a beloved family member and thus consoled the family. This man, Zara Yaqob's student, is the author of the second Hatata.
5 Abb 234: what you can eat.
6 Abb 234: except by their established created order.
7 Abb 234 omits: As the ancestors said', 'It is not good for a man to live alone', for a man needs a wife. The setup to the quotation is probably from Matthew 5:21, which has በከመ ተብህለ ለቀደምት (as it was said to the ancient ones). But the point about living alone is from Genesis 2:18. By combining the Old Testament quotation with the New Testament one, the author rhetorically gives status to his own 'new' ideas.
8 ኂሩት (Generosity, Goodness [in Ge'ez]), a common Ethiopian girl's name.

<small>Abb215 24v</small>
<small>Sum 21</small>

Lord Habtu said to me, 'Certainly! From today onwards she is not my servant, but your servant'.

I said, 'not my servant, but my wife! Because husband and wife are equals in marriage.[1] We shouldn't call them master and servant, because 'they are one flesh'[2] and one life"!'

<small>Litt Ed 23</small>

Lord Habtu replied, 'You're a man of God, do as you wish!'

We called the servant, and I asked her, 'Would you like to be my wife?'

She replied, 'Whatever my master wishes'.[3]

Lord Habtu said to her, 'I would love it.[4]

She said to me, 'It would be great for me. Where will I find a man better than you?'

She and I then said to Lord Habtu, 'Bless us, our father!'

He said, 'God bless you and keep you, and may he give you health and love for the length of your days, and may he give you children along with the wealth of this world, and may he keep evil things away from you!'

<small>Abb234 24v</small>

And we said, 'Amen! Amen!'

And so Hirut became my wife, and she really loved me, and she was so happy because she had been despised in Habtu's house, and the people there had made her suffer constantly.[5] Because she loved me, I set in my heart the desire to please her in every way I could. I believe no other marriage has been as strong in love and blessed by God as ours.

<small>Abb215 25r</small>

I [still] had two ounces of gold, left from the three I took with me when I fled from Aksum. In addition, working as a scribe, I had acquired cows, goats, and clothes. I built a small house in Lord Habtu's neighbourhood, and I lived there with my wife in [a state of] love. She spun cotton thread day and night [for sale].[6] I wrote [letters and manuscripts for pay] and taught Habtu's sons and other children[7] who lived there. Lord Habtu gave me a container[8] of *teff* each month for teaching his sons.

---

1 Although the author's idea of women's equality is uncommon, it is not unique in Geʿez texts. For instance, in the Ethiopian commentary on Genesis 2:22, the biblical passage about Eve being taken from Adam's side, the scholars interpret as meaningful the place on his body from which she came. If she had come from his head, she would be superior; if from his feet, she would be inferior. Since she is from his side, she is equal and precious.

2 Genesis 2:24, Matthew 19:6, Mark 10:8, etc.

3 As a servant and a girl, she was required to give obedient answers like this.

4 አነሰ አፈቅድ (As for me, I desire [it]).

5 Abb 234: had troubled her.

6 Spinning cotton was a common trade for women in Ethiopia.

7 ወለካልአን ሕፃናት, which could include girls. Girls from the elite were always taught to read.

8 ቀሡት, which is a container of uncertain size, often used for mead but also for grain.

I lived the good life like this in [a state of] love with my wife, although she did not bear me a child. Later, she did become pregnant and bore me a son on Monday, 18 October, 1638.¹ We rejoiced together in our son. I named him after my father: Betsega Habta Egziabher.²

Chapter 20: My Surviving Wicked Enemies, War, and Famine

Three years later, [the European Catholic] Bishop³ Efons[, that is, Afonso Mendez,] returned to his country.⁴ Then, all his enemies became powerful and his friends were driven out as well as him.

During those times[, in the 1640s], in all the regions, teachers were sought after who could teach and sustain the ancient teaching [of the Orthodox faith]. My relatives in Aksum sought me out[, asking me] to return to my previous teaching position and to teach the sacred books in Aksum as before. That's because people [mistakenly] assumed that I had fled out of fear of the persecution that arose because of Bishop⁵ Efons [and so now I could return].

They sent for me, saying, 'Return to us, for your enemies have vanished and your friends have been saved!'

---

1 አመ ፲ለጥቅምት በዕለተ ሰኑይ አምልደተ ክርስቶስ ፲፻፮፻፴፩ወ፴ወ፩ (the second day of the week [i.e., Monday], 10th of Ṭəqəmt, 1631 years after the birth of Christ). A secondary hand has properly corrected the numeral of the date from the 10th to the 11th because the 11th of that month in 1631 was a Monday and the 10th was not. The base hand of Abb 215 originally wrote ፲ለጥቅምት (10th of Ṭəqəmt), and a secondary hand overwrote the ለ with ፩ and added interlinearly a ለ, so that it reads ፲፩ለጥቅምት (11th of Ṭəqəmt). Abb 234 has the same date as the base hand of Abb 215. Littmann choose to follow the secondary hand of Abb 215 reading of the 11th.

2 በጸጋ ሀብት አግዚአብሔር (By the grace of the riches of God). This is a richly allusive name in the Ethiopian tradition. First, his 'father' is 'Habtu' (the second part of his son's name). Second, his son is a gift 'by the grace of' that richness (Habtu) and God.

3 Strictly, he was appointed the Patriarch of the EOTC, but the author refers to him with a lesser title: አቡነ (literally, 'our father'). Abb 234 omits አቡነ.

4 Afonso Mendes did not leave Ethiopia in 1641 but in 1633, when the Ethiopian emperor banished him and other Jesuits. However, 1641 marked the year when all European Catholic missionaries in Ethiopia were gone. The author seems to have assumed that the patriarch would be one of the last to leave, not the first. This error is more likely made by an Ethiopian in the late 1600s than by a Catholic priest in the 1800s, who would be familiar with the details of his predecessors' mission.

5 Abb 234 omits: bishop.

I replied, 'I have no enemies, and I have no friends, except this man of God my Lord Habtu, his children, and my wife. I will never leave them! All of you, live in peace, but it wouldn't do for me to return to you!'

[Meanwhile,] that hypocrite, who had previously accused me before King Susenyos, my enemy Walda Yohannes, he returned to the Egyptian faith[, that is, the Ethiopian Orthodox Church] after Bishop Efons had gone.[1] But, he had no faith except that which suited him for the moment. Very cunningly he went and became friendly with King Fasiladas, because kings love the crafty and hypocritical.

When Walda Yohannes heard that I was living peacefully in the Enfraz region, he again began to make accusations against me. He said, 'He is a teacher who secretly teaches foreign [Catholic] doctrine'. He said this to the Enfraz governor.

I was greatly saddened by this malice.[2] Previously he had said of me, 'He is an enemy of the foreigners[, the Catholics]', and now he said, 'He is their friend'.

With a grieving heart, I said, 'May God destroy deceitful lips!'[3]

Then, I prayed with Psalm 34 for many days, [which begins,] 'Harm them!'[4] and with Psalm 108, [which begins,] 'Don't fail to hear me!'[5]

And, God heard me! For this man [later] was appointed over many dioceses in [the province of] Dembiya, and his people[6] there hated him and killed him. His dead body was found in his house, but his killer was never found. Then, 'a stranger took his position'[7] and his possessions.

---

1 The author's enemy has not merely returned to the EOTC but has also aligned himself with the powerful Egyptian bishop's community in Ethiopia.
2 Abb 234: his evil.
3 Psalm 12:3 (11:3 LXX).
4 Psalm 35:1 (34:1 LXX). Note that the author again uses the opening of a Psalm to refer to the whole Psalm. This Psalm, a cry out for justice, is always read in the Ethiopian liturgy on Good Friday.
5 Psalm 109:1 (108:1 LXX). እግዚአ ኢትጸመሙኒ ስእለትየ (O Lord, do not be deaf to my plea).
6 'His people' were likely family members, priests, or servants, as only insiders could kill him in his own house.
7 Psalm 109:8 (108:7 LXX). The author is noting that the Psalm with which he prayed has come true. In the Psalm, a wicked man accused a good man, and so he prayed to God that the days of this wicked man be shortened and for a stranger to take his position.

In 1642,[1] a great famine came to all of Ethiopia's regions. [That divine] punishment[2] was severe because of our people's sins and the lack of neighbourly love. That is, because those who welcomed the faith of King Susenyos and Bishop Efons at first persecuted those brothers and sisters who did not accept their faith. Later, those [same brothers and sisters] who were persecuted paid back their enemies sevenfold and killed many of them.

[As a result of] all of this, everyone knew, 'there is no fear of God before their eyes, and the way of peace they have not known'.[3]

Calling them 'Christians' is meaningless because Jesus Christ commands Christians to love one another before all else and above all else. This [type of] mutual love had disappeared entirely from among those who were called Christians. They sinned against their brothers and sisters and devoured one another like they were eating a meal.[4]

[King] Fasiladas began to rule with good advice and with wisdom, but he did not persevere in goodness. Rather he became an oppressive king and persisted in persecution and violence. He hated the foreigners[, the European Catholics,] who had done good things for him, and built fortresses and beautiful castles,[5] and made his kingdom prosper through their wise work. He hated them, he persecuted them and drove them out, and he repaid evil for good. Fasiladas himself became an evildoer in every respect.[6] He unjustly killed people and multiplied his acts of adultery. After committing adultery with

Chap 13
Abb215 26v

Litt Ed 25
Abb234 26v

Abb215 27r

---

1 ወበፐየወ፻የወሷወዴ ዓመት አምልደተ ክርስቶስ (1635, in the Ethiopian Calendar). After civil wars, there is often a famine due to farmers not planting. Records about famines for this period are thin, as King Fasilädäs (r. 1632–1667) had no surviving chronicle and the Jesuits were no longer reporting on events in Ethiopia.

2 መቅሠፍት (punishment, whipping, torment, wrath, *but also* divine punishment).

3 Romans 3:17–18. These two quotations come at the end of a long passage in which St. Paul argues that there is no one who is righteous. '

4 Abb 234 omits: and devoured one another like they were eating a meal. An allusion to Psalm 53:4 (52:5 LXX), 'Those who eat my people like eating bread, did not call upon God'.

5 ሎቱ ... አብያተ ሠናያተ (for him . . . good houses). As the word for 'castle' includes the word for 'house'—ቤተ መንግሥት (*betä mangəśt*, house of the king)—we assume that the house 'for him', the king, is a castle.

6 Abb 234: he became a violent man. This negative evaluation of King Fasilädäs is unusual and striking. Generally, he is only lauded for bringing back the Ethiopian Orthodox faith; for instance, a famous poetic phrase associated with him is ፋሲለደስ ይንገሥ የሮም ሃይማኖት ይርክስ የአስከንድርያ ሃይማኖት ይመለስ (May Fasilädäs rule, may the faith of Rome be considered unclean, and may the faith of Alexandria return). But the author is focused throughout this section on justice and fairness, so it was bad for the king to persecute those who had helped them.

women, he killed them.¹ He sent his soldiers, who were violent oppressors, and they plundered the provinces and the homes of the poor. For God gave an evil king to evil human beings.²

Because of the [Ethiopian] king's sins and the [Ethiopian] people's sins, another famine [then] fell upon them as a divine punishment. After the famine, a plague came, and many died. Others were terrified, yet fear did not lead them to their salvation³ because they persisted in their foolishness and their hatred.⁴

[As a result,] a good number said, 'God's punishment fell upon us because of you all, who banished Bishop Efons'.

Sum 23

While others said, '[No, it's] because of those who denied the previous Orthodox Faith and defiled the Church,⁵ [it's] because of this that divine punishment fell upon us!'

Thus, they were divided among themselves, and they fought. They failed

Abb234 27r
Abb215 27v

to understand that they deserved divine punishment [for a different reason:] because they had abandoned neighbourly love and had broken that rule of righteousness—which God had established for all creation,⁶ because of human tenets. They had violated [God's] natural laws due to human laws⁷ derived from this or that religion.

[The Book of] Isaiah and the Gospel 'spoke rightly' about them, [saying,] 'These people honour me with their mouth, but in their hearts they are far away from me, in vain they worship me, teaching as doctrine human tenets'.⁸

John, [in his First Letter,] also said, 'whoever says, "I live in the light," and hates their neighbour, is a liar and remains in darkness to this day. But whoever loves their neighbour lives in the light and there is no cause for stumbling with them. Whoever hates their neighbour lives in darkness, and

---

1 Other known Ge'ez sources do not record such actions, but such contemporary views may have been erased over time by a grateful nation.
2 This is a common Ethiopian explanation for national suffering—that God caused it due to the people's wickedness—based on the story about the worldly king the Israelites want (1 Samuel 8).
3 ወአኮ ለድኂን (but it was not for salvation).
4 Abb 234 omits: they persisted in their foolishness and their hatred.
5 Abb 234 omits: and defiled the church.
6 Abb 234: God's command.
7 Abb 234: they had violated the word of God which says in our minds, 'do not kill, do not do to others what you do not want them to do to you', due to their precepts.
8 Isaiah 29:13 LXX, and Matthew 15:8–9, Mark 7:6–7. Also, the author changes the quotation and uses በአፉሆሙ (with their mouths), rather than በከናፍሪሆሙ (with their lips).

they do not know where they are going, because darkness has blinded their eyes'.[1]

This prophecy was fulfilled by our nation's population: they do not know where they are going, they fight with each other about their beliefs[2] because they do not [even] know what they believe, and they live in darkness.

As for us, after our gold ran out during the famine, we sold our cows and clothes. As a result, praise God, we were not hungry like others. Rather, we ourselves ate and [also] fed the hungry and sick throughout the two years of famine and plague, and we did not suffer.

The saying [in Psalms] was fulfilled in us, 'They shall not be put to shame in evil times, and they will be satisfied in times of famine'.[3] We worshipped God who did countless good things for us.

Abb234 27v

Abb215 28r

Chapter 21: My Patron Dying and My Teaching His Sons

Chap 14

A year later, [in 1645,] Lord Habtu died, and we mourned deeply and lamented greatly for him.

Litt Ed 26

Before he died, he called us all and said [to me], 'Look, I am about to die. May God protect you and bless you! Be the father to my children!'

He gave me two oxen and a mule, and to my wife he gave two cows, with their calves. Then, he said to us, 'Pray for my soul!'

He died in God's peace. May God give his blessed soul rest![4] We buried him with great honour.

Abb234 28r

His first-born son, whose name was Walda Michael, loved me as his father and listened to my advice. He had a wife by the name of Walatta Petros, known as Fantaya.[5] She was from among the nobles of the region,

Abb215 28v

---

1 1 John 2:9–11. The author quotes from the Ge'ez Bible, but adds the phrase, ሐሳዊ ውእቱ (he is a liar), which does not appear in the Greek or the Latin. The First Letter of John is the first text that a student reads in the EOTC educational system once they have learned their letters.

2 Abb 234: belief.

3 Psalm 37:19 (36:19 LXX).

4 This resembles the common prayer for the dead in the EOTC and other Orthodox traditions, which prayer is አዕርፍ እግዚአ ነፍስ ገብርክ (give rest, Lord, to the soul of your [male] servant).

5 ወለተ ጴጥሮስ ወተሰምየት ፈንታየ (Wälättä Ṗeṭros [Daughter of (Saint) Peter (in Ge'ez)]), and she was named Fantayä [My Portion (in Amharic)]). Both are common names. Habtu's son, who is wealthy, has unsurprisingly married nobility.

and a doer of good works, full of neighbourly love and humble. She loved us as a mother loves her children.¹

The two other sons of Habtu, Tesemma and Metekku, grew up. They both had learned to read the Psalter. Metekku[, that is, Walda Heywat,] had also learned to write [and work] as a scribe and had mastered grammar and the scriptures.² So, he bonded with me in knowledge and great love. He knew all my secrets, [my beliefs,]³ and there was nothing that I hid from him.⁴

Sum 24

Because of his love, I wrote this short work following his repeated requests.

Chapter 22: My Son, His Wife, and Their Children

Chap 15

My son[, Betsega Habta Egziabher, who went by the name Habtu,] grew up to become a handsome young man.

When he was twenty years old, I knew that he was inadvertently doing wrong, not knowing that it was the [kind of] sin that indicates the desire for marriage.⁵

Abb234 28v

I frequently reprimanded him, saying, 'this act is not right because it violates the creator's established order for us. Rather, you should marry a woman and live according to our nature's order'.⁶

Abb215 29r

He replied, 'Sure, give me a wife!'

I searched and found a beautiful young woman, whose name was Medhanit.⁷ She was the daughter of the head of the cattle herders, who was from the village of Lamge.⁸ My son was well pleased with her. Her father

---

1 Although she is, in effect, the author's daughter-in-law, she is mother over them because she and her husband have inherited Habtu's position and oversee all the servants.
2 Abb 234 omits: and the scriptures. That is, the student's educational progress mirrors that of his teacher, the author.
3 That is, he did not hide his unusual philosophical musings. However, this is also likely to be a biblical allusion to the relationship between a spiritual mentor and mentee. In 2 Timothy 3:10, Saint Paul tells Saint Timothy, 'you know all about my teaching, my way of life'.
4 Abb 234 omits: and there was nothing that I hid from him.
5 Abb. 234: he was sinning in his flesh by spilling his seed because of the pleasure that he would get from it. Abb 234 is explicit that the act is masturbation. Abb 215 was explicit, but the phrase has been erased.
6 Abb 234: as is proper.
7 መድኃኒት (Salvation [in Ge'ez]; Healing Medicine [in Amharic]), a common Ethiopian girl's name.
8 ላምጌ (cowbell). This is still a village today in the Qwarit District of Western Gojjam.

gave her fifteen cattle[1] as well as clothes, so she became my son's wife and we all lived together in [a state of] love.

After two years, she bore a son. I called him Yetbarak, meaning [in Amharic], 'May God be blessed'![2] Then, she bore a second son, and I called him Destaye.[3] Next, she bore a daughter, and I called her Eseteye.[4] I praised God who had satisfied me from out of all his goodness.

Chapter 23: My Writing This Book

As for me, I lived with human beings, seeming like a Christian to them. But, in my heart, I did not believe—except in God the creator of everything and the protector of everything, as he had given me to know.

And I thought and said [to myself], 'Is it a sin before God for me to appear to be a believer when I am not, and in this way deceive human beings?'

I said [to myself], '[No,] people are willing to deceive others and if I reveal the truth to them they won't listen to me, rather they will insult and persecute me. There is no benefit in revealing my thoughts to them; on the contrary, [it does] great harm'.

Because of this, I lived with people as if I was like them,[5] and I dwelled with God in the way that he had given me to know.

But, so that those who come after me will understand me, I wanted to write this book, which I will keep concealed until my death.

If, after my death, a wise and inquisitive[6] person were found, I would ask them to join their mind with mine [and continue the work]. [I would say to them,] 'Look, I began my inquiry, [about concepts] which have not been explored before. Complete what I have begun, so that our nation's people might gain wisdom with God's help and come to know the truth.[7] [Complete the work so] that they may not believe lies, trust in violence, or go from one

---

1 Both families give marriage gifts to the other family in Ethiopian culture. But this gift by her father to the couple is unusually lavish and a sign of his care for her.
2 Abb 234 omits: meaning, 'May God be blessed'. This is a common Ethiopian boy's name.
3 ደስታየ (My Delight [in Amharic]), a common Ethiopian boy's name.
4 ዕሴትየ (My Reward [in Ge'ez]), a common Ethiopian boy's name.
5 Abb 234 adds: except their evil deeds.
6 Abb 234 omits: and inquisitive.
7 Abb 234: In the same way all people, if they are able, should arrive gradually at knowledge of the truth.

meaningless thing to another,¹ but rather might understand truth,² love their brothers and sisters, and avoid fighting with one another because of their meaningless beliefs,³ as they have done so far'.

If a wise person is found who understands this book, and concepts even more excellent than it contains, and that person is willing to teach and write⁴ [more, add to it], may God give them the desire of their heart. May God fulfil his good will for them and satisfy them from with his limitless goodness just as he satisfied me. May God make them rejoice and bless them on the earth, just as he made me rejoice and blessed me through to this very day.

As for the one who slanders me because of [my writing in] this book, and does not want to understand how to be better,⁵ may God reward that person according to their actions! Amen.

Coda: The Completion of the Book

[Walda Heywat adds the following coda:]

Zara Yacob, who was [also called] Warqe, wrote this book in the sixty-eighth year of his life, when Fasiladas had died and Yohannes [I] reigned.⁶

After he wrote this book,⁷ Zara Yacob lived in virtuous old age for twenty-five more years,⁸ loving God our creator, and glorifying him day and night. Meanwhile, he became very honoured [by everyone around him]. He [lived to] see his great grandchildren; [because] as for his son [Betsega Habta Egziabher, who was also called] Habtu, he had five sons and four daughters with his wife, Medhanit.

Zara Yacob, who is [also called] Warqe, lived until he was ninety-three years old, never falling ill. He died with great hope in God our creator. His wife died four years later, and she was buried with her husband. May God graciously receive their souls [to live] in peace forever and forever!

---

1 A paraphrase of Psalm 62:10 (61:9 LXX).
2 Abb 234: They might understand the Creator's wisdom, and set their hope on his mercy and truth, and pray to him with a pure heart when they suffer.
3 Abb 234: they themselves would not fight with one another because of their beliefs.
4 Abb 234: like me.
5 Abb 234 omits: and does not want to understand how to be better.
6 The Ethiopian king Fasiladas died in October 1667; his fourth son, King Yohannes I, reigned from then until 1682. The author was born in August 1600.
7 Abb 234 omits: book.
8 That is, he died at the age of 93.

His great grandchildren became very honoured [as well] in our region, and they were blessed with their father's blessing. Indeed, their house was not big enough to contain all their cattle, so some of them went down to the lowlands,¹ to their mother's relatives, and lived there.

[As it says in Psalms,] 'Behold! The one who respectfully fears God is blessed like this!'²

May God bless us with the same blessings as those of my father, Habtu, and with the same blessings as those of my teacher, Zara Yacob.

Now I am [also] very old [and near death]. [As the Psalmist says,] 'I was a young man and I have grown old, yet I have never seen a righteous person rejected, nor their children lack food, but they live amidst blessings forever'.³

I, Walda Heywat, who is called Metekku, added this short piece to my teacher's book, so that you may know the beautiful end of his life.⁴

Regarding my wisdom, which God gave me to understand and that Zara Yaqob taught me for fifty-nine years,⁵ I also have written a book, one of knowledge and advice for all Ethiopia's children.

May God give them understanding and wisdom⁶ and love, and may he bless them forever and ever. Amen!

The end of this book.⁷

---

1 ቆላ (lowlands), in Amharic. That is, the area of Gojjam from which the son's wife came, Lamge.
2 Psalm 128:4 (127:5 LXX).
3 Psalms 37:25–26 (36:25–26 LXX).
4 Abb 234 omits: to my teacher's book, so that you may know the beautiful end of his life.
5 Since children begin school between the age of four and seven, we may infer that Walda Heywat, at the time of the writing of this coda, is in his sixties.
6 Abb 234 omits: and wisdom.
7 Abb. 234: May God bless, with the [same] blessing [as that he gave to] Zara Yaqob, his servant Walda Giyorgis, who enabled this book to be written down so that God's blessing would always be with him, and also bless his scribe Walda Yosef, forever and ever. Amen! Let it be, let it be.

Ralph Lee with Mehari Worku and Wendy Laura Belcher
Translation of the *Hatata Walda Heywat*

Prologue by the Scribe

In the name of God, creator of everything, the one who embraces all things,[1] preserves all things, and protects all things![2] Who was and is and will be, from before the world existed and for eternity, the only perfect being, whose greatness is limitless.[3]

Litt Ed 29
Abb215 31r
Sum 27

I[, Walda Heywat's disciple, now] copy down a book of wisdom,[4] inquiry, philosophy, and counsel[5] that a great teacher of our nation composed, whose name was Walda Heywat.

May the blessing of his God, and the wisdom of our glorious creator's mysteries, and the observing of his righteous laws remain with all the children of Ethiopia, now and forever, Amen!

[Walda Heywat spoke or wrote the following:]

Part I: Inquiries

Chapter 1: On the Importance of Performing Inquiries

You have heard the saying, according to the ancients, 'Give a wise person an opportunity and they will become wiser'.[6]

So, I decided to [give wise people an opportunity and] write about what God taught me during my long life. [I wrote] about what I had examined uprightly with my intelligence, so that this book would be a guide, [full] of instruction and understanding, for our children who come after us. [I wrote

---

1 ኦኃዜ ኵሉ (the holder of everything, but also: all-embracing, omnipotent, almighty).
2 The HWH text is found in one handwritten parchment manuscript, which we shorthand as Abb 215.
3 Opening with lyrical praise for God is the standard way of beginning any Geʿez text; for instance, see መጽሐፈ ምሥጢር (The Book of Mystery).
4 It is unclear whether the unnamed scribe is writing down what he has heard aloud from Walda Heywat or copying a written document composed by Walda Heywat.
5 መጽሐፈ ጥበብ ወሐተታ ወፍልስፍና ወተግሣጽ (a book of wisdom, inquiry, philosophy, and instruction).
6 Proverbs 9:9.

https://doi.org/10.1515/9783110781922-006

so] that [this book] would be a reason for the wise to inquire into and comprehend God's works, so they could stack up wisdom upon their wisdom.

Abb215 31v

As for me, I don't write what I have heard others say. Indeed, I have never accepted others' teaching without inquiring into it and understanding whether it is good. I only write what appears true to me after inquiring into it and understanding it. [I do so] in God's presence, whom I implore with much prayer and pleading to reveal the truth to me and give me understanding of the mystery of how he created human beings as understanding beings[1] and placed them among the other creatures who live in this world.

Listen, my friend[2] who reads this book of mine, know that I wrote it with great [and reverent] fear of God, which totally prevents me from lying. Yet, I have no fear of human beings. I am never ashamed in their presence, and I never associate with those who write and teach useless things and lies.

If anyone says to me, 'Do you alone know the truth, and all except you don't know the truth?'[3]

I would say to them, 'I'm not the only one who knows the truth. Many

Abb215 32r
Litt Ed 30

have known her[4] and loved her like me, but they did not dare to teach the truth openly, because they feared the slanderous insults of those who cannot see [the truth] and feared excommunication from their fearful community'.

The rest of human beings don't understand [the truth in the first place].

Sum 28

They don't seek [the truth] or make inquiries to perceive what is true and what is false. Rather, they accept and believe what they have heard from their ancestors without inquiring into it.

As a result, Christians' children are Christians, and Muslims' children are Muslims, and Jews' children are Jews. [For them,] there is no other reason for their faith than this: that they are the children of their ancestors. They heard in their infancy that their ancestors' faith was true, and they believed in it without inquiring into it or understanding it. All of them fight for their own faith, insisting that it is true. But it is impossible for all faiths of humankind to

---

1 ለባዊ (rational, intelligent, one who reasons). Such Ge'ez words are based on the root ልብ (heart), as in Ge'ez and other Semitic languages, the seat of both thought and emotion is the heart. We have translated such words differently according to context, with such variations as 'rational', 'faculty of reason', 'rational being(s)', 'understanding being(s)', 'intelligent', or 'wise'.

2 እኁየ (my brother).

3 A classic aspect of Ethiopian biblical commentary is the question-and-answer format, organized around an invented someone who asks a question, which is then answered at length. The author of this Hatata uses this form throughout.

4 the soul, the mind, human nature, wisdom, truth, and many other abstract qualities are feminine. This text here treats 'truth' as feminine.

be true because they contradict each other. They could, however, all be false, because there are lots of lies but only one truth.¹

Chapter 2: My Inquiry regarding the Risks and Benefits of Inquiry

All truth and wisdom are from God, and without God all 'wisdom is drowned'.²

Just as the sun is the source of light, so God is the source of wisdom; and just as breath is the fountain of life, so God is the fountain of all truth.

Those who don't meditate on God with a pure mind, purified from all worldly stubbornness,³ will not find wisdom and will be incapable of understanding truth.

Lift up your mind,⁴ my friend, to this perfect being who created you as an understanding being. Look to God with the insight of your intelligence⁵ and comprehend with the light of the knowledge that your creator has revealed to you.

Don't listen to the voice of those who vilify you and call you a denier of the creator when you reject the doctrine that they teach. For they don't know the creator, and there is no wisdom in them.

As for you, never believe what human beings teach you without you yourself investigating every single thing that they teach you and distinguishing truth from lies. For human beings are capable of lying, and you don't know whether what they have taught you is true or false.

Likewise, never believe what is written in books except that content which you have scrutinized and found to be truthful. For human beings who write books are capable of writing what is false. But if you scrutinise books, you will quickly find in them perverted wisdom which is not in harmony with our intelligence, which intelligence is given by God to us for seeking out truth.

I am not saying to you, however, that all human beings and all books are false in every respect, rather that they are capable of being false. So, you cannot tell whether what they declare is true or false, unless you yourself

---

1 This 'one truth' is not God but one common reality.
2 A slight paraphrase of Psalm 107:27 (106:27 LXX).
3 ግዛፈዝ ዓለም (the thickness *or* stubbornness of this world)
4 አልዕል አእኁየ ሕሊናኸ (lift up your mind, my dear brother), which resonates with other expressions in the EOTC liturgy, such as the line አጽንዑ ሕሊና ልብሀሙ (strengthen *or* secure the mind of your heart).
5 በዓይነ ልቡናኸ (with the eyes of your intelligence).

Sum 29 scrutinize what is said and what is written. That way, you may thoroughly know what you should trust and that way you may understand God's work.

Indeed, inquiry is the door through which we enter into wisdom. And intelligence is the God-given key for us to unlock this door, enter into his chamber of mysteries, and be graciously granted gifts from his treasure house of wisdom.

Abb215 33v We should then scrutinize everything that human beings teach us and what is written in books. If we should find truth, let's accept it with joy and gladness. If we should find falsehood, let's reject it and mercilessly eradicate it. For falsehood is not from the Lord, the God of truth, rather it is from error and human deceit.

Chapter 3: My Inquiry regarding the Goodness of Creation

The foundation of all faith, all wisdom, and all truth is this: to believe that there is a God, creator of all, guardian of all, perfect being and infinite, who was and is and will be forever.

All of humanity's teachers and every nation's books agree on this truth.[1] As for us, we should believe [in this truth.] If we investigate the matter, our intelligence demonstrates to us that it is true, and cannot be a lie. For we who live today, but did not exist yesterday and will disappear tomorrow, we are created creatures.

All that we see in this world is the same, it is [all] fleeting and created.
Abb215 34r Without a creator, how is it possible for a created creature to exist? For all creation is limited and weak and has no power whatsoever to create [anything] out of that which does not exist. So, there must be one being who existed before all creation, without beginning or end,[2] 'who created all that exists' out of that which does not exist, whether tangible or intangible, 'visible or invisible'.[3]

After creating everything, God did not abandon what he created. Rather, he takes care of it and nourishes it, suiting his care to every creature's needs. Also, he leads everything on the path he made.

---

1 It seems unlikely that a European, who would be very aware of the many works of atheistic philosophy, would state that no books assert there is no God. In the next few paragraphs, the author similarly states that everyone believes in angels and demons.
2 አንበለ ጥንት ወኢተፍጻሜት (without beginning or end), a phrase from a hymn ዚቅ (Ziq). This famous chant is sung on the Feast of St. Michael the Archangel (June 16 in the 1600s). The phrase also alludes to Christ in Hebrews 7:3.
3 ዘያስተርእ ወዘኢያስተርእ (visible or invisible), quoting Colossians 1:16, which phrase is used in the Nicene Creed (Prayer of the Faith).

There is no error in him, who created everything with great wisdom. He designed all species, in ways appropriate for their different natures. He led them on diverse paths, on which they might be perfected over all the days of their existence and [in their] acts of divine service, within the limits prescribed by the law of their nature.

Litt Ed 32

Don't listen to fools! They say daily, 'this or that is not good', or, 'it would have been better if this or that had not been created'.

But all that God has made is excellent in the very way he made it. For all creation has a purpose, which we should seek out for our own benefit. For God created all things to be useful, and he laid them out in front of human eyes, so that humanity [might be inspired to] seek and understand the wisdom with which God created, and to find those things' value, that was purposed in them to for their benefit.

Abb215 34v

How many things seemed useless to the ancients, but later their use was found? How many things seem useless to us [now], but later their purpose will be found?

In the same way, everything was created for the benefit of human beings or to beautify this world, the dwelling place for the one, that is humanity, who is greater than all [other] creatures. For human beings are greater than all the world's other creatures, and as understanding beings they approach their creator's image.[1] Everything that exists in this world was created for the adornment of humanity's dwelling place.

Sum 30

Chapter 4: My Inquiry regarding the Nature of Spirits and Souls

When I say 'human beings' to you, my friend,[2] [you must] understand [that I mean] human souls—and their spiritual existence and their intangible nature, which thinks and understands. [I don't mean] their fleshly nature, because that is [of the] earth[3] and it can do nothing by itself. Rather, when the body's soul departs, the fleshly nature falls away like a dry piece of wood.

Abb215 35r

---

1 An allusion to Genesis 1:27. Also, in EOTC theology, humanity is greater than the rest of creation, but it is also a microcosm of creation, encompassing all aspects of the rest, in the way that a church dome is a microcosm of the structure of the whole church building.
2 አመ ዕበለከ ሰብእ አእጐየ (when I say to you 'human being', my dear brother).
3 An allusion to Genesis 3:19.

It is certain that we have a spiritual and rational soul, because we think and we understand. By contrast, the thickness of our fleshly nature cannot think or understand, unlike the soul within our flesh, which thinks and understands.

Regarding [our] spiritual nature, I assume that there are other spirits greater than human souls, namely, angels and demons, because all human beings believe in their existence. Their nature is superior among God's creatures. But, because they are invisible to us, our intelligence is silent about this belief [in them], and gives us no explanation whatsoever about them and we cannot know [the truth of] the matter for sure.

We can be certain, however, that there are spirits inferior to human souls, which are the spirits of tame and wild animals.[1] Regarding tame and wild animals, since they don't converse in human language, we cannot know the extent of the intellect of spirits like these, or whether they have knowledge of their creator or not, but it seems to me that they don't have reason.

Consequently, the spirit of tame and wild animals is distinct from the human soul. Just as in the [hierarchal] order of creation, the life of tame and wild animals is greater than the life of plants and trees—which don't move around but rather germinate,[2] mature, and die in one place—in the same way the human soul is greater than animal souls. The human soul is appointed to the highest rank of creation's order, the very nearest to the creator.

Also, we don't know if the spirits of tame and wild animals are mortal or immortal. The human soul is immortal, because intelligence is her essence. Our soul's intelligence is the shining splendour of light which emanates from the creator God's essence. This light will not perish, rather it returns to God, and can never be destroyed.

Thus, the rational soul's[3] life must be eternal, otherwise all human existence would be futile and inferior, and God would not be wise but a mocker in creating humanity. So then, we should believe without doubt that our soul is immortal.

Just as the human soul emerged as brilliant from the womb of God her creator, so shall she return to him after this life. Because our intelligence demonstrates to us that this is so, then this teaching [about the soul] delights

---

1 In EOTC theology, human beings have both ደመ ነፍስ (life force) and መንፈስ (souls), while animals have only the former. The author challenges this view in the next paragraph.
2 ይትወለዱ (are born or come forth).
3 ነፍስ ነባቢት (the speaking soul).

our mind, strengthens us with indestructible hope, and beautifies our whole life and becomes the foundation for all good deeds and all truth.

Chapter 5: My Inquiry regarding Religious Faith

Concerning what remains—human teachings and books—we should not believe them hastily, without inquiry. Rather we should [only] accept these teachings intentionally, after extensive investigation, as long as we see them as being in harmony with our intelligence. That is to say, our intelligence will be the measure of whether we should believe in them, and what our intelligence affirms as untrue we should not believe. Neither should we hastily say, 'It's a lie!'—for we don't know whether it's true or false. Instead, because of this [ignorance] let's say, 'We won't believe it because we don't understand it'.[1]

If people say to me, 'Why don't you believe everything that is written in books, as those before us did?'

I would reply to them, 'Because books are written by human beings who are capable of writing lies'.

If people further say to me, 'Why don't you believe?'

I would reply to them, 'Tell me why you believe? After all, no reason is needed for not believing, but it is needed for believing. What reason do you have to believe in everything that is written? You have no reason except this alone: that you have heard from human mouths that what's written is true. But don't you understand? [Just] because they tell you, "What's written is true", doesn't mean they [actually] know whether it's true or false. Rather, just as you heard this from them, they too heard it from those before them. In the same way, all those ancestors believed in human words, even though they might have been lies, and not in God's words. [And regarding that speech,] God does not speak to you except through the voice of your intelligence'.[2]

If people say to me, 'It's not like that! Rather, God has spoken to human beings and revealed his truth to them!'

---

[1] ኢነአምና እስመ ኢነአምሮ (we don't believe it because we don't know it), a catchy and memorable rhyming phrase in Ge'ez.
[2] በቃለ ሰብእ ... በቃለ እግዚአብሔር ... በቃለ ልቡና (in the word *or* voice *or* speech of human beings ... in the word *or* voice *or* speech of God ... in the word *or* voice *or* speech of intelligence). The author is playing with a philosophically rich term in the Ethiopian tradition: ቃል (word, voice, speech, meaning).

I would reply to them, 'How do *you* know that God has spoken with human beings and revealed his truth to them? Isn't it rather that you heard it from human mouths, who testified that *they* heard it from [other] human mouths? Must you always believe human words, even though they could be lies? Whether it's true or false, you believe [it] unthinkingly'.

So, inquire! Don't say in your hearts, 'We are steadfast in our religion, which cannot be false!' Pay attention! For human beings lie about religious matters, because religions are utterly inconsistent. Human beings don't give reasonable explanations about what's right for us to believe. So, they put an inquiring heart into a total quandary.

Look, one tells us, 'Believe in the religion of Alexandria!'

Another tells us, 'Believe in the religion of Rome!'

And a third tells us, 'Believe in the religion of Moses!'

And a fourth tells us, 'Believe in Mohammed's religion, Islam!'

Further, Indians have a different religion!

So do Himyarites and Sabeans,[1] and [many] other peoples.

They all say, 'Our religion is from God!'

But how can God, who is righteous in all his actions, reveal one religion to one group,[2] and another to another group? And how can all these different religions be from God? Which of them is true, requiring us to believe in it?

Tell me, if you know, because I don't know! I will only believe what God has revealed to me [if it comes] through the light of my intelligence. That way I won't be misled in my religious faith.

If someone should say to me, 'Unless you believe, God's judgement will fall on you!'

I will say to them, 'God can't order me to believe in lies. And he can't judge me for a religious faith that I have rejected because it doesn't seem true to me.[3] For he gave me the light of my intelligence to distinguish good from evil, and truth from lies. This intelligent light reveals absolutely nothing as to whether all human religions are true, but it does clarify for me that all religions arise from human error and not from God. Thus, for this reason I have rejected them [all]!'

---

1 ወለሰብአ ሐምር ወለሰብአ ሳባ (and the people of Homor and the people of Saba), with Ḥimyar being unusually spelled as Ḫomor. The people of Yemen have referred to themselves as 'the sons of Himyar and Saba' since antiquity. Here the author is likely recalling the Old South Arabian pantheon, which was once honoured in the Aksumite Empire as well and known in the Aksum of the author's youth through ruins and inscriptions.

2 That is, to the faith's founders.

3 That is, the faith of Christianity.

Chapter 6: My Inquiry regarding Questions of Faith and God's Care

However, everyone who disagrees with me, they're all permitted to keep their religion. They can believe what they want, and trust what is written in books, while declaring that these 'books were written by the Spirit of God'[1] and so they cannot be lies.

Nevertheless, let such believers understand that I write this book myself[,[2] it was not written by the Spirit of God]. But, it seems as though God's Spirit is with me, guiding me to write the truth and keeping me away from all deceptiveness in my writing. For I write after careful and lengthy inquiry and after prayer and purifying my heart before God. I won't write anything which is inconsistent with our intelligence, but only what is present in the heart of all human beings. Because of this, what I write cannot be false.[3]

Also, I don't write this book to put 'a stumbling block in the path' of believers.[4] Rather, I write it to turn the wise and intelligent toward inquiry, through which they may 'seek and find' truth.[5] For inquiring into everything is beautiful wisdom. It glorifies our creator, who graciously gave us a rational soul and an inquiring intelligence to make [just] such inquiries.

It's not God's will [for us] to believe without inquiry. Nor is it in accordance with a rational creature's nature. Because of this, we should not believe in our ancestors' faith without examining it or understanding whether their faith is true. For, God didn't give intelligence only to our ancestors.[6] On the contrary, he gave us that which is even greater than theirs.

Abb215 38v

---

1 2 Timothy 3:16, which has ወኵሉ መጽሐፍ ዘበመንፈስ እግዚአብሔር ተጽሕፈ. (All scripture [the body of sacred texts in the Christian religion] is written by the Spirit of God).
2 አነሂ እጽሐፍ ዘንተ መጽሐፈ. (I write *or* write down *or* inscribe *or* describe this book myself). The author might be referring to the mechanical process of applying ink to paper to record his thoughts or, if he developed his ideas orally first, he might be referring to the composition process as a whole.
3 This author is more assertive than the author of HZY, likely because he is following in someone else's footsteps and thus feels protected by precedent.
4 A stock phrase from Psalm 140:5 (139:6(5) LXX); 2 Corinthians 6:3. Note that the author has cited the Ge'ez Bible, using ዕቅፍት (stumbling block) and not followed the LXX and other versions based on it, which have the slightly different 'snare' or 'trap'. The author's rhetorical point depends on 'block' not 'snare', suggesting an intimate, lived knowledge, through memorization, of the Ge'ez Psalms specifically.
5 Matthew 7:7; Luke 11:9.
6 That is, it is not only ancient texts like the Bible that are correct, having wisdom and knowledge.

How do we show that our ancestor's faith is true unless we examine it and understand it from beginning to end? So, we must always walk in the light of our intelligence, which is the light of God.

Above all things, this light, which does not lie, demonstrates to us that there is a God, who is creator of everything, and who embraces all things. We should believe in him and worship him in love and awe.

Moreover, our intelligence ascertains that God, who created everything, has not abandoned his creation after bringing her forth from that which does not exist.

On the contrary, just as he made everything with great wisdom, so he will preserve everything with great care, nourish everything, guide everything, be mindful of everything,[1] and be gracious to everything.

As for us, we should always give thanks to him with all our heart's power. We must trust in his generosity. Let us pray to him day and night to protect us, to be gracious to us, to give us everything that we need in life, and to enlighten our intelligence to understand his holy will, so that we may perform and fulfil his holy will diligently in all the days of our service in this world.[2]

Let us plead with sorrowful hearts that he pardon our faults and forgive the sins we committed in ignorance when we were young.[3]

Let us repent, turn back, and approach him with our pure minds, for he loves us.

Even though I am small, insignificant, and detestable before him, my creator does not reject me because of this. For his infinite greatness is sufficient for all, great and small. There isn't a worm among all the earth's tiny worms, nor a tree among the wilderness' [many] trees, nor grass among the field's [many] grasses that God does not think about and watch over. How could he not always think about and watch over me, his rational creature?

---

[1] ወለኵሉ ይሔሊ. (he thinks of all things). The verb here may be inspired by the intercessory prayer of the Divine Liturgy: በእንተ ኵሉ ዓለም ናስተበቊዕ ከመ እግዚአብሔር ያቅድም ሐልዮ ወሐሊ. ለለአሐዱ አሐዱ ጻሕቆ ዘይሣኒ ወዘይኄይስ (concerning the entire world, we pray that the Lord might first consider, and keep in mind, the desires of each person, [considering] what is good and better for them).

[2] Probably a paraphrase of Colossians 1:9, which concerns knowing and fulfilling God's will. This idea also appears in ትምህርተ ኅቡአት (Mystagogia), a short text that is memorized and recited every day by the EOTC clergy.

[3] A paraphrase of Psalm 25:7 (24:7 LXX), in which the author asks God to forgive the sins of his youth.

'As a father has compassion on his children, so God has compassion on us', his creatures.¹

[Such tender care] is not in any way hard for God, among all his thoughts and all his caring actions for this world. For all things take place according to his blessed will. He can simultaneously direct thousands or tens of thousands² of worlds without difficulty and without tiring. Surrounding and protecting them is as nothing for him.

Chapter 7: My Inquiry regarding Loving One Another and Cooperation

Even more, my intelligence tells me that my soul was created as intelligent so that she may know her creator, and glorify and give thanks to him at all times, and serve in acts of divine service³ that the creator has prepared for her. Also, [so that] my soul may seek and understand God's will in every action that she does, and worship him without deceit as long as she lives her life in this body.

After this life, she will return to her creator, and he will make her exalted and blessed according to his will.

As for me, until I'm able to remain persistent in this act of divine service, I must seek, know, and fulfil God's will for me, and improve my actions. For this is why God created me as an understanding being.

Moreover, because God did not create me alone, but rather put me with other creatures like me, who are equal with me, I must join with them in mutual love and aid. I must not hate them or do anything evil to them, because God commanded me to serve together with them, to love my broth-

---

1 Psalm 103:13 (102:13 LXX). The verb in this verse can be spelled in two different ways: either ይምሁር (as found in the manuscript) or ይምሕር. these two h's—ሁ and ሕ—are often interchanged in writing, so manuscripts of the Psalms can have either spelling. At the same time, these two spellings can have different meanings, based on their roots: ይምሁር (he teaches) and ይምሕር (he is merciful), following the LXX. Someone trained in the EOTC tradition of scholarship would almost certainly have both meanings in mind as they wrote.
2 አእላፈ አእላፋት ወትአልፊተ አእላፋት (thousands of thousands and tens of thousands of thousands).
3 ቅኔ (submitting), but here meaning the service of life itself as well as manual labour, worshipping God, and such creative labour as writing the poetry of the same name: ቅኔ (qəne).

ers and sisters[1] who serve with me, and to help them as much as I can, just as I would want for all human beings to love and help me.[2]

This rational teaching is clearly based[3] because human beings cannot be born, grow up, or labour on their own without the help of others.

Our creator's will is clear on this matter, for he placed human beings in this holy service, that they might join with each other, love and help one another, and so that everyone gets everything they need to live.

This faith[, of mutual love,] that our intelligence reveals to us is greater [wisdom] than all the hidden mysteries, which have no use whatsoever for improving our actions in life or perfecting our created nature. Let us persevere in this faith, and we shall find a great reward with God and with human beings.

Chapter 8: My Inquiry regarding Humanity as the Ruler of Creation

God's work within all creation is wonderful. 'His thoughts are profound'[4] and his wisdom is ineffable. Only a tiny part of his design is revealed to us.

We are unable to understand, because of all the [diverse] ways he created and guided all his creatures.

We should not say to God, 'Why did you do this or do that?'

Just as 'the thing formed does not say to the potter [who formed it], "why did you make me like this?"'[5]

So, a creature should not say to her creator, 'why did you create me like this?'

But we should worship him and all his holy ways, which we are unable to understand, because our intelligence tells us that God is wise and that his plan is incorruptible. Since he made everything with great wisdom we should believe and be persuaded that all that he does is good, as it is essential for making this world beautiful and fulfilling all creation's needs.

We see many creatures that seem useless or corrupt, or created without purpose or wisdom, or whose creation has no value. But this is because we

---

1 The word አኃው (brothers) is not limited in meaning to men or family relationships but should be understood as including friends and other community members too.
2 An allusion to Matthew 5:43, Luke 19:18, John 2:8, and Mark 12:31.
3 ጥዩቅ (certain *or* penetrating). The root of this word means that it is certain due to observation or investigation, not mere intuition.
4 Psalm 92:5 (91:5 LXX).
5 Romans 9:20–21, based on Isaiah 29:16

don't understand the creator's wisdom, he who made everything to be good, and who created everything in a purposeful way. Still more, we don't understand the precious *act* of creation.   Abb215 41v

We should wonder at and glorify the creator in all his actions, even things that we don't understand. Let us praise him, because he created us and put us among these beautiful and wonderous creatures and made us superior to all of them.

He graciously granted us intelligence and wisdom that he did not grant to other creatures, only us! He appointed us to oversee and 'rule over' all creation.[1]

If God had not created other things below us we would not have known our superiority.   Litt Ed 38

Now, since we are superior to animals and the plants of the field, we should praise our creator who made us superior, crowned us with glory, and appointed us from among all his handiwork. He also 'made us master of all that is under our feet'.[2] For humanity is the ruler of this world, and commands all and rules over all things.

Other creatures [either] obey and serve human beings or they tremble and flee from their presence. But humanity has no ruler except God alone. Therefore, human beings should worship him who appointed and exalted them over all his works.   Abb215 42r / Sum 35

They should serve him with all their heart and fulfil his whole will, which he reveals to human beings through the illumination of their intelligence, by which he showed them good and evil. For, just as we know the creator through the illumination of our intelligence; with the same intelligence, we know his will for us.

Let us keep in mind that he is our Lord, and we are his handiwork; he can treat us according to his good will for us. So, we should praise him every day because of the good things that he has made for us. Let us bow our heads when he disciplines us and puts us to the test. Let us beg him to make the service of our labour easy and to turn our hearts to him in wisdom and love.

---

1 Genesis 1:28; Genesis 9:2.
2 Psalm 8:6 (8:6 LXX). When quoting from Psalms, the HWH author often changed the pronouns to suit his rhetorical purpose. Here, he personalized the Psalm, from 'you . . . him' to 'he . . . us'. Alternately, here and throughout, the author may simply be reflecting the Ge'ez Bible version with which he was familiar.

Chapter 9: My Inquiry regarding the Consequences of Violating the Established Order of the Creator

In our hardship and suffering, with which God is pleased to test us in this life of divine service, we should be patient, and we should plead with him to strengthen our trust of him, and 'we should humbly bow our heads under his holy hand'.[1]

If someone says, 'In what way is "God merciful and compassionate"?[2]—he punishes us and is angry with his creatures!'

I would say to them, 'it's not God who punishes us in his anger, for God is perfect in nature'. He is never angry, and no one can make him angry, nor is his delight ever unsettled. Rather, it is we who bring punishment upon ourselves when we violate the laws which the creator established for us and all creation alike.

Therefore, violating the law brings down judgement upon us, [judgement] prescribed by the creator's wisdom for the protection of every created thing, within its boundaries.[3] Just as one who burns their hand in a fire suffers but is unable to blame God who created fire [to burn] like this,[4] one who violates God's law, established for all creation, will receive judgement commensurate with their violation of the law.

This making judgement commensurate with the violation of the law, was established with the creator's good counsel. It's needed to better this world and to protect all creatures within their prescribed boundaries.

So, God does not punish us in anger but rather because our actions are out of harmony with the laws governing our nature and that bring disaster upon us.[5] Besides, we should understand that God is righteous, and he safeguards righteousness in all his actions and toward all creatures, and his judgement is commensurate with human sin.

---

1 An allusion to 1 Peter 5:6. The author has changed the pronouns to personalize the scriptural allusion.
2 Psalm 103:8 (102:8 LXX), and many other biblical passages.
3 That is, humanity is punished to protect creation, each part of which has its own place (e.g., water ends at the earth, the earth ends at the sky). According to the EOTC commentary on Genesis 6, human actions often harm the rest of creation.
4 An allusion to Sirach 15:16, a famous passage on God giving people a choice between putting their hands in fire or water, often cited when commenting on free will.
5 The author is challenging the common view that God punishes humanity for sin due to his anger, arguing that God has no anger. Rather, calamity is the natural consequence of the human violation of God's laws for creation.

When human beings conceive sin in their hearts[1] and carry it out by their evil will, at that time they don't understand that from that moment [of sin] forward they will deserve judgement commensurate with the sin they committed. This judgement will not be neglected but will happen at the established time, whether [that is] right away or much later. Human beings may forget the sin that they committed and may not remember the debt recorded against them, but God's righteousness will not neglect it, [nor be satisfied] until the judgement is commensurate with the sin.

So, when punishment comes on us we should humble ourselves with a repentant heart and turn back to our creator with our whole will. We should praise him constantly, because 'his name is praised and glorified through all that he brings on us. All his judgements are righteous, and he is just and fair in all he does for us, and there is no injustice in him'.[2]

Chapter 10: My Inquiry regarding the Suffering of the Innocent and Reincarnation

If someone says, 'God's righteousness [actually] doesn't apportion judgement according to a person's sin in this world. For we see evil and violent human beings enjoying themselves, while the humble and righteous are troubled by all kinds of hardships. The strong terrify, oppress, and rob the poor. The poor weep and no one helps them; they cry out to God but he does not hear them. Also, we see children who fall sick before they even know how to do evil. All of this shows us that God's righteousness is not accomplished on earth'.

Regarding that, I would say to them, 'We must bow down in silence to God's good will because we cannot understand his righteous ways, and we cannot understand why he punishes human beings who seem righteous to us. But we surely know that God is always righteous in all his actions; there is no injustice in him; and its impossible for him to punish human beings unjustly'.

Therefore, let's not complain when he punishes us, but let's humble ourselves, and bow down to our Lord who punishes us to save us. He doesn't punish us to destroy us but to cleanse us from the sins that we have committed, to turn us back to him, and to make us worthy of the reward that he has prepared for us in his wisdom. Or [he does it] so that he might restore crea-

---

1 An allusion to James 1:15.
2 Daniel 3:26–27, from the Prayer of Azariah that is also found in the Ge'ez Psalter (a collection of the biblical Psalms and other short works), as one of the fifteen biblical Canticles. Here, the author has made changes to the word order and pronouns.

tion's beauty and sustain this world. For all creation is connected together: when one thing is twisted, God torments it as well as the other things connected to it.[1]

There are those who say, 'Human souls are angels who have sinned in God's presence['.[2] They say, ']Due to this sin, they deserve judgement commensurate with the sins that they have committed. Human beings' bodies are their prisons. They are imprisoned in a body until they complete their penance. God created thousands and thousands of angels, and as the wise ancients suggest, those angels sinned in their thinking and they deserved judgement, so they were imprisoned in human bodies until their penance was complete'.

[They say that] 'Later, the angels will return to their creator and to their spiritual service. If they sin again, they will again be imprisoned [in a human body]. As long as the angels live in human bodies, they won't remember anything about their previous life. That way, they won't break their chains and kill their own bodies out of longing for their previous [heavenly] existence'.

[They say that] 'God created this beautiful prison, which is the human body, for sinful angels.[3] While they are imprisoned in a body, they will animate it with life until they leave that body. On that day, because of the dignity of the one who was imprisoned in it, that prison will be destroyed so that it can't be used by others'.

Moreover, they say that 'because angels' sins are not all equal—the sins of one are greater and those of another less—so they will be imprisoned in human bodies [for a lifespan] in proportion to their sins. So, one will live in this body for just a few days and another for many years. The ones who sinned only a little will be set free [by dying straight away] or they will die in infancy; those who sinned more [than a little] will die during adolescence or in forgetful old age; and those who sinned much more than those, adding still

---

1 The author continues to emphasize that God does not single human beings out to punish them but rather that they are subject to certain rules (whose violation has consequences) and that they are bodies in a connected material world (which affects them in ways that look like punishment).

2 The source of this idea could not be identified. 1 Enoch, part of the Ethiopian Canon, states that 'the children of God', who are often understood to be angels, took wives from among 'the children of men' but not that the resulting children were angels. The ideas in the following about reincarnation can be found in popular Ge'ez texts, such as በረላም ወይደስፍ፡ (Barlaam and Josaphat), a tenth-century composition translated into Ge'ez and loosely based on the life of the Buddha but turning him into a Christian saint.

3 ለመልአክ አባሲ. (for a *or* the sinful angel); in using the singular, the author may be thinking of the most famous sinful angel, Satan, who was reputedly very beautiful.

more to their sins in this life, they will be imprisoned for many years in a vile existence and their life [in a body] will be long and agonizing'.

These wise ancients spoke like this, and to strengthen their point they added that if our souls had not sinned in a previous existence, they would not have been condemned to live in this world.[1] For God cannot judge a soul other than in proportion to its sin.

After I had inquired into this teaching, I found that [truly] understanding it was beyond the limits of our understanding, and we cannot know whether it is true or false.

Chapter 11: My Inquiry and Prayer regarding Temptation and the Testing of the Faithful

More excellent than this teaching [about human suffering] is the one my wise teacher Zara Yaqob taught.[2] The temptations and troubles that happen to human beings in this world are to test them, so that they will be worthy of the reward that their creator will graciously grant them. In fact, no wages are due to anyone who does not work,[3] and no one is worthy of reward who has not been faithful during a period of testing.

Litt Ed 41
Abb215 45v

Just as silver is tested in a furnace to be refined and purified, so human beings are tested with troubles and temptations.[4] Those who are patient during a period of testing, who praise God when experiencing troubles, who humble themselves in worship and thanksgiving, and who at all times serve God, they will be worthy of the reward that does not perish.[5] The one who does not know the sovereignty of the Most High, who denies God during a period of testing and who curses him in a period of temptation, will be punished, just as is fitting for any rebellious child and any servant who denies his Lord.

---

1 That is, in this theory, when an innocent baby suffers in this life, that's because they bring a debt of sin from a previous life and body.
2 See HZY, Chapter 16.
3 An allusion to Matthew 10:10; ይደልዎ ዐሳቡ ለዘይትቀነይ (the one who works deserves his wage). The author has stated the verse's corollary, in the negative: those who do not work do not deserve a wage.
4 This analogy—of metal's purification through fire as like the godliness produced through suffering—is found throughout the Bible, notably in 1 Peter 1:7, Proverbs 17:3, and Isaiah 48:10.
5 This is an allusion to 1 Peter, which talks about trials and suffering for purification, and also the crown of glory that never fades as a reward for the faithful.

Prayer:

I give thanks to you, O Lord[1] my King,
    and I always glorify my God.
I trust in you,
    and I bow down to your holy good will.
You are my God and my Lord!
As servants' eyes [look] towards their master's hand [for grace],
    so my eyes always [look] towards you.[2]
Do to me as you please because your will is righteous forever.
Bowing to your sovereignty,
    I only ask and entreat you[3] with all my heart
    not to lengthen the days of my testing or make them a burden.
That way, the foolishness of the many,
    who worship you when you are gracious to them
    but curse you when you test them, will not fall upon my soul.
Give strength to my soul,[4]
    and establish her firmly, so that she will never shake.
I won't say to you, 'Don't test me!'
Rather make me fight for what is right[5] and to be patient,
    when it pleases you to test your understanding creature as she deserves it.
Secure me so that I will not stumble or ever deny you,
    and make me glorify you always
[Both] when you are gracious to me with your blessing
    and when you test me according to your holy good will.
Because you are my Lord and my God,
    from before the world and for ever.[6]

---

1 Psalm 9:1 (9:1 LXX).
2 Psalm 123:2 (122:2 LXX). A *Ta'ammera Maryam* story (PEMM ID 1160) also cites this passage in a similar genre; that is, in a prayer created for the context.
3 The author has personalized a phrase frequently used in the liturgy, for instance, in the genre of intercessory prayer known as መስተብቍዕ (Mästäbqʷəʾ). The original phrase is ንስአለከ ወናስተበቍዐከ (we ask and entreat you).
4 Psalm 30:8 (29:7 LXX). The author's point, ሀባ ኃይለ ለነፍስየ (give strength to my soul), depends on the wording of the Ge'ez, which is ሀባ ኃይለ ለሕይወትየ (give strength to my life) The LXX is quite different.
5 አትጋደል (struggle).
6 The author concludes the poem with the traditional ending from the liturgy, ወአስከ ለዓለም (forever *or* for eternity).

Chapter 12: My Inquiry regarding Prayer and the Prayerless Human Soul

Concerning prayer, we should always pray to God our creator so that we receive what we need for our lives and so that he graciously grants us understanding and wisdom to make our actions beautiful. [We should do so] because prayer is fitting, and suits the nature of our understanding souls.

If someone says, 'Prayer is not needed because God knows all our needs. So, after he created us with those needs, he should give us what we need without us asking him'.

I would reply to such people, 'Prayer was not established for us to make known to God our needs, which he understands perfectly. On the contrary, prayer was established so that we could be worthy to receive God's blessing; so that we could know from whom we receive what we need for our life, so that we would recognise that everything is from the Lord our God; so that we would worship him and glorify him; and so that we would always be near him in our thought and worship. For God created us for his glory, and he doesn't need anything from us'.

In this matter [of prayer], human beings are distinct from the animals. For animals don't know from whom they have received what they need, while human beings know God, the Creator, who hears their requests and 'grants the request of the one who prays'.[1]

Moreover, prayer joins and unites our spirit with our creator. It glorifies him, and affirms to us that he is the creator of all, the one who embraces all things, and the fountain of all riches and all grace. However, we are but creatures: we are poor, we are pitiful, and we are devoid of all goodness; we are weak, and we have no help except from God alone.

Because of this, the human soul without prayer falls from her superior status and becomes numbered among the animal orders, which have no understanding,[2] and even comes to look like the animals. The prayerless soul is not worthy of her creator's blessing.

For the prayerless soul has denied and ignored the Creator, has refused to come close to him, and has withdrawn from the fountain of all blessing. The prayerless soul has 'preferred the curse'[3] and has hated the giver of life.

---

1 An allusion to 1 Samuel 2:9 (2:9 LXX), which is part of a biblical section that appears as one of the Biblical Canticles, 'The Prayer of Hanna', in the Ge'ez Psalter.
2 An allusion to Psalm 32: 9 (31:9 LXX). The author has expanded the original biblical verse, which is limited to 'the horse and the mule', to reference all animals.
3 Psalm 109:17 (108:17 LXX).

So the prayerless soul falls, cast down into darkness, to where there is no 'sun of righteousness'.[1]

The prayerless soul has not wanted to live in the creator like a branch on a tree trunk. Like branches that are cut off from their trunk have no life, so our spirit cannot live unless it draws near to its creator, and 'lives in him'[2] with prayer, worship, and constant thanksgiving.[3]

Chapter 13: My Inquiry regarding Justice, Self-Preservation, and Neighbours

When human beings draw near to their creator and cling to him[4] through prayer and worship, they should not be distant from their neighbour. For it's God's command that they live with other human beings and share their lives with them.

God didn't create human beings 'to live alone',[5] rather he created them with a longing to live with other human beings. Indeed, human beings cannot live alone, but each person needs the help of others. All human beings should help one another, and those who withdraw from the company of human society violate their creator's established order.

As for you, don't commend those who withdraw themselves from human company to live as hermits in wilderness caves,[6] because they don't know the creator's will, he who commanded all human beings to help one another. One who lives in solitude is useless to human society; it's 'as if they were already dead'.[7] God will not accept the service of human beings who rebel against walking the path he leads them on, and who refuse 'the acts of divine service prepared' for them.[8]

---

1 Malachi 4:2 (4:2 LXX).
2 An extended allusion to the Gospel of John 15:1–11, in which Jesus refers to himself as the 'true vine' and the disciples as 'the branches'. The Gospel of John is memorized by many in Ethiopia; some monks recite it weekly or even daily.
3 Many biblical passages express these ideas, but perhaps 1 Thessalonians 5:18 most clearly.
4 ወክነረ ስቅለ ኅቦሁ (live as ones clinging to him or live crucified with him). can mean either 'one who clings' or 'crucified'. The idea of the believer being 'crucified with Christ' is expressed in several NT verses, including Romans 6:6, 1 Corinthians 2:2, Galatians 2:19, Galatians 5:24.
5 An allusion to Genesis 2:18.
6 HW's mentor ZY did retreat to a cave, but only because he was persecuted into exile.
7 Psalm 143:3 (142:3 LXX). ከመ ምውት ትካት (like one long dead).
8 Allusion to Ephesians 2:10.

Moreover, God created all human beings as equals, like siblings, children of one father. That father is our creator, the Father of all. Because of this [equality], we should love one another. Also, we should keep this eternal law that God wrote on 'the tablet of our heart',[1] which says, 'Love others as yourself',[2] and 'do to them as you want them to do to you',[3] and 'don't do to them as you don't want them to do to you'. By keeping this fundamental rule, all righteousness and the perfection of all our actions will be gained.

Don't be impressed with the teaching of those inferior in wisdom, who say [things like], 'I don't know who to call "neighbour", except our relatives, our neighbours, our friends, and our fellow believers'.

Don't say what they say, since all human beings are our 'neighbours', whether they are good or evil; whether Christians, Muslims, Jews, or pagans. All of them are our equals and all of them are our siblings because we are all children of one Father, and we are all one creator's creatures.

Because of this, we should love one another and do as much good for everyone as we can, and we should not do evil to anyone. Moreover, we should be patient with human beings' ignorance, and sins, and forgive their errors which have caused us grief, because we ourselves are sinners and we want our sins to be forgiven.

If someone says to me, 'What should we do with those who wish evil upon us?'

I would reply, 'We should reject their evil with all our ability, without repaying their evils with evil. For 'vengeance is the Lord's',[4] who is the only judge of everyone. If we cannot push away the evil that they devised for us without inflicting harm on them, only then should we preserve our life and existence in every way that we can. We should reject their force with our strength, their deceit with our cunning, their intrigue with our [good] counsel, and their spear with our spear. For God has given us intelligence and strength to protect our life and existence and to save us from evil human beings' snares and deceit.

If we can't [push it away], we should be patient and 'leave our [worried] thoughts to God'.[5] Let us leave our judgement and our revenge to him.

---

1 An allusion to 2 Corinthians 3:3.
2 Romans 13:9, Galatians 5:14.
3 Matthew 7:12, Luke 6:31.
4 Deuteronomy 32:35, Romans 12:19.
5 Psalm 55:22 (54:23 LXX). The author quotes the Ge'ez Bible, which refers to ሕሊናህ (your thoughts), while the LXX versions refer to τὴν μέριμνάν σου (your cares).

We should also plead with him to save us and free us from human oppression.[1] Despite the difficult task [of leaving things up to God], we should never treat anyone badly, whether in word or deed.

On the contrary, we should strictly abstain from all lies, slander, verbal abuse, theft, adultery, beating, and murder[2]—indeed, from all evil actions which grieve and destroy our neighbours or their possessions. Since all these actions oppose the creator's established order, they destroy all the laws of nature, and they extinguish the love and harmony needed for human beings to live together.

Part II: Advice

Chapter 14: Loving Your Neighbour

Just as a gnawing mouse spoils valuable fine linen garments but is utterly unnourished by them, so a slanderous tongue that destroys a good name does not benefit from that act. And look, 'a good name is more valuable than' fine linen garments or any other possession.[3]

Just as hail destroys mature grain but shatters when it falls, so the slander that comes out of a human being's mouth puts their neighbour to shame but also ruins the slanderer.

Just as fire can burn up the house of someone who starts a fire, so the anger of a human being can burn them up from the inside.

My dear child! Don't ever be angry yourself, or you'll bitterly regret it. 'Don't let the sun go down on your anger'.[4] Be someone who repents over your mistakes. When you sin against your neighbour, don't be slow to turn around, but get up straight away and be good to them in compensation for the evil that you have done. Reconcile with your neighbour so that there may be peace and so that God will bless [you and your neighbour].

Be a peaceful person with everyone,[5] and 'let your mouth speak no evil'.[6] Be tender and a comfort to the distressed and sad, and God will reward you

---

1 Allusion to Psalm 72:14 (71:14 LXX).
2 Although the Ten Commandments appear in the OT, the list here is similar to those in the NT: Mark 7:21, Ephesians 4:31, Colossians 3:8. 1 Timothy 6:4, 1 Peter 2:1.
3 Proverbs 22:1; Ecclesiastes 7:1.
4 Ephesians 4:26.
5 Paraphrase of Romans 12:18.
6 Ephesians 4:29.

with good things. Remember to give alms, and if you have bread, share it with your hungry brothers and sisters and friends, and God will nourish you from [all] his good things. If you have the power, rescue your persecuted brothers and sisters, and God will rescue you, and will not let sinners rule over your land.[1] If you have wisdom, have compassion for those[2] lacking understanding, and God will give you understanding of his mysteries, and he will reveal to you his hidden wisdom.

When you can, be willing to delight everyone, because the Lord our 'God is love'.[3] The one who lives in mutual affection with their neighbour, and pleasing them, will live with God and God with them.[4] Mutual love improves all human life. It relieves our suffering, it seasons and sweetens our whole life as it transforms this world into the kingdom of heaven. Moreover, 'we should not love with word and speech alone, but with actions and truth'.[5]

Let's not be like those Christians of our country who teach the love of Jesus Christ with their mouths but have no love in their hearts. They excommunicate each other, insult each another, and kill each another because of their religion. This 'love' is not from God and is absolutely useless. So, let's not love one another like those hypocrites, whose mouths speak truth and love, but 'beneath their tongues is snake's venom',[6] and their hearts are fixated on hatred and quarrelling.

Similarly, let's not love like those who love [only] their fellow believers and hate strangers and those who don't share their faith. Their 'love' is not love at all.

We must understand and take seriously that all human beings are created equal.[7] They are all children of God. We are wrong when we hate others because of their religion. Everyone is allowed to believe what seems true to them.[8] Religion doesn't become established in human hearts through force or [the threat of] excommunication, nor is it corrected [that way]. Only

---

1 An allusion to Psalm 125:3 (124:3 LXX). The author has made the usual change in pronoun to 'you'.
2 መሐሮሙ (have compassion on them). See the previous note about this spelling and መህሮሙ (teach them).
3 1 John 4:8.
4 There are many allusions in this sentence to John 14 and the mutual indwelling of God in believers.
5 1 John 3:18.
6 Psalm 140:3 (139:3 LXX).
7 ኩሎሙ ሰብእ ዕሩያን እሙንቱ በተፈጥሮቶሙ (all human beings are equal in their nature).
8 ዘኮነ ብውሕ ለኩሉ ለለጰጰ ይእሙኑ በከመ ይመስሎሙ ጽድቀ (which is permitted for anyone to believe, each one as it seems true to them).

wisdom and learning do. Just as we should not hate others because of their knowledge, so we should not hate them because of their religion.

Chapter 15: Accepting Other Cultures

In all your conduct towards human beings, check your heart['s motivations] in the presence of God. Do to others what you would want them to do to you, and don't do to others what you wouldn't want them to do to you. For such love and mutual love is the fundamental command that God gave us and wrote on the tablets of everyone's heart.

You, my friend, if you 'desire to see good days',[1] be in harmony with everyone, in love and peace. To achieve this goal, the wisdom of the ancients is beneficial: 'When you live among your own [people], live according to the customs of your homeland, but should you go to a foreign land, be like them'.[2] For it is truly wise to live in peace with everyone and to avoid endless quarrelling and insults between you and others.

Don't disparage anything as impure except that which is contrary to the laws that God established for all creation. Any action that doesn't violate natural law is pure and has nothing impure in its motivation.[3] Although everything was pure when created, that's no longer the case among human beings. Actions can be good according to one's own country's customs, but not good in another. If you don't keep the customs of the country that you live in, you violate love, and you cause quarrels and insults.[4]

Don't do anything which is not good according to that [country's] custom. Don't say, 'this action [of mine] is not offensive'! Rather, on the contrary, praise the customs of the country that you are living in. Be united with the people of that country, and pray that God will be gracious to everyone according to their character, customs, and actions.

Nevertheless, don't give up your understanding of God-given wisdom on account of this [acceptance of others]. On the contrary, guard what the illu-

---

1 Psalm 34:12 (33: 13 LXX); 1 Peter 3:10. The author has changed the pronoun.
2 This is a proverb frequently quoted by Ethiopian preachers. Although it is similar in meaning (but not wording) to the advice given by Saint Ambrose to Saint Augustine about 'when in Rome', none of these early Latin texts were translated into Ge'ez.
3 ወአልቦ ርኩስ ውስተ ጠባይዑ (and has no impurity in its nature).
4 The author seems to have in mind the country's many religions, ethnic groups, cultural practices, and schools of thought (this last being especially true in the 1600s), recommending that people not stand firm on unimportant principles.

mination of your intelligence has revealed to you while living in harmony with a people's customs for as long as you lived with them.

Purify your heart and mind, and from one day to the next, perfect your actions, so that you may find favour with your creator, who wants you to be perfect.

Chapter 16: Honouring One's Parents and Elders

As a child and young adult, honour and love your parents because the time will come when you want to have the honour and love of your children. Revere God who commands you to 'honour your father and mother'.[1] Keep this commandment with great care and love your parents with all your heart.

Don't distress your parents for any reason. That way their mouths won't curse you and their hearts won't be sad. Also, God won't hear their curses and reject you.

Help your parents and delight them with all your good actions. A time will come when you will want the help of your children and teenagers, to care for you and feed you in your forgetful old age. On that day [of need,] God will well reward you. If you are harsh and cruel to your parents and elders, God will impose misfortune on you in your forgetful old age, and your children and teenagers will rightly avenge your sin against your elders. Then you will weep bitterly and repent pointlessly.

There was an old man whose eyes were blind.[2] One day, he and his son quarrelled with each other. His son was a wicked person and, as they quarrelled, he angrily grabbed his father's leg and started to drag him along, over stones and thorns, his father weeping and wailing in a feeble voice.

When they reached a place that the old man recognised [from his youth], he cried out and said to his son, 'Let go of me for one moment and listen to me!'

His son let go of him and said, 'Have your say!'

The old man said, wailing bitterly, 'I was wicked in my youth and quarrelled with my father just as you have done with me today. In my rage, I struck my father and dragged him to this very place. Today, God has avenged

---

1 This command is given in Exodus 20:12 but reiterated throughout the Bible, including Deuteronomy 5:16, Matthew 15:4, Mark 7:10 and 10:19, Luke 18:20, and Ephesians 6:2.
2 This is a famous folktale in Ethiopia still today. What the son does to his father sometimes changes in the story (e.g., making him eat from a broken wooden bowl or abandoning him on a hillside to die by himself).

[my father] and paid me back with the misfortune I deserved. Now, let me go, and don't make your punishment more severe than mine. You won't escape your punishment—it will certainly befall you!'

This story shows that God rewards everyone according to their actions, and that God avenges a child's wickedness against their parents and elders.

My child, be patient and skilled in dealing with your parents' infirmities and prickly nature. Don't ever distress them with any of your actions, but please them in every way that you can, so that they may bless you with their joyful hearts. God will add his blessings to theirs.

'God will deliver you from the day of evil',[1] protect you, make you happy on this earth, and help you on your sick bed as well as in your forgetful old age.

Listen to the advice of your elders and don't despise their wisdom. Don't be careless in their presence, that way they won't be distressed by you. Rather, always honour them with your humble words and amiable behaviour.

[However,] just put this in your heart: you must question and test [what the elders say]. You must 'hold on to what is good'.[2]

Chapter 17: On the Importance of Learning

Don't tire of learning, and don't ever abandon it your whole life long.

Never say, 'I have learned plenty—what I've learned is enough for me'.

For, even if you learned everything human beings can teach you, there would still be much more that you don't know. Preserve what you learn so that you will discover many ways to serve. Don't confine yourself to one teaching, as that would be lazy.

Instead, observe the bee collecting [nectar from] the flowers of the field: It doesn't rest on only one flower, nor [even] in a single field, but it wanders and gathers from all [types of] flowers. It produces two natural elements: honey and wax. The first, through drinking it, is the delight of the day, while the second, through its illumination, is the light of the night.[3]

Likewise, if you collect wisdom from all teachings, you will produce two natural elements: honey, [that is,] good actions which are sweet and give joy to

---

[1] Psalm 41:1 (40:1 LXX); Ephesians 6:13; but with the author's usual pronoun change from 'he' to 'you' for rhetorical purposes.

[2] 1 Thessalonians 5:21.

[3] The author is poetically describing ጠጅ (*tej*), Ethiopia's mead or honey wine, and ጧፍ (*tʷaf*), Ethiopia's slender candles made of beeswax.

your heart; and wax, [that is,] your learnedness, which illuminates your mind, so that you will be a light for the earth's blind and those lacking wisdom. You will drive darkness out of the hearts of those sleeping through the night of their ignorance and those lost in the darkness of their foolishness.

Chapter 18: Hard Work and Its Fruits

Cherish working with your hands, as much as harmonizes with your way of life, and grow skilful at it, so that you may profit [from it].

Don't be ashamed of working with your hands,[1] because it is God's commandment. Unless all human beings work with their hands, humanity will be ruined, and its livelihood destroyed.

Don't say, 'Working with one's hands is [only] appropriate for the poor, as well as farmers, blacksmiths, builders, and the peasantry.[2] It's not appropriate for the great and honourable'.[3] For such reasoning [against manual labour] comes from a proud heart.

Aren't life's necessities equally sought after by each person? Since life's necessities are not attained without working with one's hands, so each and every person is required to work hard [with their hands] to meet their needs.

Abb215 54v

Sum 44

Don't say, 'I am rich, so I can eat and drink without working hard'. For such reasoning comes from a wicked laziness, and it destroys the creator's established order. God said, 'You shall eat the fruit of your hard work'.[4] Eating from another's labour while having the ability to work is to be a thief and a robber.

Get used to working with your hands starting when you're young and diligently eliminate laziness, for lazy people don't deserve God's blessing. Do your work so that at just the right time you may get what you, your family, and your dependent poor need.

---

1 The author is giving advice unusual for his class, celebrating the value of working with one's hands. He is advising his likely audience, noble students and clergy, against their prejudices.
2 ውሉደ ገበር (children of the peasants). Regarding the inclusion of blacksmiths, those who performed crafts were generally seen as inferior in highland Ethiopia and were often outsiders.
3 ውሉደ አበይት ወክቡራት (children of the great and of the nobles).
4 Psalm 128:2 (127:2 LXX).

Don't let your heart sink when the fruit of your labour is wasted or destroyed.[1] Rather, persevere in your work and pray to God to bless your labour and make it fruitful. Don't work like animals, 'which have no understanding'.[2] Rather, adapt your work, using your wisdom to increase efficiency and profits, and to lessen your fatigue.

When God blesses your labour and you harvest its fruit, worship him with all your heart and rejoice with your whole household. Eat, drink, and feast with joy and gladness! Persevere in your work so that you may add more fruit to your past labour's fruit, and more profit to your past labour's profit.

Never say, 'I have enough!' Nor should you say, 'this morsel is enough for my life, why should I bother?'[3] Such talk is laziness!

Furthermore, obtain as much as you can without injustice. Rather, rejoice in all your possessions gained 'through the sweat of your brow',[4] and you will resemble our creator.[5] Just as the creator, through his power and wisdom, produced from nothing every good thing that we can see for [sustaining] life in this world, so will you, by your labour and wisdom, produce from his work good fruit for the life of you and your neighbour.

Chapter 19: The Management of Wealth and Drinking

Don't live your life like a miser, because misers are doubly poor: poor because of what they don't have and poor because of what they do have. It's as if they really have nothing. Misers won't eat or drink or enjoy what they have, rather they lock up their treasures and live in poverty even though they have wealth.

This behaviour is incredibly stupid. It is the severe torment[6] God has ordained for stubborn hearted people. Misers don't enjoy their wealth and they don't make their neighbour glad [with it]. Throughout their life, they render their wealth useless. Therefore, God 'swallows up their wisdom'[7] and enslaves them to toil and 'accumulating wealth, without them knowing

---

1 Farmers' crops are regularly destroyed by animals, insects, rain, hail, and drought.
2 Psalm 32:9 (33:9 LXX). This is the second time the author is citing this verse.
3 This is a criticism of the asceticism of monks, who live on little.
4 Genesis 3:19. Here, በላሐ ገጽh (by the sweat of your face).
5 An allusion, perhaps, to Colossians 3:10.
6 ወአኩይ መቅሠፍት (and degrading passions *or* suffering). Romans 1:26.
7 Psalm 107:27 (106:27 LXX); this is the second time the author has used this verse.

whose it will finally be'.[1] These misers are 'stewards' for those who are not their relatives[2] and even for their enemies, without ever enjoying the fruit of their labour.[3]

As for you, keep away from such miserly foolishness. Be wise for your own good and enjoy your wealth as long as you live. Don't hoard your wealth for those who are not your relatives or for coming generations, because your God-given inheritance on earth is for you 'to eat, drink, and enjoy things'[4] for as long as you should live. When you die, you won't take any of it with you and all that you have hoarded will then be useless to you.

Sum 45

Abb215 56r

So, if you are wise, you won't abstain from the blessings that God your creator has given you: eat, drink, and enjoy yourself!

On the other hand, don't ever go beyond what you need, because excess ruins your health and reduces your enjoyment to nothing. Never drink to the point of drunkenness because drunkenness destroys intelligence, the understanding that makes us superior to the animals, who have no understanding. Drunkenness destroys our human nature and makes us lower than the animals—whether tame or wild. Drunkards don't deserve to be regarded as human beings.

Chapter 20: Food and Fasting

Choose food that gives you good health and prepare it with skill.[5] Wash it carefully so that it's tasty and healthy, for God has given you the intelligence for this. He created food to be tasty so that we would desire its flavour [and enjoy it], and worship our creator who graciously gives us countless good things.

Litt Ed 50

Abb215 56v

Let's not be like those fools who think that God forbids us from eating the food he created for [our] good health. Let them fast and abandon their

---

1 Psalm 39:6 (38:6 LXX).
2 This Ge'ez phrase reflects a common Amharic expression about a stingy person: ሁቡቱን ባዕድ በላው (a foreigner has eaten his wealth). It may be that the Amharic expression originated from Ge'ez, with the author translating familiar Amharic proverbs into Ge'ez here and several times below.
3 An allusion to Sirach 14:4, ዘይቄቅያ ለነፍሱ ይዘግብ ለባዕድ ([the miser] who deprives himself collects for others). This became a common proverb in Amharic.
4 Luke 12: 19; see also Isaiah 22:13; 1 Corinthians 15:32.
5 Later, the author directly addresses women readers, so he has a woman reader in mind here too when giving advice on food preparation. In Ethiopia, men do not generally cook, although men would have a say in what they eat and how it is prepared.

creator's blessing.¹ Look, [by their fasting] in this way, they accept judgement on their foolishness, because they refuse to understand the depth of God's wisdom, falling for human slander against food.

Don't give weight to their words when they say to you, 'We must fast!'

Just [agree and] say to them, 'By all means!' For it's better to give the impression that you're like them.

You will do well if you eat when you are hungry, and drink when you are thirsty, because this is the will of God your creator, who created you with the need to eat and drink.

Nothing is forbidden in all his creation, and no food is forbidden, except that which destroys our life. Nor is food forbidden on any [specific] day of our life—instead, our need to eat is equal on all our days.² The people who established the fasting laws did not inquire into or understand the creator's wisdom.

Chapter 21: Cleanliness, Clothes, and Homes

Don't seek to wear luxurious clothes, for that is vain. Wear clean, white clothes, and not dirty clothes, which spoil one's health, producing sores and scabs on your skin. Wash your clothes thoroughly and frequently because God has made plenty of water for you.³

Don't lie down or sleep on the ground, leaves, or damp grass, because it spoils your health and produces sores on your skin.⁴ Lie down or sleep on a bed, one that is [at least] three feet⁵ above the ground in cold regions and five or six feet⁶ in the lowlands.

Always pursue cleanliness of your body and soul, and don't be like the animals, which have no intelligence. Don't imitate the animals, because God

---

1 Again, the author is critiquing the asceticism of monks, who deliberately eat tasteless food or refrain from eating.
2 Traditionally, EOTC members fast on Wednesdays and Fridays as well as during the seven fasting seasons (including Lent and Advent).
3 The author is expressing common cultural values about cleanliness. For instance, white cotton clothing is the preferred clothing in highland Ethiopia, which also has plenty of water.
4 Again, the author is expressing common cultural values. While many sleep on leaves or grass in rural areas, this is frequently advised against as well.
5 ፪ በእመት (two cubits).
6 ፫ አው ፬ በእመት (three or four cubits).

gave you the intelligence for all these matters. As you are more intelligent than the animals, so also make your way of life better than theirs.

Build yourself a spacious and well-lit house.¹ Also, use your abundant wisdom to make it beautiful. Don't live in a pit like a hyena!²

Take pleasure in the good things that God has given you, and don't be stingy. Finally, don't be lazy, but make your food, clothes, and house, indeed your whole way of life, excellent.

Chapter 22: Charity and the Lazy

Don't be harsh with your neighbour. If you have great wealth, then give it out generously; if you have only a little, then [still] share it with those who are needy like you or even poorer than you. Then, the blessing of God will dwell in you. For he created the rich and the poor, the strong and the weak, together to help each other and to strengthen our love for each other.

But, discern between the poor who are weak and the poor who are lazy. Give to the weak what you have,³ but tell the lazy, 'Go and work! Eat what you produce!'⁴

Don't listen to the lazy when they weep and say to you, 'We're going to die of hunger!'⁵ For this is the creator's established order: 'let those who don't want to work starve' and perish in poverty.⁶ As for you, it would be better for you to throw your possessions into the sea⁷ than to give them to the lazy and

---

1 In the past, people often built round homes with just one window. The author is expressing a common cultural value of building homes with at least two windows, especially ones facing east.
2 The author is critiquing the asceticism of hermits, who often live apart from human society in caves.
3 ዘትርከብ ውስተ እዴከ (what is found in your hand). Specifying 'in your hand' is a typical Ethiopian formulation; for instance, see the proverb በእጅ ያለ ወርቅ ከመዳብ ይቆጠራል (gold that you have in your hand is treated as copper).
4 ወተሴስዮ ፍሬ ግማከሙ (you shall eat the fruit of your labour), from Psalm 128:2 (127:2 LXX).
5 ንመውት በረኃብ, which the author may have formulated based on the common Amharic expression of በረሀብ ሞትኩ (I have died of hunger).
6 2 Thessalonians 3:10.
7 This phrase—a direct address referencing throwing, possessions, and water in the context of the poor—matches up the metaphors in multiple biblical verses, from 1 Corinthians 13:3 (about giving all one's possessions to feed the poor) to Ecclesiastes 11:1 (about casting one's bread upon the waters). It is an example of the author's richly allusive creative process, and fearless adaptation of scripture to argue an opposite point.

enable them to persist in their laziness. Without mercy, push the lazy away from you because they disobey the creator's law.

Chapter 23: Slander, Adultery, and Theft

The slander that comes out of a person's mouth is like a plague, which causes a [whole] generation of human beings to perish, and is like a serpent, which is 'full of deadly poison'.[1] So then, beware of slander, because many evils and countless miseries spring from slander.

Don't listen to anyone who slanders their brother or sister, even if you like what you hear. For you yourself don't want other people to slander you. So, you should stay away from slander, [yours or theirs,] for surely it is plunder that our tongue steals from our neighbour's [good] name.

Just as a thief deserves judgement because they have stolen someone's possessions, likewise the slanderer deserves harsh judgement because they have stolen their neighbour's good name and destroyed it.

As for you, watch your mouth and tongue, even when you talk with your friends, because your tongue is more evil than all your enemies [put together]. When words come out of your mouth, they may seem delicious to you. But afterwards, they might burn like raging flames in dry straw,[2] and nothing you can do will extinguish them.

You must weigh all your words on wisdom's scales before they leave your mind[3] [and then your mouth]. Otherwise, after you have spoken them in ignorance, your repentance will be useless. Remember, there is no speech that is better than silence; indeed, silence is better than all speech.[4] 'A talkative person can't be righteous on earth'.[5]

A man went to one of the ancient sages and asked him, 'O wise man, what should I do to be at peace with all people?'

---

1 Allusion to James 3:8.
2 A paraphrase of James 3:5–8, which warns that the tongue is as dangerous as a fire. A common Amharic expression arises from the same verse: የሰው ምላስ እሳት ነው or አንደበት እሳት ነው (the human tongue is fire).
3 ይወጣ እምልብህ (they come out of your heart).
4 Talkativeness is often warned against in the monastic literature; see, for instance, Arsenius' remarks in the *Apophthegmata Patrum* (Collection of the Desert Fathers), translated into Ge'ez in the 1200s as ዜና አበው ቅዱሳን (The History of the Holy Fathers).
5 Psalm 140:11 (139:12 LXX).

The wise man didn't say anything, but he put one of his hands on his mouth and his other hand on his penis.[1]

With these gestures, he signalled three of the causes of conflict between one person and another. The first cause is the tongue, which communicates with indecent, foolish, abusive, and slanderous speech, and produces countless conflicts. The second cause, which makes everyone fight, is the penis, which proliferates adultery.[2] It brings unrestrained murder and war. The third cause is the hands, when they stretch out to take others' possessions.

As for you, if you are going to be wise, diligently guard your mouth and tongue. Don't say anything that doesn't benefit you, and don't be talkative or speak hastily. Moreover, guard your hands and restrain them from stretching out to take others' possessions. For stealing is a terrible sin and is extremely shameful for one [who is aiming to be wise].

Just as you don't want to lose any of your possessions, so you must not cause the loss of [any of] your neighbour's possessions. Don't ruin what results from another's labour, in case your actions cause them grief, and they curse you, calling out to God, and God punishes you. If you have lost or destroyed any of another's possessions, whether accidentally or deliberately, or if what you owe your neighbour is in your hands, don't delay, for any reason whatsoever, but repay your entire debt, so that you are not punished together with thieves. Shun human punishment or you won't escape God's judgement.

Strive diligently to control your genitals. For if you don't, limitless evil will overtake you, since there is no peace for the adulterer nor mercy from either human beings or God.[3] Don't raise your eyes to [look at and] lust after someone's wife, because others' wives are a disastrous snare. For a husband's own wife is enough for him, and a wife's own husband is enough for her.

Turn away from adultery, which does you no good. It seems sweet to you at first, but later, you'll find it's more bitter than a serpent's venom. Don't listen to your body's desires, the ones drawing you to another husband's wife or another wife's husband, for it is a theft worthy of punishment.

---

1 The author is paraphrasing a sentence from the Geʻez book አንቅጸ ፈላስፋ (Sayings of the Philosophers), Chapter 3.
2 The author seems to be concerned primarily with the desires of married people (rather than sexual sin in general), as most people were married from a young age and single people were rare.
3 Someone who commits adultery will be ostracized by the community so the cost to the individual is tremendous.

Chapter 24: Celibacy, Marriage, and Sex

Litt Ed 53

If you don't have a wife, marry one! If you don't have a husband, get married! For it's the creator's commandment [for us to marry], as he created men and women with the desire to marry.

Don't be like those fools who despise marriage. Don't extol monks who enter the monastic life in their prime. For, this kind of monasticism [while young] violates the creator's established order, and conflicts with our natural disposition.[1]

Marriage is a great and holy service, one that reveals the creator's wisdom more any other of his handiworks. Based on this, I wanted to write about it here. For marriage is more beautiful and more magnificent than all of creation's mysteries. More than the rest of these mysteries,[2] marriage benefits generations of humanity and their whole way of life. Marriage shows the creator's wisdom, and the mystery of marriage 'glorifies the one who has gloriously glorified himself'.[3]

But human beings have not understood the world's beauty. Rather, they have belittled it and treated it with contempt, like scum. Indeed, human beings are worthless, 'they are liars who cheat on the scales'.[4] They honour

Abb215 60v

abandoning the world and[, by becoming monks,] they abandon the true honour [of marriage].

Just as a lush tree that bears fruit is better than a dry and withered tree, so marriage is better than monasticism. The scales of human judgement deceive them, and they honour monasticism over marriage.

---

1 The author's disapproval of (celibate) monks is not an atypical attitude for (married) clergy in the EOTC. Many discourage young men from becoming monks, as it is a high calling in which one should not fail.

2 'Mystery' here should also be understood as 'sacrament'. The Orthodox Churches have seven sacraments, of which one is marriage.

3 ይሰብሕ ለዘስቡሕ ተሰብሐ (it [the mystery of marriage] glorifies he who has gloriously glorified himself), from Exodus 15:1 as it appears in the Ge'ez Psalter's First Song of Moses (i.e., Exodus 15:1–19). The texts of the Psalter's fourteen biblical canticles differ from the same texts as found in biblical manuscripts. This verse about God's glory—እኩብሕ ለእግዚአብሔር ስቡሕ ዘተሰብሐ (we will glorify the Lord, who has gloriously glorified himself)—is sung again and again by the congregation during the Good Friday liturgy.

4 Psalm 62:9 (61:9 LXX). The author here uses a typical Ethiopian theological expression for humanity: ኩሉ ደቂቀ እጓለ እመሕያው (all the children of the mother of the living). This formulation, emphasizing that we all come from one mother, is used throughout Ethiopian Christian literature, including in Ge'ez translations of the Bible, where Hebrew and Greek have just 'sons of men' or 'men'.

Don't listen to those human beings; just remember that in marriage a person becomes a creator in the likeness of their creator and fulfils the counsel and glorious wisdom of the Most High. If marriage is not holier than monasticism, then God would not have commanded human beings to marry.

Couldn't the creator have shown human beings another way to bear children[, a way that did not require two people, one] without marriage? He [did not and thus] hasn't required monasticism [of human beings]. Rather, he created a man and a woman to be united in the established order of marriage.

So we should not disdain marriage, or regard the creator's institution of marriage as less than a human institution like monasticism.[1] Marriage arises from natural law and from the creator's will. For the creator established marriage, fortified it, made it beautiful, and rewarded it with a sweetness greater than every sweetness of this world. He drew humanity into this married way of life through a hidden and irresistible power, so that human life might not be destroyed and its generations not perish.

All God's ways are 'righteous and upright',[2] and all God's wisdom is wonderful! Ignorantly, human beings instituted monasticism, which violates the primary law of our created nature. 'They devised a scheme for that which they cannot hold in check'.[3] For a monk has left the path that God created [for humanity], and a monk has absolutely no power to carry out that scheme [of celibacy]. For it's not his creator's will [to be celibate], and so every day we see monks inflamed and consumed with bodily lust, and they sin by doing what is unnatural for them.[4]

As for you, observe the established order that your creator set for you. Don't love monasticism or long to be a monk when you are young. Don't praise monasticism or celebrate those able to keep their virginity, because they are violating and thwarting the creator's established order.

---

1 ሥርዓተ ፈጣሪ ... ሥርዓተ ሰብእ (the creator's established order ... the human order).
2 The author has ፍናዊሁ ለእግዚአብሔር ጽድቅ ወርቱዕ (the ways of the lord are righteous and upright), which seems to have been inspired by Psalm 19:9 (18:10 LXX), which in the Ge'ez Bible is ፍትሐ ለእግዚአብሔር ጽድቅ ወርቱዕ ኅቡረ (the judgement of the Lord is righteous and upright altogether).
3 Psalm 21:11 (20:11 LXX).
4 ወይኤብሱ በዘኢኮነ ፍጥረቶሙ (they sin by doing what is not according to their nature). This phrase here likely refers to celibacy itself as 'unnatural', but the word also refers to sexual acts outside of marriage, including homosexual acts. The word 'unnatural' comes up four times in the HWH, in different contexts.

Rather, marry a woman at a suitable time. When your body reaches maturity and displays the need for marriage, don't delay.[1] Rather marry quickly so that you don't sin by doing what is unnatural. Don't lose marriage's rewards, which your creator prepared for you, and don't put off its blessings.

Turn aside from adultery—don't go from one woman to another. Also, a woman should not lust for man after man, because this is adultery, which brings no benefit but rather is contrary to the creator's established order for the descendants of Eve.

Don't seek to marry a famous or beautiful woman, otherwise, feelings of superiority will take her over. For mutual love in marriage can't happen if a woman feels superior [to the man]. [Likewise], a woman shouldn't seek to marry a mighty or important man, otherwise, he will despise her and go after other women. For mutual love is better than great wealth and all the honour of this world.

Also, because a woman's [physical] maturity arrives sooner than a man's, and she ages more quickly, it's better for you to marry a woman about eight to ten years younger.

After you are married, as husband and wife, you should love one another with all your heart, because you are no longer two but 'one flesh'.[2] From then on, neither of you should lust after another man or another woman. As much as you can, give pleasure to one another, with mutual care and perfect love.

Beautify your whole life together and make your covenant of marriage delightful and rejoice in it. For this pleasure is allowed for you both, and it is pure and pleasing to God, who commanded marriage and sex. In his great wisdom, God created this drive in our flesh that makes the sweetness of sex blossom. This sweetness is astonishing and impossible to understand. We shouldn't defile it by doing that which is unnatural[: celibacy]. Rather, let us marvel at this sweetness, and make it holy, in the way our creator has shown: which is marriage of one man with one woman.[3] Let us worship God who prepared this delight for our mortal bodies.

---

1 He seems to be recommending marriage for men by sixteen or seventeen. Later, however, he recommends marrying women a decade younger, so perhaps he has is recommending marriage for men in their twenties.
2 Genesis 2:24; Mark 10:8, etc.
3 That is, men should not have more than one wife; women should not have more than one husband.

What tongue can proclaim[1] and what hand can write down our creator's wonders? Just as God produced from soil delicious food to eat that gives power to life—because even though we seek to eat food for its taste, it strengthens our life—in the same way God created in the soil of our flesh an astonishing drive, one that germinates a sweetness greater than any other sweetness, and reproduces a human seed greater than any other of creation's works.

Through seeking this delicious taste on the path established for us, we multiply our seed in our likeness. Every work of God is amazing, and his great wisdom is ineffable. Although human beings are marvellous, they have not realized [this fact] and have imitated 'the animals [in their lust], becoming like them'.[2] They became wicked, worse than animals, when they sought this delicious taste by [doing] what is unnatural for human beings, despised the creator's wisdom, and rebelled against following God's law.

My friend, don't stray from the path that your creator is leading you on and live in the covenant of marriage with your one wife. Turn away from adultery, from spilling your seed in a way that is unnatural,[3] and [also] from [the celibacy of] dead monasticism,[4] since all of this is departing from nature's path and from the creator's will.

Be intimate sexually with your wife, in wonder and praise for your creator. When you enter her, don't seek the sweetness of sex just for yourself but make it sweet also for your wife. Don't deprive her of her share [of this sweetness] that God gave for her. For her sake, don't perform quickly but wait awhile until she takes her pleasure in it, so that she isn't left behind you, and her pleasure is not lessened. If you don't perform this [attentive] love for her, she will be grieved and reject you, and your marriage will no longer deserve God's blessing.

---

1 This sentence አይ ልሳን ዘይክል ነቢበ (what tongue can proclaim) is from the Ethiopian hymn ውዳሴ ማርያም ዘሠሉስ (The Praise of Mary for Tuesday).
2 Psalm 49:12 (48:12 LXX); see also Psalm 49:20 (48:21 LXX). The author has adapted the verse, which uses animals to depict the fleeting nature of our existence, to make a point about our animal desires. The Ge'ez Bible has ወሰብአ እንዘ ክቡር ውእቱ ኢያአመረ ወኮነ ከመ እንስሳ ዘአልቦ ልቡ ወተመሰሎሙ (and an honoured person did not understand, and he became like senseless animals and resembled them).
3 Jubilees 41:4–5; Genesis 38:9–10. The Bible has edicts against the sin of Onan, a man spilling his seed on the ground rather than in a woman's body.
4 Monks are supposed to be dead to the world; it is said መነኮስ ብሂል ምውት (a monk means a dead one). However, the author is flipping this positive into a negative through his *qene* wording: እምንክስና ምውት (from dead monasticism).

Don't listen to those who say to you, 'sex is unclean, it has a smell that corrupts, and a darkness that has no benefit'. Those who speak like this deny their creator. Only, don't have sex too often, without moderation, so that you won't be weakened, since our nature has its limits, and we should not exceed them.

Chapter 25: Divorce and Remarrying

It is love that makes all things beautiful. So, persevere in it.

Don't be like many husbands and wives who love their spouses for just a little while[1] and then hate being married. They become a burden to each other, and they yearn for another marriage, one that seems better for them, or, hating [any] marriage, they want to get divorced.

Don't be like them, because they have made a big mistake. As for you, strengthen your heart and persevere in your first marriage, the one in which God has joined you together. That will be better for you than getting divorced and remarrying.

Humanity's shallow nature suggests to a husband or a wife that another spouse would suit them better, but this is an error. Both of you,[2] [husband and wife,] don't follow this lustful thought, which isn't good for you and will never benefit you. Rather, it will embitter you, make your life a burden, and lead you into adultery.

Indeed, persevere in your first marriage with all your ability and make it into a beautiful thing. Neither of you will gain anything from changing one spouse for another. Rather, you will gain by improving [your] first marriage, [the one] in which God's will united you. Don't let your lust separate 'what God has joined together'.[3] [Stay married] so that the judgement God has set for the arrogant—who won't follow the path God leads them on—won't fall upon you.

---

1 ወኢትኩን ከመ ብዙኃን አምታት እለ ያፈቅሩ ብአሲቶሙ ወከመ ብዙኃት አንስት እለ ያፈቅራ አምታቲሆን ሕዳጠ ዘመነ (don't be like many husbands who love their wives and many wives who love their husbands for just a little while).

2 The author has chosen to speak to partners together, not just husbands, seeing them both as responsible for the protection of their marriage.

3 Mark 10:9; Matthew 19:6. The author has adjusted the original for his rhetorical purpose, here by one word. He has ወዘግዚአብሔር አስተፃመረ ኢይፍልጥ ፍትወትክሙ (what God has joined together, let not your lust separate), while Mark 10:9 has ዘእግዚአብሔር አንከ አስተፃመረ ሰብእ ኢይፍልጥ (what God has joined together, let not man separate).

This [very judgement] happened to one of my foolish relatives.

Sum 51

He married a wife when he was young and lived peacefully with her for ten years. Then he saw another woman and thought, 'This woman is better for me than my wife'. So, he divorced his first wife and married the second.

But the second wife's behaviour was very wicked and after just a few days they quarrelled with each other. When he wanted to divorce this second wife, she went and made false accusations against him to a local official. After a lengthy court case, my relative was put in chains and paid everything he owned as a fine.[1]

Two years later, he married yet another woman, and she became quarrelsome and too talkative. One day he felt like hitting her, but she beat him to it. She threw a piece of wood at him, which flew into and got embedded in his right eye and blinded him. To this day, my one-eyed relative lives with this woman, who torments him day and night. Meanwhile, we all laugh at him.

Abb215 64v

He, however, bears it patiently, and says, 'I brought this upon myself. My first wife was good, but I didn't want to live peacefully with her. I married a second wife who destroyed my possessions and my third destroyed my eye. So, if I should marry a fourth wife, she might kill me!'

As for you, don't be like him! Don't think that if you divorce a wicked wife that you will find a good one. It's better if you get used to the wife God gave you. Also, you can make her better through your advice, your example, and your tenderness. For tenderness improves every aspect of life, while bitterness ruins it.

Litt Ed 57

Chapter 26: Winning Your Spouse's Love

Gain strength together against each other's coarse nature and hidden faults. For nowhere in all the world can a faultless man or woman be found. A wise man said it well, 'If there ever was a human being who was faultless, he would never have died'.[2]

Abb215 65r

As for you men, keep in mind that a woman is a 'weak creature' lacking knowledge.[3] So be strong in the face of her blemished nature and talkative-

---

1 That is, they restrained the man until he paid his fines, which would usually take up to a few months. While those who offended the king might be put in prison, ordinary offenders would not go to prison.
2 We were not able to identify this wise man; it is said among Ethiopians and other Christian traditions that if Adam had been perfect, he would not have died.
3 1 Peter 3:7.

ness. Ignore her anger with good humour, and never argue with her. If you regularly do this, your life will be easy.

As for you women, do as much as you can to make your husband happy. Prepare food and drink that pleases him, and beautify his house and whole life. For your husband can't love you if you don't love him, and if you really do love him, he'll be incapable of despising you.

Once, a man had a lazy and stubborn wife.[1] So, he hated her and began going to another woman. This made his wife jealous, and she went to a potion maker, and said to him, 'My husband hates me, so create a potion that will make him love me'.

He replied, 'Sure, just go and pluck three hairs from a lion's forehead and bring them to me. They're essential for this potion'.

She went away, thinking to herself, 'How can I possibly get close to a lion without it eating me?'

She caught a sheep and then took it with her into the wilderness.

Soon a lion ran up to eat her. So, she left the sheep behind and fled. The lion stopped chasing her because it had something to eat.

The next day she did the same thing, and she kept on doing it day after day, for she was gripped by jealousy regarding her husband.

When the lion saw that this woman kept bringing him food, he stopped being hostile and loved her. Whenever she came with a sheep, the lion received her with joy, wagging its tail, greeting her like a dog, and playing with her.

So, she plucked three hairs and brought them to the potion maker.

She said, 'Look, I have brought you what you need for the potion'.

He replied, 'How were you able to pluck these hairs [from a lion]?'

She told him everything that had happened.

He said, 'Go, and do the same thing for your husband, just like you did for the lion, and your husband will love you. Do you expect your husband to be more obstinate than a lion? By giving food, you gained a lion's love; you will gain your husband's love in the same way'.

So, she went and began following the potion maker's advice, and did everything to please her husband. She persevered, and after [just] a few days, that man thought in his heart, 'How can I love another woman rather than my wife, when she is good, and better for me than they are?'

So, he returned to her and loved her greatly.

---

[1] The story that follows is a common Ethiopian folktale, often told by priests preaching about marriage.

Chapter 27: Children and Abortion

As for you, my children who are married, 'love one another',[1] and don't quarrel with one another. Rather, keep renewing your love and joy by comforting each other and talking playfully with each other. Don't renounce your faith or your marriage vows, not even once, so that you won't be punished as adulterers.

Live in mutual love and put your hope in God. to give you good children, for [they are] 'a gift from God, a reward from the womb's fruit'.[2] This is the primary purpose of marriage, and the primary reason why God commands a man and a woman to get married. It is for the sake of bearing children.

So, those who seek in any way to abort a foetus, to cause it to come before its time, commit a great sin and they will be judged as murderers.[3] Be careful never to associate with those who plot to do this abominable thing, because they have 'departed from all righteousness' and all mercy.[4]

Abb215 66v

Chapter 28: Raising Good Children

As for you, [my own children,] give thanks to God when he gives you children. Enjoy them, and love them as a part of yourself. Bring them up carefully and wisely, and take care of them and all their needs in life. From their childhood, show them the path that God would have them follow; and teach them that which they should understand and do.

Sum 53

Don't be a bad example, in case they learn to do evil from you. Model wisdom and good works, so that they may become wise and improve their

Abb215 67r

---

[1] John 13:34.
[2] An allusion to Psalm 127:3 (126:3). The author quotes from the Ge'ez Bible, which speaks of children as ጸጋሁ ለአግዚአብሔር (a gift from God). The LXX is different, speaking of them as κληρονομία (an inheritance).
[3] Abortion (with herbal aids) was practiced in Ethiopia but not religiously condoned. Many books in Ge'ez condemned abortion, notably 1 Enoch 69:12 (19:27–28 in the Ethiopian numbering) ወሐምስ ስሙ፡ ካስድያዕ ዝንቱ ውእቱ ዘአርአየ ለውሉደ ሰብእ . . . (ወ)ዘባጠታተ ጾሳዕ በማኅፀን ከመ ይደቅ (And the name of the fifth one is Kasdeyae: [this is] the one who showed the sons of men . . . the blows [with which to attack] the embryo in the womb so that it miscarries) (Knibb 1978a, 202; 1978b, 161–162). See also the ራእየ ማርያም (Vision of Maryam), in which Mary sees those who did abortions in hell.
[4] Allusion to Psalm 43:1 (42:1 LXX), 1 Timothy 1:9, 6:5. The author alludes to the Ge'ez Bible's phrase አምሕዝብ ወቱአን አምጽድቅ (from people departed from righteousness), which differs a bit from the LXX's ἐξ ἔθνους οὐχ ὁσίου (from a godless nation).

conduct. While your children are still young, don't let their angry behaviour or fiery nature exasperate you. For they don't yet understand [how] to distinguish good from evil. Be patient [with them], and strengthen your hearts, for you grew to adulthood just as they do. So you should bring your children up patiently and tirelessly.

'Renounce rage, and abandon anger'.[1] Don't be like those fools who become angry with their children, beating them when they accidentally break a pot or spill a cup of water,[2] when it is not their fault, but remaining silent when they are [deliberately] wicked. Be patient with your children when they accidentally and unintentionally ruin your possessions.

Rebuke them and beat them when you see evil, arrogance, disobedience, hostility, or laziness in their hearts; or when they blaspheme, abuse, or curse; or when they steal, rob, and seize others' possessions; or when they have sex outside of marriage—or do any similar evil things. On the very day is the most effective time to rebuke, admonish, and beat them, so that they won't develop evil habits because you are silent [about them]. Unless you rebuke them when they are young, they will grow up with evil habits, and so they won't listen to your rebuke when they're adults.

There once was a man, a robber, who lived in the wilderness, and he robbed and killed people who travelled that way.[3] The king heard [about him] and sent his soldiers after him. They caught him and sent him in chains to the king, who sentenced him to death.

As the soldiers took him to behead him with a sword, the robber's elderly father followed him, weeping. When the robber saw his father, he begged to speak with his father before he died. But, when he got close to his father, the robber wanted to hit him but couldn't, because his hands were tied, so he started to bite him, [hurting him] with painful bites.

All the people who were there cried out, saying, 'Truly this robber deserves death, for he even wants to kill his [own] father!'

The robber replied, saying, 'It's not me who deserves death, but my father! When I began to steal grain and bread in my youth, he praised me instead of rebuking me and I grew accustomed to robbery. Because of his

---

[1] Psalm 37:8 (36:8 LXX). The Psalm is addressed to an individual, but here the command is plural.

[2] Spilling water causes more work in a place where women must carry water long distances.

[3] This story, titled በእንቁላሉ ጊዜ በቀጣሽኝ (If You Had Punished Me at the Time of the Egg), is a popular folktale in Ethiopia to this day, often told by parents to their children. The modern version has a mother, not a father, and she encourages her son when he steals eggs.

praise I became a robber and [now] I have come to this hour of [my] death. If my father had rebuked me at the right time, I would not have arrived at this punishment'.

The robber said this, and then his head was cut off. Everyone who [saw this and] had children became afraid [of not rebuking their children]. Sum 54

As for you, fear for your children, and bring them up in the [reverent] fear of God and knowledge of the right thing to do. When you rebuke your children, don't do so in anger, with blasphemous words, or [calling down] curses.

Rather, rebuke them with wise words and [good] advice, so that they may know that you rebuked them for their sake and benefit. Teach them and always help them to understand, [by] speaking skilfully, in parables and stories, and with examples from others. That way your children will be turned away from evil and learn to do good. Litt Ed 60
Abb215 68v

Moreover, teach them with words from texts, teachings, and Scripture. Also teach them through manual labour, and everything else that will benefit them.

Don't get tired, and don't ever lose heart. Look, all your laborious toil, and all your exhausting trouble, and all your enduring patience that you will expend in raising your children, it will all be credited to you by God, and he will give you a great reward. Then your children will comfort you in your forgetful old age. They will lower your grey hair into the grave, [full of] indestructible peace and hope.

If you neglect bringing up your children well, they will become wicked, and God will judge you. When you are old, you will weep bitter tears over their wickedness. Your children won't listen to you. Rather, they will neglect you, just as you neglected raising, teaching, and improving them when they were young. Act early to prevent this torment! Plead with God to make your children wise and their character good. Instruct them with the right words, and you will rejoice in a prosperous old age and be at ease. Abb215 69r

Chapter 29: Living with the Customs of Your Time

A person's earthly life is made up of testing and temptation. One cannot improve their life without patience and wisdom: 'A patient person is better than a powerful one, and a wise person is better than an angry one'.[1]

---

1 An allusion to Proverbs 16:32 (16:33 LXX).

During your hardships, persevere with patience. While 'patience is bitter' at the time, later it is sweeter than honey or sugar.[1] Never forget that 'there is a time for everything',[2] and the right thing done at the wrong time will be contemptible and result in disaster.

Learning the right time to do things is great wisdom, greater than all knowledge. As for you, become familiar with this wisdom.

Live with others as befits the times and your country's customs. Don't talk like foolish old people who always say, 'The old days were good, and these days are evil'. For every time has evil and good together. If we understand world history, we will find something in every time that is more evil than in ours.

They once asked a wise man, 'What about the times?'

And he replied, 'the times are yours, and if you are good yourselves, the times will be good, but if you yourselves are bad, then the times will be bad'.

As for you, be good, and your times will be good to you. Don't blame the customs of your times. Rather, let time pass, along with its wisdom, because 'a generation comes and a generation goes',[3] and every generation will live according to the wisdom the creator has shown.[4] No one should turn a generation away from the path on which the Lord of all ages has led it.

As for you, adjust your actions to the customs of your time. Accept them peacefully, and plead with God to lead those who come after you on a better path. Don't be sad on account of the wickedness of your time, and don't be bitter about your people's wickedness. Rather be on your guard. Let it all pass with ease.

[Just] laugh at the perversion of immoral human beings. For if you 'reproach them severely, they will hate you', and hold you in contempt.[5] But, if you make fun of them, and mock them wisely, they will be ashamed and they will turn from their immorality.

---

1 This is a common proverb in Ethiopia; in Amharic ትዕግሥት መሪራ ናት ። ፍሬዋ ግን ጣፋጭ ነው (patience is bitter, but her fruit is sweet). The proverb is very old, found in Arabic texts as long ago as the 800s (Zakeri 2006).
2 Ecclesiastes 3:1–8.
3 Ecclesiastes 1:4.
4 In Ethiopia, a generation (people born in a fifteen-year period or so or bounded by important historic events) has a specific culture, ethos, and aims; the author's 'generations' therefore may not be a generic reference to time.
5 An allusion to Proverbs 9:8 (9:9 LXX).

Chapter 30: Trust and Caution

Don't trust everyone whom you encounter. For the one who trusts everyone is a fool.

'Test everything and hold on to what is good'.[1]

Protect yourself once from your enemies, but a thousand times from your friends.[2] For your friends [can] reveal your secrets. 'While a secret remains in your heart, it is shackled by your will, but if you reveal it by speaking, it is you who will be shackled by its snare'.[3]

Don't depend on the gifts of others. Rather, depend on your own wisdom, and your own hard work and what it produces. Above all, depend on God's gifts and blessings, and don't depend on your friends, as tomorrow they may become your enemies. Have confidence in your own hard work, which will never escape your control.

Love those who are in your community and are close to you. Make them believe that you have confidence in them, but don't completely trust anyone. In all your encounters with human beings, think first and plan [at least] one way out from their traps should they wish you evil.

Abb215 70v

Be vigilant because not everyone who seems good is good, and those who behave well towards you once, will not always behave so. Therefore, be careful not to fall into anyone's traps, and [reverently] fear God so that you don't hurt any of them. 'Don't repay the evil done to you with evil',[4] rather 'give your [vengeful] thoughts to God'[5] and let human beings' 'evil recoil on them'.[6]

Litt Ed 62

Never say in your heart, 'I will punish my enemies for the evil they have done to me'. For such acts are pointless. They won't benefit your life with others and will produce conflict and unending hatred. It's better for you to hide all the sadness caused by others.

Sum 56

---

1 1 Thessalonians 5:21. The author changes the quotation from the plural into the second person singular masculine. This is the second time he has quoted this verse.
2 Possibly an allusion to Micah 7:5.
3 This is a direct quotation from አንጋረ ፈላስፋ (The Sayings of the Philosophers) (1960, 11). The author has used the word ሕውር in its Amharic sense, meaning 'shackled'. In the *Sayings*, the word means 'confounded'.
4 1 Peter 3:9.
5 Psalm 55:22 (54:22 LXX). The author quotes the Ge'ez Bible, which refers to ሕሊናህ (your thoughts), while the LXX versions refer to τὴν μέριμνάν σου (your cares).
6 Psalm 7:16 (7:16 LXX).

Chapter 31: Pride and Anger

Subdue the anger that forms in your heart, because anger destroys wisdom, and is not in harmony with the creator's will. He commanded human beings to live together on earth and to love and help one another. Angry human beings can't live together in peace—they fight one another all day, and they curse, beat, and kill each other.

Don't be like them, rather beautify your life by being wise, by secluding yourself [from angry conflict], and by not mistreating or oppressing others. You will find life's sweetness in a secluded and humble life.

So, turn away from being conceited, don't let your heart be proud, and don't live with important people or associate with the renowned.

Don't seek to be honoured more than others. Rather, live equitably with and secluded from human beings, and you will find great peace.

Someone who takes a walk on a low plain doesn't fear falling. But someone who goes up on a roof does. So, the measure by which that person elevated themselves is the measure by which their fall will be humiliating and shattering.

Likewise, the one who lives secluded from human beings will not be disgraced, but the one who is esteemed [by others] or who elevates themselves above others will be put to shame—disgraced, dishonoured. Everyone will be intensely jealous of the esteemed person and full of hatred for him.

Chapter 32: The Abuse of Authority

Don't seek to oversee others, for to be the person in charge is a terrible affliction and those who are appointed to office are harshly judged. If you are put in charge of others, don't treat them with a heavy hand, or mistreat them with your power. Instead, be fair to everyone, high or low, rich, or poor, and without being timid in others' presence, but administering justice with righteousness and impartiality.

Don't subjugate others with bitter servitude or enslavement. Instead, protect them as if they were your own children. Then they will love you instead of being afraid of you, and you will find peace among them and blessings from God. If you mistreat those who live under your power, be afraid. For they will curse you in their hearts, crying out to God, who listens swiftly to the poor's lament. Watch out! God will reserve harsh judgement for you, which will happen at the time he has set, and you won't be able to avert it [then,] even through great repentance.¹ Then you will search for someone to help you but you won't find anyone, and you will cry out to God but he won't hear you.

Never say, 'Today, I'll enjoy myself, doing whatever I want, and later let whatever is coming happen to me'. For the day of judgement, which is more bitter than death, will inevitability arrive, and then, you will repent pointlessly and speak to no effect.

You will be just like Antiochus [in the book of Maccabees], the lawless king who did evil things with a proud heart and whom God punished severely.² His [living] body was just like a decomposing corpse, tormented by worms eating him. On the verge of death, he said, 'Today I have recalled all the evil things that I did to the children of Israel'. Antiochus died in bitter torment and sorrow because God's judgement relentlessly hunted him down.

As for you, be afraid if you do evil things to others. For God will fully pay you back [for them], and you will bear all the heavy burdens that you laid on so many. This burden will severely weigh you down forever. You will never be able to toss it from your back.

Chapter 33: Rewards for Good Deeds

God does not allow evil to go unbalanced by judgement, nor does God allow good works to go unbalanced by reward.

Consequently, tirelessly do good to everyone. For God will accept all of your good works, and he will count them, measure them out, and store them close to him for you, to repay you at the established time. You might forget the good that you have done, but God will never forget it.

So, don't be lazy about doing as much good for everyone as you can. When you see those who are in distress, comfort them; when you see those who are hungry, feed them; when you see those who are naked, clothe them: be a help to everyone, each one according to their needs.³

---

1 This sentence reflects the Ethiopian concept, held among Christians and Muslims, of ጋፍ (gəf), the idea that some people carry a large cosmic debt due to their bad behaviour, such as abusing the poor, mistreating animals, wasting resources, and so on.
2 The story of King Antiochus is probably summarized from መጽሐፈ ዮሴፍ ወልደ ኮርዮን (The Book of Joseph, the Son of Koryon), Chapter 15, but originally occurs in the LXX books of Maccabees. The Book of Joseph is a source for another Ge'ez book, often called the 'Ethiopic Maccabees', which is quite different than the LXX Maccabees.
3 See Matthew 25:35–45.

Make joy and happiness rise like the sun in each heart, if only for a single hour. Comfort the suffering and the poor, take care of them regularly [throughout the day]; ease their suffering, and suffer with them. Heal them and help them as much as you can, so that you will receive help and comfort when you are ill or suffering.

Chapter 34: Embracing Death Joyfully

As for you, when you are sick, persevere despite the severity of your suffering. Don't be shaken. Rather trust in God, who sees and counts all your anguished suffering so that he may reward you richly in keeping with your perseverance. And if he doesn't reward you in this world, he will reward you after your death, when you go to him.

Don't fear leaving this life behind, because death is liberation. When God chooses to release you from this prison, so that you can go to be with him, thank him. It's better for you to be set free from this putrid bondage.

You will fly free, shining like an angel in the lap of your creator. There you will know and understand all the mysteries of this world and the beauty of the order of the heavens and the earth.[1] You will live a full life without hardship or suffering, you will rejoice with complete delight, and you will find unending and limitless blessings.

Don't love this wretched world, where you must live until you have completed your labours and your testing. For you don't have the authority to leave this world of your [own] will, but only of your creator's will, who made you do these labours. When the time comes for you to be freed, and God chooses to set you free from your chains, bow down to him and worship him, and run to him with joy and hope.

For, look, he will reward you with a [heavenly] life superior to any life in this world. Just ask him to give you a peaceful death, and to let you depart peacefully from this world, trusting him.

Don't fear any of the things that evil human beings fear—those who rebel against travelling the path that the creator leads them on through this world and who refuse to serve in the acts of divine service prepared for everyone.

---

1 In ancient Christian traditions and the EOTC traditional cosmology, there are seven heavens, each with different denizens and a different name. God's throne is in the highest heaven, the seventh one.

They have no insight into God's work, and they don't keep the natural laws that their intelligence taught them.

As for you, my friend who has accepted my advice and delighted in it, don't be fearful when the time of your death comes, because it is better for you to go to your creator.

You, you who knows that the immortal soul is better than the mortal body, why do you fear death? Isn't freedom better than bondage? Isn't joy better than mourning? Isn't [spiritual] life lovelier than [physical] death? In the same way, it's better for your soul to be set free from her physical chains than to remain chained. Just as someone emerges from prison and sees the shining sun, which delights and warms them, likewise our soul emerges from our flesh and sees God's light and rejoices—set ablaze with the love of her creator. She will look back, see the desolation of this world, and wonder at herself, 'How was it possible for me to love that shameful bondage? And how did I fear the death that set me free and brought me to this blessed state, forever and ever! Amen.[1]

Coda: Some Final Words

Look, I have written these few morsels with God's help.

My friend, you who reads this book of mine, if you have wisdom, you also must write down what God gave you to understand![2]

Don't be like 'a lamp which they put under a basket'.[3] Rather, shine forth your wisdom to instruct and correct our country's children, so that wisdom may multiply, and sin and the ignorance of righteous acts may cease on our earth.

For our country's children don't know our creator's arm is raised [to punish]. If they had known, they would have shunned useless things. For, in our days, rivalry has taken hold of our foolish people, and they kill each

---

1 Strictly, the 'Amen' is not narratively required. But the author, having grown up hearing the phrase ለዓለመ ዓለም አሜን (forever and ever, amen) in the liturgy every day, either unconsciously provides the full liturgical phrase or consciously wants to give a liturgical ending to the book.
2 He is recommending that the reader do what he did, following in his teacher's footsteps.
3 Matthew 5:15, Luke 8:16.

Sum 59   other due to their [humanly inspired] religions, not understanding their creator's rules.¹

[With the words of Isaiah, I pray:]
Lord, apart from you, we know no other and we call on your name alone.²
We have not abandoned your teaching for human teaching.
For your commandments shine light on earth.³
Give us peace, since you have given us everything.⁴
Give us life, with the dew of your blessing,⁵ and save us, so that we may worship you in righteousness and truth.
For glory and honour are due to you—now, always, forever and ever. Amen!

This book is complete!

---

1 The author is referencing the religious conflicts among Roman Catholics, Orthodox Christians, and Muslims.

2 Isaiah 26:13. The author's prayer here is an adapted version of the beautiful Prayer of Isaiah, in Isaiah 26:9–20. This prayer appears as the twelfth biblical canticle in the Ge'ez Psalter and is also found in the መሐሪን አብ (Father, Have Mercy) prayer in the መጽሐፈ ሰዓታት (Liturgy of the Hours). The text here differs slightly with the addition of the word ባሕቲቶ (only).

3 Isaiah 26:9. This verse also appears in the አግዚአ ኵሉ (Lord of All) section of the አንቀጸ ብርሃን (The Gate of Light).

4 Isaiah 26:12.

5 Isaiah 26:19. 'Dew of your blessing' has long been a metaphor used to describe rain in Ethiopia.

Jeremy R. Brown, Ralph Lee, and Mehari Worku

Appendix 1: Chart of Differences between Abb 215 and Abb 234 of *Hatata Zara Yaqob*

The *Hatata Zara Yaqob* appears in two manuscripts, known as Abb 215 and Abb 234. The differences between them aid us in answering scholarly questions about the philosophical works; thus, we have provided a chart documenting these differences. We have not documented marginalia in Latin, minor changes of a character or two that do not change the meaning, nor spelling differences (unless they are significant variations in proper nouns).

We have worked from the high-resolution colour digital copies that the BNF placed online in 2022, which reveal much that was not clear before, as explained in the Manuscripts of the Text section.

The English translations provided in the appendix may not exactly match that in the body of our translations, as they are intended to be more literal in order to compare the two manuscripts more clearly. Sometimes, the English translation cannot reveal what is different about the wording; this requires careful consultation of the Geʽez.

Chapter numbers used in the chart are the manuscript's original numbers, not our innovations.

Codes used:

[]	Explanatory text inserted by us, the translators, appears in square brackets—such as the word [sic].
()	Text inserted into the manuscript by the base hand (original scribe) appears in parentheses ().
{}	Text inserted by the secondary hand appears in curved brackets {}.
<>	Text marked for erasure by the scribe appears in angle brackets <>.
<. . .>	Text that has actually been erased by the scribe appears in angle brackets with ellipses <. . .>.
italics	Notes from the editor appear in italics.

Appendix 1: Chart of Differences

	Abb 215			Abb 234	
	Folio	Literal Translation		Folio	Literal Translation
Chapter 1					
በስመ እግዚአብሐር ጸድቅ ባሕቲቱ እጽሕፍ ገድለ ዘርአ ያዕቆብ ምስለ ጥበቡ ወነተታሁ ዘደረሰ ምአለሁ እንዘ ይብል	1r	In the Name of God, who alone is righteous, I, Walda Heywat, shall write down the life story, wisdom, and philosophical inquiry of Zara Yaqob, which he himself composed. Zara Yaqob saying:	*Minus*		
እስመ ናሁ ወጠንኩ	1r	Now I begin	*Minus*		
እጽሕፍ	1r	I will write	እዌጥን እጽሐፍ	2r	I will begin to write
ወርቄ	1v	Wärqe	ወርቅየ	2r	Wärqyä
ኀበ ቤተ ትምህርት	1v	to school	*Minus*		
ፈነውኩ	1v	You sent him	ትፌንዎ	2v	You send him
፫አውራኅ	1v	3 months	፫ዓመተአውራኅ	2v	3 <years> months
{ወደቁ}	1v	{I fell}	ወደቁ	2v	I fell
ወኢያመርኩ ከመ	2r	And I don't know	ወኢየአምር	2v	And I wasn't shown
ቤተ መምህርየ	2r	My teacher's house	ቤተ ትምህርት	3r	The school
መምህራነ ብሔርነ	2r	<Our country's teachers> *scribal repetition marked for deletion*	*Does not have repetition*	3r	
(፪)ዓመት	2r	(two) years	፪ዓመት	3r	Two years
Chapter 2			**Abb 234**		
አዓቢ.	2v	I was better	<ወቢይ> አዐቢ.	3v	<better> I was better
ወእሰነዓው	2v	And I was on friendly terms	እስመ አነ እሰነዓው	3v	Because I was on friendly terms
ዝኑቱ ሠናይ ወዝኑቱ እኩይ	2v	This is good and this is bad.	ዝኑቱ እኩይ ወዝኑቱ ሠናይ	3v	This is bad and this is good.
ወእግዚአብሐር	2v	And God	ወባሕቱ እግዚአብሐር	3v-4r	But God

(continued)

	Abb 215			Abb 234	
	Folio	Literal Translation		Folio	Literal Translation
እምካህናቲሃ ለአክሱም ዘስሙ ወልደ ዮሐንስ	2v	From among the priests of Aksum, his name was Walda Yohannes.	ወእምካህናቲሃ ለአክሱም ውእቱ <ወ>ዘስሙ ወልደ ዮሐንስ	4r	And he was from among the priests of Aksum, <and> his name was Walda Yohannes.
[ወንቅትሎ ለንጉሥ] ወንስድዶሙ ለፍኖጅ ወበዘይመስሎ ለዝንቱ አስተዋደዩኒ ብዙኃ ወአንስ አአመርኩ ዞንተ በጊዜ ወፈራህኩ	3r	{So we should kill the king,} and expel the foreigners. And he made many other similar false accusations against me. As soon as I found this out, I became afraid.	ወንቅትሎ ለንጉሥ ወንስድዶሙ ለሱራንጂ በዝንቱ ወበዘይመስሎ አስተዋደዩ ወአንስ ሰማዕኩ ዞንተ በጊዜ ወፈራሁኩ	4r	So we should kill the king, and expel the foreigners. And they made many other similar false accusations against me. As soon as I heard about this, I became afraid.
እምአብዕልተ ሀገር	3r	from the wealthy in town	እምዑአብአልተ ሀገር	4r	from the wealthy in town
ሸዋ	3r	Šäwa region, in Amharic	ሰዋ	4r	Sewa region, in Geʿez
ወሰበ ኮንኩ ለባሕቲትየ	3v	And when I was alone	ወአመ ኮንኩ ባሕታዊ	4v	And when I was a hermit
ወተሰፈውኩ በእግዚአብሔር ዘይሰምዓኒ	3v	And I trusted in God who hears me	ወተሰፈውኩ ከመ እግዚአብሔር ይሰምዓኒ	4v	And I trusted that God hears me
Chapter 3			**Abb 234**		
ጸሎት	3v	Prayer	ጸሎትየ	5r	My prayer
ወባሕቱ አኮ ፍራንጅ ባሕቲቶሙ ወሰብአ ብሔርኒ የአከዩ	4r	And it was not just the foreigners alone, but as for the nation's people, they were even more evil	ወባሕቱ አኮ ፍራንጂ እስመ ሰብአ ብሔርኒ የአከዩ	5r	And it was not just the foreigners, for our own people, they were even more evil
ግብጻውያንስ ክሕዱ ሃይማኖተ ርትዕት ዘመንበረ ጴጥሮስ ወአጽራሪ እግዚአብሔር እሙንቱ	4r	The Egyptians have denied the orthodox faith of Peter's See, and they are the Lord's enemies.	ግብጻውያንስ ክሕዱ ሃይማኖተ ርትዕት ወአዕራሪ እግዚአብሔር	5r	The Egyptians have denied the orthodox faith, and they are the Lord's enemies.

(continued)

Abb 215			Abb 234		
	Folio	Literal Translation		Folio	Literal Translation
ወካማሁ ግብጻውያን ይገብሩ በእንተ ሃይማኖቶሙ	4r	And the Egyptians did the same on account of their own faith	ወከማዝ ግብጻውያን ይገብሩ	5r	And the Egyptians did likewise.
በቅዱስ ስም ዚአሁ	4r	In his holy name	በስም ዚአሁ	5r	In his name
ወጸለይኩ ወአቤ	4r	And I prayed and said	ወአቤ	5r	And I said
ነበርኩ እንዘ አጼሊ	4v	I continued praying	ጸለይኩ	5v	I prayed
ወእምአይቴ መጻእኩ	4v	And from where did I come?	Minus	5v	
ሶበ ተፈጠርኩ	4v	When I was created	አመ ተፈጠርኩ	6r	At the time I was created
እስመ (እም) አልቦ ፈጣሪ	5r	Because (if) there were no creator	እስመ አልቦ ፈጣሪ	6r	Because there is no creator
ፈጣሪየ ይሰምዓኒ ሶበ ጸለይኩ ኃቤሁ	5r	My creator will listen to me when I pray to him	ፈጣሪ ይሰምዓኒ ሶበ አጼሊ ኃቤሁ	6v	The creator will listen to me when I pray to him
ወአፍቀርኩዎ ለፈጣሪየ	5r	And I loved my creator	ወአፍቀርኩዎ ለፈጣሪ	6v	And I loved our creator
Chapter 4			**Abb 234**		
ወይነግሩኒ ጽድቀ	5v	And they will tell me the truth	Minus	6v	
እስመ ኩሉ ሰብእ	5v	Because everyone	ወኩሉ ሰብእ	6v	And everyone
ወየማሁ ፍራንጅ ይቤሉብሉን	5v	And now, the foreigners say to us	ወየምኒ {ፍራንጂ} ይብሉን	7r	And even now, {the foreigners} say to us
በእንተ ብዙኃ ነገረ ሃይማኖትን	6r	About many things concerning our creed	Minus	7r	
ወውእቱ ፈትሐ	6r	And he himself judged	ወፈትሐ	7r	And he judged
ኩሉ {ሰብእ}	6r	Every{one}	ኩሉ ሰብእ	7v	Everyone
ለአጥፍአተ ነፍሶሙ	6v	To destroy themselves	ለአማስኖተ ነፍሶሙ	7v	To ruin themselves
ወመስለኒ	6v	And it seemed to me	ወይመስለኒ	7v	And it seems to me
{እስመ ረገ0 ልቦሙ[sic]}	6v	{Indeed their hearts are 'curdled'}	እስመ ረገ0 ልቦሙ	7v	Indeed their hearts are 'curdled'
ወአሐተቱ	6v	Furthermore, they never investigated	ወኢየሐትቱ	7v	Furthermore, they never investigate

Appendix 1: Chart of Differences — 165

(continued)

	Abb 215			Abb 234	
	Folio	Literal Translation		Folio	Literal Translation
ወቅብዓ ኃጥአንስ ወሐሳውያን መምህራን	6v	The oil of sinners and false teachers	ወቅብዓ ኃጥአንስ ወሐሳውያን	7v	The oil of sinners and liars
አሌቡ ከመ ፈጣሪ ዘየዓቢ አምኲሉ ፍጥረት	6v	I understand that there is a creator who is greater than all the creation	አሌቡ ከመ ፈጣሪ ዓቢይ ውእቱ አምኲሉ ፍጥረት	7v-8r	I understand that the creator is greater than all the creation
{ልባውያን}	6v	{Rational beings}	ልባውያን	8r	Rational beings
ወአም ንጼሊ ኃቤሁ ይሰምዓን	6v	And when we pray to him, he hears us	ወአም እጼሊ ኃቤሁ ይሰምዓኒ	8r	And when I pray to him, he hears me
ዳእሙ ከመ አኃሥሥ ወአለቡ ኪያሁ ወጥበቢሁ በፍና እንተ ፈጠረኒ	7r	Rather, so that I would seek him, and understand him and his wisdom in creating me in the way he did	አላ ከመ አኃሥሥ ኪያሁ ወጥበቢ በዘፈጠረኒ	8r	Rather, so that I would seek him, and his wisdom with which he created me
ወጥቀ ያፈቅራ ወይፈቅድ ያአምር	7r	And they love her greatly, and they desire to know	ወጥቀ ያፈቅር ያአምር	8r	And they greatly love to know
ወባሕቱ ዕፁብ ውእቱ ዝንቱ ነገር ወኢይትረከብ እንበለ በዓቢይ ፃማ ወትዕግሥት	7r	But this matter is difficult, and will not be found without great toil and patience	ወባሕቱ ዕፁብ ውእቱ ወኢይትረከብ እንበለ በፃማ ወበዓቢይ ትዕግሥት	8r	But this is difficult, and will not be found without toil and great patience
ይትካሐሉ እስከ ይረከቡ ኲነኔ ዘይደልፕ ለአከፎ	7rv	They can be, until they receive the judgement that their evil deserves	ይትከሀሉ	8v	They can be
ለሕዊን	7v	To be	ከመ ይኩን	8v	To be
በሐሳበ ከዋክብት	7v	In astrology	በእንተ ምንት የአምኑ በሐሳበ ከዋክብት	8v-9r	Why do they believe in astrology?
ዳእሙ የአምኑ እስመ ሰምዕዖ አምቀደምቶሙ	8r	Rather they believe because they heard it from their ancestors	እንበለ እስመ ሰምዑ ሰምዑ አምቀደምቶሙ	9r	But because they heard <heard> it from their ancestors.
አለ ይፈቅዳ ይምልክዎሙ ለሕዝብ	8r	Those who want to rule the people	አለ ፈቅዳ ይምልኩ ሰብአ	9r	Those who wanted to rule the people
ኢኃተቱ አሚነ አበዊሆሙ አላ ተወክፏ	8r	They did not inquire into the belief of their fathers, who accepted it	ኢሐተቱ አላ ተወከፉ አሚነ አባዊሆሙ	9r	They did not inquire, rather they accepted the faith of their fathers

(continued)

	Abb 215			Abb 234	
	Folio	Literal Translation		Folio	Literal Translation
ወዓዲ አጽንዕዋ እንዚ ይዌስኩ ታሪካተ ዘተእምርታት	8r	And also they strengthened it, adding [to it] with stories of signs	ወዓዲ አጽንዕዋ ለሐሰት እንዚ ይዌስኩ ላዕሊሃ ታሪካተ ዘተእሐአምርታት	9r	And also they strengthened the lies, adding on top of it stories of signs
ለአጠይቆ ጽድቀ ሃይማኖቶሙ	8r	To prove the truth of their religion	ከመ ያጽንዑ ሃይማኖቶሙ	9r	In order to strengthen their religion
ወሱታፌ ምስለ ሐሳውያን	8r	And a collaborator with liars	Minus	9r	
Chapter 5			**Abb 234**		
ይትከሡት ጽድቅ ፍጡነ	8r	Truth will quickly be revealed	ይትከሡት ጽድቅ	9r	Truth will be revealed
ነጺሮ ሥርዓተ ወሕገጋተ ፍጥረት	8r	To perceive the creation's established order and laws	ወባሥርዓተ ፍጥረት ዘኩሎት ለልቡናን	9r	And into the ordering of creation, which is clear to our intelligence
ዘተገብሩ ይቤሉ	8v	Which they allege were done	ዘተገብሩ	9v	Which were done
እስመ ይትረከብ ውስተ መጻሕፍተ ሙሴ ጥበበ ሕስም	8v	For in the books of Moses is found detestable wisdom	እስመ ውእቱ ይረከብ በመጻሕፍተ ሙሴ	9v	For this is found in the books of Moses
ሥርዓት ወሕገጋተ ፍጥረት	8v	Creation's established order and laws	ሥርዓተ ፍጥረት	9v	Creation's established order
እስመ በፈቃደ ፈጣሪ ወባሥርዓተ ፍጥረት ተአዘዘ	8v	So, the Creator's will, and the creation's established order commanded	እስመ ሥርዓተ ፍጥረት ይኤዝዝ	9v	So, the creation's established order commands
ወዝንቱ ሩካቤ ዘሥርዓ እግዚአብሔር ውስተ ሕገ ፍጥረቱ ለሕሰብእ	8v	This union which God established in the law of his creation for mankind	ወዝንቱ ሩካቤ ሕገ ፈጣሪ ውእቱ	9v	This union is the law of the creator
ግብረ እደዊሁ	8v	The work of his hands	ሥርዓቶ	9v	His precepts
ልቡናን ያጤይቀነ	8v	Our intelligence assures us	ልቡናን ያጤይቅ	9v	Our intelligence makes certain

(continued)

	Abb 215			Abb 234	
	Folio	Literal Translation		Folio	Literal Translation
ይብለነ ወያጤይቀነ ከመ አውስበ አምሥርዓተ ፈጣሪ ውእቱ	8v	It tells us and assures us that marriage is part of the creator's established order	ይብለነ ከመ አውስቦ ሕገ ፈጣሪ ውእቱ	9v	It tells us that marriage is the creator's law
ሶበ ትቤ ይኄይስ ምንኩስና	9r	When it says, 'monasticism is better'	ትብል ምንኩስና ይኄይስ	10r	It says, 'monasticism is better'
ነቢበ ሐሰት ወኢኮነት አምአግዚአብሔር	9r	It's telling a lie, and it is not from God	ወዝንቱኒ ሐሰት ውእቱ	10r	And this is a lie
ወይክልኑ ምክረ ሰብእ ያስተሣንዮ ለግብረ አግዚአብሔር	9r	Or can human deliberation improve on the work of God?	Minus		
ወከማሁ	9r	In the same way	ወዓዲ	10r	Also
አምኀበ እግዚአብሔር {ተወከፍኩ}	9r	{I received} from God	አምእግዚአብሔር ተወከፍኩ	10r	I received from God
ትምህርት {መሀመድ} ኢይክል ይኩን አምእግዚአብሔር አስመ ዘትወለድ ሰብእ ተባዕት ወአንስት	9r	{Mohammed's} instruction cannot be from God. For, human beings, born male and female	ዘይትወለዳ ሰብእ ተባእት ወአንስት	10r	Human beings, born male and female
ሕገ ፍጥረት	9r	Creation's law	ሕገ ፈጣሪ	10r	The creator's law
ወሕጋታ ፍጥረት	9r	And the creation's laws	ወይትቃረን ጥበቡ	10r	And opposes his wisdom
ፈጣሪነ	9v	Our Creator	ፈጣሪ	10v	The creator
ወኵሉ ዘያርአየነ	9v	And all that it shows us	ወዘያርአየነ	10v	And that which it shows us
ያጤይቀነ	9v	It affirms to us	ይብለነ	10v	It tells us
በሠናይ ጥበብ	9v	With virtuous wisdom	በዓቢይ ጥበብ	10v	With great wisdom
ወለወሊደ ውሉድ	10r	And for the bearing of children	ወለወሊድ	11r	And for childbearing
ኵሎ ዘይትገሥሥ	10r	Anything that she touches	ኵሎ ዘገሠሠት	11r	Anything that she touched

(continued)

	Abb 215			Abb 234	
	Folio	Literal Translation		Folio	Literal Translation
ወያበጥል ሕገ ተራድኦ ወይከልአ አልህቆ ውሉድ	10r	And it annuls the law of mutual help and impedes the raising of children	እስመ ‹ወ›ያበጥል ተራድአ ወ.. ውሉድ ወሐጺነ ውሉድ	11r	Because <and> it annuls the law of mutual help < and … of children> and the raising of children
ወበእንተ[ዝ] ዝንቱ ሕገ ሙሴ ኢይከል ይኩን እምፈጣሬ ብአሲት	10r	There{for} this 'Law of Moses' cannot be from the Creator of women	ወበእንተዝ ዛቲ ሕገ ሙሴ ኢትክል ወኢአ ‹እምእግዚአብሔር› እምፈጣሬ ብአሲት	11r	Therefore this 'Law of Moses' cannot come <from God> from the creator of women
ልቡና ‹ልቡና›ነ ይብለነ ይኩን መፍትው ንቅብሮሙ ለአኃዊነ	10r	Our intelligence <our intelligence> tells us, 'it is necessary to bury our brothers'	ልቡናን ይብለነ ከመ ንቅብሮሙ ለአኃዊነ	11r	Our intelligence tells us to bury our brothers
ለኰሎ ‹ኩ›ፍጥረት	10r	For all creation	ለፍጥረት	11r	For the creation
ይቤ ወንጌል ዘኢየኃድግ አቡሁ ወእሞ ብእሲቶ ወወሉዶ ኢኮነ ድልወ ለእግዚአብሔር	10r-10v	The Gospel says, 'he who does not leave his father and mother, his wife and children will not be worthy of God'	ይቤ ወንጌል ከመ ዘየኃድግ አቡሁ ወእሞ ወብእሲቶ ወወሉዶ ድልው ውእቱ ለእግዚአብሔር	11r-11v	The Gospel says that he who leaves his father and his mother, his wife and his children is worthy of God
ያርእየነ	10v	It shows us	ይብለነ	11v	It tells us
ዓቢይ አበሳ	10v	Great sin	ዓቢይ አመፃ	11v	Great rebellion
ሥርዓተ ፈጣሪ ወሕጋተ ፍጥረት	10v	The creator's established order and the creation's laws	ሥርዓተ ፍጥረት	11v	The creation's established order
ወዓዲ እስላም	10v	Also Muslims	ወእስላም	11v	And Muslims
ኢይከል ይፃእ እምፈጣሬ ሰብእ ዘፈጠረነ ዕሩያን ከመ አኃው በዝኅቡሎ ለፈጣሪ አቡነ	10v	It cannot come out from the Creator of humans who made us equal, like brothers, that we call the creator our father	ኢይከን እምፈጣሬ ዘፈጠረ ሰብእ ዕሩያን እስመ ሰብእ ‹ኀ› አኁሁ ውእቱ ለሰብእ በዝኅቡሎ ለእግዚአብሔር አቡነ	11v	It cannot be from the creator who created humans equal because a person is a brother to another person, that we call God our father
ወከማሁ እግዚአብሔር ኢኤዝዝ ነገረ ከንቱ ወኢይብል	11r	Likewise, God will not command pointless things, and will not say,...	ወከማሁኬ እግዚአብሔር ኢይብል	12r	Likewise, God will not say,...

(continued)

	Abb 215			Abb 234	
	Folio	Literal Translation		Folio	Literal Translation
ዮም ብላዕ ወጌሠም ኢትብላዕ ወሥጋሂ ኢትብላዕ ዮም ወጌሠም ሐኢትብላዕ በከመ ይመስሎሙ ለአለ የዓቅቡ ሕጋጋተ አጽዋም በነብ ክርስቲያን ወለአስላምሂ ኢይቤሎሙ እግዚአብሔር ብልዑ ሌሊተ	11r	Eat today and don't eat tomorrow, don't eat meat today but <do not> eat it tomorrow', as it seems [he would say] to those who keep the Christian fasting laws. Also, God did not say to the Muslims, 'eat during the night'	ዮም ኢትብላዕ ወበካልዕ ዕለት ብላዕ ወዮም ሥጋ ኢትብላዕ ወበካልዕ ዕለት ብላዕ ሌሊት ብላዕ	12r	Don't eat today but on another day eat. Don't eat meat today but eat it on another day. Eat during the night
ልቡና ይሜህረነ ይኩነነ ብውሕ ንብላዕ ኩሎ ዘኢያምስን ጥዒናን ወፍጥረተነ	11r	Our intelligence teaches us that we are permitted to eat everything that does not harm our health or our constitution	ልቡናን ዘገዐነ ፈጣሪ ይብለነ ከመ ንብላዕ ኩሎ ዘኢያማስን ፍጥረተነ	12r	Our intelligence with which the creator bestowed us tells us to eat everything that does not harm our constitution
ለመፍቅደ ሕይወትነ	11r	For the sustenance of our life	ለሕይወትነ	12r	For our life
ወሕገ ጾም ውጹአ ውኡቱ አምሥርዓተ ፈጣሪ ዘፈጠረ ወመባዕተ ለሕይወት ሰብእ ወፈቀደ ንብልያሙ ወናእኮቶ ወኢይደልወነ ንትሐረም እምበረከቱ	11r	The fasting law lies outside the established order of the creator, who also created food for human life. He desired that we eat them, and that we give thanks to him, and we should not reject his blessing.	ወኢይክል እምእግዚአብሔር ይኩን ሕግ ዘጾም ወዘካልአ ሕርመት እንበለ ዳዕሙ ሕርመት እምዘያማስን ፍጥረተ ሰብእ እስመ እግዚአብሔር ኢያዝዝ ከንቶ ወእምድኃረ ፈጠረ መባዕተ ለሕይወተ ሰብእ ይፈቅድ ከመ ንብልያሙ ወናእኩቶ ወአኮ ከመ ንትሐረም እምበረከቱ	12r	The fasting law and other abstinences, except the abstinence from that which corrupts human nature, cannot be from God. Because God does not command useless things and after he created food for human life, he wants us to eat them and worship him and not to reject his blessing.

(continued)

Abb 215			Abb 234		
	Folio	Literal Translation		Folio	Literal Translation
ወለእመቦ ዘይብሉኒ ለአሙቶ ፍትወተ ሥጋ ተሠርዓ ሕጎ ጾም	11r	And if there are those who tell me that the fasting law was established for the mortification of the flesh	ወለእመቦ ዘይብል ለአሚዊተ ፍትወተ ሥጋ ተሠርዐ ጾም	12r	And if there is one who says fasting was established for the mortification of the desires of the flesh
እንበለ በሥርዓት እሙር ዘሠርዓ ውእቱ ፈጣሪ በፍካሬ ሕጋዊ	11v	Except in the well-known order which the creator himself established in lawful intercourse.	እንበለ በሥርዓት ዘሠርዐ ፈጣሪ ዘውእቱ ሩካቤ ወአውስቦ ሕጋዊ	12v	Except in the order which the creator established which is intercourse and lawful marriage
ፈጣሪነ	11v	Our creator	ጠቢብ ፈጣሪ	12v	The wise creator
ዳእሙ ተከለ ዘንተ ፍትወተ ውስተ ሥጋ ሰብእ ከመ ይኩን መሠረት ሕይወቱ ለዝ ዓለም	11v	But rather he planted this craving in human flesh as the foundation of life in this world	አላ ከመ ዝንቱ ፍትወት ይኩን ሕይወት ዝዓለም	12v	But so that this craving would be for the life of this world
ወያቀምኮ ኵሎ ፍጥረተ ውስተ ፍና ዘተሠርዓ ላቲ	11v	And he sets all creation on the path which was established for it	ወያቅም ፍጥረተ ሰብእ ውስተ ጥበበ ፈጣሪ ወውስተ ኵሉ ሥርዓት ፍጥረት	12v	And he sets human nature in the wisdom of the creator and in all of creation's established order
እምውሳኔሃ	11v	Beyond its limits	እምውሳኔ ፍጥረት	12v	Beyond the limits of creation
በመጠነ መፍቅድነ	11v	In the measure of our need	እመጠን	12v	With measure
በከመ ኢአብሰ ዘበልዓ በመጠነ መፍቅዳ በዕለተ እሑድ	11v	Just as one who eats according to the measure of his need on Sunday doesn't sin	በከመ ዘበልዐ ወሰትየ በመጠነ መፍቅዳ በዕለተ እሑድ ኢአብሰ	12v	Just as one who eats and drinks according to the measure of his need on Sunday doesn't sin
ወበመዕል ፶ ከማሁ ኢይኤብስ ዘይበልዕ በዕለተ ዓርብ ወበመዕለ እምቅድመ ፋሲክ	11v	And during the 50 days [of the Easter fast], likewise he who eats on Friday and on the day before Easter does not sin	እፎ ይኤብስ ዘይበልዕ ከማሁ በዕለተ ዓርብ	12v	How does he sin who likewise eats on Friday?

(continued)

Abb 215			Abb 234		
	Folio	Literal Translation		Folio	Literal Translation
ኢለበዉ ውስተ ግብረ እግዚአብሔር ሶበ ሠርዑ ሕገ ጾም ወይሔስዉ እንዘ ይብሉ	11v-12r	They did not comprehend the inner working of God when they established the fasting laws, and they lie saying...	ይሔስዉ ሶበ ይብሉ	12v	They lie when they say...
እስመ እግዚአብሔር ፈጣሪነ ወሀበነ መባልዕተ ሲሳየነ ከመ ንሴሰዩ ወኢከመ ንትሐረም እምኔሁ	12r	Yet God our creator gave food for our nourishment, for us to eat from it and not to abstain from it	እስመ ውእቱ ፈጣሪ መሀቦሙ ሲሳዮሙ ለሰብእ ከመ ይብልዕዎ ወኢከመ ይትሐረሙ እምኔሁ	12v	Yet that creator gave people their nourishment to eat and not to abstain from it
Chapter 6			**Abb 234**		
፩ሕዝብ ለሕይወት ወለሞት ፩ደ ለምሕረት ወ፩ደ ለኩነኔ	12r	One people for life and one for death, one for mercy and one for judgment	፩ሕዝብ ለሕይወት ወ፩ደ ለሞት	13r	One people for life and one for death
ይሜህረነ	12r	It teaches us	ይብለነ	13r	It tells us
ወበዝንቱ መዋዕል	12r	In these days	ወዮምኒ	13r	But today
ወንሕነሂ ከመዝ ከመ ዘንብል	12v	We say the same thing	ወንሕነሂ ከማሁ ንብሎሙ	13r	And we likewise say to them
እንበለ {ኅበ}	12v	Except {for}	እንበለ ኅበ	13r	Except for
ኅበ ሙ በጽሐ እምአሉ ኮሎሙ	12v	To whom of all these it reached	ኅበ ሙ እምአሉ ኮሎሙ በጽሐ	13r	*Same meaning, transposition of clauses*
ኢኀደገ ሰብአ ይሰነዓዉ በሐሰት	12v	He did not abandon people to agree with lies	ገብረ ከመ ሰብአ ኢይሰነዓዉ በሐሰት	13v	He acted so that people would not agree with lies
ይመስል ጽድቀ ዝንቱ ነገር	12v	This one thing seems like the truth	ይመስል ጽድቀ	13v	It seems like the truth
ወኮሉ ሰብአ ኢይክሉ ይሰነዓዉ በሐሰት በከመ ኢይሰነዓዉ	12v	All people cannot agree with one another in a lie, just as none of them agrees	ወይእዜኒ ይትዓወቅ ሐሰት እስመ ሰብአ ኢይሰነዓዉ	13v	So now lies are known, because people do not agree

(continued)

	Abb 215			Abb 234	
	Folio	Literal Translation		Folio	Literal Translation
ወከመ ኢይክል ይትረከብ ፍጡር እንበለ ፈጣሪ	13r	And that it is not possible to find a created being without a Creator	ወከመ ኢይትረከብ ፍጡር እን[በ]በ ፈጣሪ	13v	And that a created being without a Creator cannot be found
እስመ ሀሎ ውስቴቶሙ ሐሰት ምስለ ጽድቅ ተቶሲሓ በእንተዝ ኢ.ንሰማዕ ቦሙ	13r	Because lie exists in them mingled together with truth, consequently we do not agree with one another in them	እስመ ሐሰት ውእቱ ኢ.ንሰማዕ ቦቱ	13v	Because it is a lie, we do not agree with one another in it
እንዘ ይሬስዩ	13r	While making	አም ይሬስዩ	13v	When they make
ሃይማኖተ ሰብእ ወለአመኒ ኢኮነት እምእግዚአብሔር ትትፈቀድ ሎሙ ለሰብእ ወታገብር ሠናየተ እስመ ታፈርሆሙ ለአኩያን ከመ ኢይግበሩ እከየ ወትናዝዘሙ ለሠናያን	13r	Even if people's religion is not from God, it is desirable for them. It makes [people] do good, because it terrifies the wicked into not doing evil, and it consoles the good ones	ሃይማኖተ ሰብእ ኢኮ እምእግዚአብሔር ወጊሕቱ ኮነ ሠናየ እስመ ያገብር ሠናየተ ወያፈርሆሙ ለአኩያን ከመ ኢይግበሩ እከየ ወያስተፌሥሓሙ ለሠናያን	13v–14r	People's religion is not from God, yet it is still good. For it makes [people] do good. It terrifies the wicked in order not to do wickedness and it cheers the good ones
ዘይመስሎ {ወልዶ}	13r	Whom he supposes to be {his son}	እንዘ ይመስሎ ወልዶ	14r	Supposing him to be his son
ሃይማኖትየ ዘማ ይእቲ	13v	My religion was adulterous	ሃይማኖት ዘማ	14r	Religion was adulterous
ተከዝኩ ‹ቡ›በእንቲአሃ	13v	I grieved because of this	አቴክዝ በእንቲአሃ	14r	I am grieving because of this
ሰብአ ብሔርነ አፍለሱ	13v	Our country's people have banished	ሰብእ አፍለሱ	14r	People have banished
Chapter 7			**Abb 234**		
ያስሕትዎሙ ለሕዝበ ዚአሁ	13v	So that they might deceive his people	ያስሕትዎሙ ለሕዝበ ‹ዚአሁ› በስመ ዚአሁ	14v	So that they might deceive his people <his> in his name
እግዚአብሔር	14r	God	ፈጣሪ	14v	The creator

(continued)

	Abb 215			Abb 234	
	Folio	Literal Translation		Folio	Literal Translation
ከመ ንርአይ ቦቱ ዘኮነ ለነ መፍትወ ውስተ ኵሉ መፍቅዳተ ፍጥረት	14r	To see with it what is best for us from among all the attractions of the creation	ከመ ቦቱ ንርአይ ጥበበ ውስተ መፍቅዳተ ፍጥረት	14v	With it to see his wisdom among the attractions of the creation
ወለጽድቅሰ ኢንረክባ በትምህርታተ ሰብእ	14r	And the truth, however, we will not find it in human teachings	ወአኮ ዘንረክባ ለጽድቅ በትምህርተ ሰብእ	14v	It is not that we find truth in human teaching
ወለአመሰ ናበድሪ ለሐሰት አምጽድቅ	14r	And if we choose lie over truth	ወለአመሰ ኢንፈቅዳ ለጽድቅ	14v	If we do not want the truth
ወኢሕግ ጠባይዓዊ ዘተሠርዓ ለኵሉ ፍጥረት	14r	Nor will the natural law that was established for all creation	ወኢሕግ ጠባይዓዊ ዘፍጥረት	14v	Nor the natural law of creation
ሥርዓተ እግዚአብሔር ይጸንዕ እምሥርዓተ ሰብእ ወበእንተዝ	14r	God's rules are stronger than the people's rules. Therefore...	Minus	14v	
እምኃየሉ ለሥርዓተ ፈጣሪ	14r	By the strength of the Creator's established order	እምኃይለ ፍጥረት	14v	By the power of creation
ወእግዚአ ፍጥረት	14v	And the Lord of creation	ወእግዚአብሔር	15r	And God
በዘኢኮነ ፍጥረቱ	14v	Which are not in his nature	Minus	15r	
ኵሎሙ {እለ} ይክስቱ	14v	All those {who} violate	ኵሎሙ እለ ይኔሥቱ	15r	All those who violate
ወኵሉ ፍኖቱ ጽድቅ ወርቱዕ	15r	And all his ways are true and just	ወኵሉ ፍኖት እግዚአብሔር ሣህል ወጽድቅ	15v	And all God's ways are merciful and true
ሞተ ሥጋነ	15r	The death of our flesh	ሞትነ	15v	Our death
ይሔምር	15r	It shows	ያጤይቅ	15v	It recognizes
አላ ወለ{ዘ}ይመጽእ ንብረት	15r	But and also for the life {that is} to come	አላ ለዘይመጽእ ንብረት	15v	But also for the life that is to come

(continued)

| \
Abb 215			Abb 234		
	Folio	Literal Translation		Folio	Literal Translation
ወበህየ ነፍሳት አለ ፈጸማ	15v-16r	And there are souls who have fulfilled	በዘንፍሳት ዘፈጸማ	15v	In which are souls who have fulfilled
ወአንበለዝ	15v	Without this	እስመ እንበለዝ	16r	Because without this
ወዓዲ ነፍስ (ትክል) ተሐሊ እግዚአብሔርየ ወትርአዮ በሕሊናሃ	15v	Also, our soul (is able to) think of God and to see him in her mind	ወዓዲ ነፍስየ ትክል ተሐሊ አምላከ ወትርአዮ ለአምላከ በሕሊናሃ	16r	Also, my soul is able to think of the Lord and to see the Lord in her mind
ወዓዲ ትክል	15v	Also it is able	ወትክል	16r	And it is able
ዳዕሙ	15v	On the contrary	አላ	16r	Rather
ቦ ዓማፂ ዘይትፌጋዕ ወቦ ጻድቅ ዘይበኪ	15v	There are violent people who live in luxury, and there are righteous people who mourn	Minus	16r	
ቡብርሃነ ልቡናሆሙ ወለአለ ዓቀቡ ሕገ ጠባይዓዊ ዘፍጥረቶሙ	15v	By the light of their intelligence, and those who observed the natural law of their nature	በልቡናሆሙ ወበሕገ ፍጥረት	16r	By their intelligence and by the natural law
ወአብደሩ	16r	And they preferred	ወያበድሩ	16r	And they prefer
ፈቃደ ፈጣሪሆሙ	16r	Seeking the will of their creator	ፈቃደ ፈጣሪ	16r	Seeking the will of the creator
Chapter 8			**Abb 234**		
ይታወቅ	16r	It is known	ይትረከብ	16v	It is discovered
ለእግዚአብሔር ፈጣሪከ	16r	To God your Creator	ለእግዚአብሔር	16v	To God
ዘኢ፡ትፈቅድ ይግበሩ ለከ	16r	What you do not want them to do to you	ዘኢ.ትፈቅድ ይግበሩ ለከ ሰብእ	16v	What you do not want people to do to you
ወዓዲ ፲ቃላተ	16r	Furthermore, the Decalogue	ወ፲ ቃላተ	16v	And the Decalogue
ይሜህረነ	16r	It teaches us	ይብለነ	16v	It tells us
ፈቃደ {ፈጣሪ} እሙንቱ	16r	They are the will of {the Creator}	ፈቃደ እግዚአብሔር እሙንቱ	16v	They are the will of God
ንፈቅድ ይግበሩ	16r	We want them to do	ንፈቅድ ከመ ሰብእ ይግብሩ	16v	We want people to do
ዘትክሃለነ	16rv	What we are able to	ለእመ ይትከሀለነ	16r	If we are able to

Appendix 1: Chart of Differences — **175**

(continued)

	Abb 215			Abb 234	
	Folio	Literal Translation		Folio	Literal Translation
ፈቃደ {ፈጣሪ} ውእቱ	16v	It is the {Creator's} will	ፈቃደ ፈጣሪ ውእቱ		It is the Creator's will
በፈቃደ ፈጣሪ	16v	By the will of the Creator	በፈቃደ እግዚአብሔር	16v	By the will of God
በፈቃሕ ቅዱስ	16v	By his sacred will	በፈቃደ ፈጣሪ	16v	By the Creator's will
ወይፈቅድ ውእቱ ፈጣሪነ ከመ ናሠንየ ለንብረትነ በአእምሮትነ	16v	This same Creator of ours wants us to improve our way of living through our knowledge	ወይፈቅድ ውእቱ ፈጣሪ ከመ ናሠንየ ለንብረትነ በአእምሮ	16v-17r	This same Creator wants us to improve our way of living through knowledge
ወሀለዉ ዓዲ ብዙኃን ካልአን ግብራት ዘይስነዓዉ. ምስለ ልቡናን ወይትፈቀዱ ለሕይወትነ አው ለንብረተ ኵሎሙ እጓለ እመሕያው ወይደልወነ ንዕቀበሙ እስመ ከመዝ ውእቱ ፈቃዱ ለፈጣሪ ወይደልወነ ናእምር ከመ እግዚአብሔር ኢፈጠረ{ነ} ፍጹማነ	16v	And there are many other deeds which are in harmony with our intelligence, and they are beneficial for our life or for the lives of all people. We should keep them because such is the will of our Creator, and we should know that God did not create {us} perfect	ወሀለዉ ብዙኅ ካልእ ነገር ዘይስነዓዉ ምስለ ልቡናን ወይትፈቀዱ ለፍጥረትነ አው ለንብረተ ኵሉ እጓል እመሕያው ዘይደልወነ ንፈጽሞሙ እስመ ፈቃደ ፈጣሪ ውእቱ ወይደልወነ ነሐሊ ከመ እግዚአብሔር ኢፈጠረነ ፍጹማነ ወአንበረነ ውእተ ዝንቱ ዓለም	17r	There are many other things which are in harmony with our intelligence, and they are beneficial for our nature or for the lives of all people. We should accomplish them because it is the will of the Creator, and we should consider that God did not create us perfect but he put us in this world
ዳዕሙ ፈጠረ{ነ}	16v	Rather he created {us}	ወባሕቱ ፈጠረነ	17r	But he created us
ውስተ ዝንቱ ዓለም	16v-17r	In this world	ውስተ ዛቲ ንብረት	17r	In this life
ወእምተከህሎ ለእግዚአብሔር ይፍጥሮን ፍጹማነ ወይረስየን ብዑኣነ ዳበ ምድር	17r	It was possible for God to create us perfect and make us blessed ones on earth	እስመ እምተከህሎ ለፈጣሪ ይፍጥሮሙ ለሰብእ ፍጹማነ ወይረስዮሙ ብጹዓነ ውስተ ዝንቱ ዓለም	17r	For it was possible for the creator to create people perfect and to make them blessed ones in this world
ወፈጠረነ	17r	But he created us	አላ ፈጠረነ	17r	Rather he created us
ይደልወነ ንስብሖ ለፈጣሪነ ወንፈጽም ፈቃደ ወንትዓገሡ እስከ አሙ ይወስደነ	17r	We should glorify our Creator, and fulfil his will, and we should be patient until he takes us	ይደልወነ ንንብር እንዘ ንሴብሖ ለፈጣሪነ ወንንብር በከመ ውእቱ ፈቀደ ወእስከ አሙ ይወስደነ	17v	We should live glorifying our Creator and live as he wills, and until he takes us

(continued)

	Abb 215			Abb 234	
	Folio	Literal Translation		Folio	Literal Translation
ወንስአል ኀበ ኄሩቱ	17r	And let us appeal to his goodness	ወዓዲ እስከ አሙ ንሕዮ ይዴልወነ ንትዓገሥ በኲሉ ምንዳቤነ ወንስአል ኀቤሁ	17v	Moreover, for as long as we live we should be patient in all our hardship, and let us appeal to him
ወዕበደነ ዘገበርን በኢያእምሮትነ	17r	And our foolishness that we have done in our ignorance	ወዕበደነ ዘንዕስነ	17v	And the foolishness of our youth
ወነፍስ ነባቢት	17r	And the soul is rational	ወነፍስ	17v	And the soul
ወኲሎ የዓቅብ ወኲሎ ይመልክ	17v	He protects all, and he rules over all	ወዘኲሎ የዓቅብ ወዘኲሎ ይአኀዝ	17v	Who protects all and who holds all
ወትስአል እምኔሁ ሠናያተ ወትድኃን እምእኩይ ወትትመሀጾን ውስተ እዴሁ ለዘኲሎ ይመልካል	17v	And to ask from him good things, and to be saved from evil, and to be protected in the hand of the one who can do all	ትጸሊ ወትስአል ሠናያተ እምኔሁ ዘኲሎ ይክል	17v	And to ask good things from him who can do all
እግዚአብሔር ዓቢይ ወልዑል ወይሬኢ ዘበታሕቱ	17v	God is great; and is Most High; and he sees what is in the depths	እስመ እግዚአብሔር ዓቢይ ወልዑል ውእቱ ወይሬኢ ዘታሕት	17v	Because God is great; and is most high; and he sees what is deep
ወይአኀዝ ኲሎ ወይሌቡ ኲሎ ወይመርሕ ኲሎ ወይሜህር ኲሎ	17v	He holds all, and he understands all, and he guides all, and he teaches all	ወይመልክ ኲሎ ወኲሎ ይሌቡ ወኲሎ ይመርሕ ወኲሎ ይሜህር	17v	He rules over all, and he understands all, and he guides all, and he teaches all
ወንስሊ. ኀቤሁ በእንተ ረኪበ መፍቅዳተ ሥጋነ	17v	And pray to him for finding the needs of our body	ወንስአል ኀቤሁ በእንተ መፍቅድተ ሥጋነ	18r	And ask him for the needs of our body
ዝንተ ኲሎ ይሜህረነ ልቡናን ዘደየ ፈጣሪ ውስተ ልበ ሰብእ	18r	Our intelligence, which our creator put into the heart of people, teaches us all these things	ዝንተ ኲሎ ይብለነ ልቡናን ዘደየ ፈጣሪ ውስተ ልበ ሰብእ	18r	Our intelligence which the creator put into the heart of people, tells us all these things
Chapter 9			**Abb 234**		
ወነበርኩ አሙ ንዕሰየ	18r	I lived in my childhood	ወነበርኩ ቅድመ	18r	I lived beforehand

(continued)

Abb 215			Abb 234		
	Folio	Literal Translation		Folio	Literal Translation
እንዘ ኢይሐሊ ወኢምንተኒ	18r	Not thinking at all	እንዘ ኢይሐሊ.	18r	Not thinking
ወአበስኩ ብዙኃ በዘኢይደልዋ	18r	And I sinned so much in what is not fitting	ወገበር ዘኢይደልዋ	18v	And I did what was not fitting
ውእተ ዓሚረ ተመየጥኩ ኃበ እግዚአብሔር ወወጠንኩ አጸሊ ኃቤሁ	18r	At that time, I turned to God, and I started to pray to him	ወውእተ አሚረ ወጠንኩ አስአል ኃበ እግዚአብሔር	18v	And at that time, I started to ask God
ወዕቤሎ ለእግዚአብሔር	18r	I said to God	ወአቢ.	18v	I said
ወዓዲ	18v	And also	ወካዕበ	18v	And again
ነደ ላዕለየ መዓተ ንጉሥ ወበዕለአመዋዕል መጽአ ኃቤየ መልአክ ንጉሥ	18v	The king's rage burned against me. One day the king's messenger came to me	ነደ መዓተ ንጉሥ ላዕለየ ወበዐ አመዋዕል መጽአ መልአክ ንጉሥ ኃቤየ	18v	*Same meaning, transposition of word order*
ተስአለኒ በእንተ ብዙኅ ነገረ ትምህርት ወመጻሕፍት	19r	He asked me about many matters of doctrine and scripture	ተስአለኒ ብዙኃ ነገረ ትምህርት	19r	He asked me many matters of doctrine
ወአአኩት{ክ}ዎ ለእግዚአብሔር	19r	And I praised God	እንዘ አአኩቶ ለእግዚአብሔር	19r	While I was praising God
ይደውከ ታፍቅሮሙ ለፍራንጅ	19r	It is fitting for you to love the foreigners	አፍቅሮሙ ለፈራንጅ	19r	Love the foreigners
ወለሰብአ ይደልዎ ይግበር ኩሎ ዘይትከሀሎ እንበለ ያምክሮ ለእግዚአብሔር	19r	Human beings should do everything that they can without asking God to help them	ወይደልወነ ንግበር ዘይትከሀለነ እንበለ ናምክሮ ለእግዚአብሔር	19r	We should do what we can without asking God to help us
ፈጣሪየ	19r	My Creator	ፈጣሪ	19v	The Creator

(continued)

	Abb 215			Abb 234	
	Folio	Literal Translation		Folio	Literal Translation
ወበአማን እብሎ ለእግዚአብሔር ደለወኒ ዘአሕመምከኒ ከመ አአምር ኵነኔክ እስመ ለበውኩ ጥቀ እንዘ ሀሎኩ ባሕቲትየ ውስተ ግብየ እምዘለበውኩ ሶበ ሀሎኩ ምስለ መምህራን	19v	Truly I say to God, 'I deserved what you caused me to suffer so that I could know your statutes'. For how much more I have understood while living alone in a cave than I understood when I lived with scholars?	Minus	19v	
ንስቲት ጥቀ ውእቱ	19v	It is very little	ንስቲት ውእቱ	19v	It is little
ወአለብዎ ምስጢራተ ፍጥረት	19v	And he made known by it [wisdom] the mysteries of creation	ከመ እለቡ ዘንተ ኵሎ	19v	So that I might understand all this
ሐልዮ በግብረ እግዚአብሔር ወበእንተ ጥበቡ	19v	Meditating on the works of God, and about his wisdom	ሐልዪ ኀበ እግዚአብሔር ወኀበ ጥበቡ	19v	Meditation on God and on his wisdom
ወጸለይኩ ኵሎ ዓሚረ በስፉሕ ልብየ	19v	I prayed all day with my outstretched heart	ወጸለይኩ በኵሉ ልብየ	19v	And I prayed with all my heart
ወዕብል ዘልፈ	20r	I always say	ወእቤ ኵሎ አሚረ	19v	I say all day
Minus	20r		ምሕረትክ ይትልወኒ በኵሉ መዋዕለ ሕይወትየ	20r	Your mercy will follow me for all the days of my life
እዴክ {ይእቲ} ዛቲ	20r	This {is} your hand	እዴክ ይእቲ ዛቲ	20r	This is your hand
Chapter 10			**Abb 234**		
ወጸሎትሰ ዘጼሊ ነግህ መሠርክ	20r-20v	And the prayer that I pray morning and evening	ወጸሎትስ ዘነግህ ወሰርክ ዘጸለይኩ ወዘጸሊ ኵሎ አሚረ በባቢይ ተስፉ	20v	And the prayer of the morning and of evening that I prayed and that I pray all days in great hope
አፈጣሪየ	20v	My dear Creator	ፈጣሪየ	20r	My Creator
ለመፍቅዳተ ሕይወት	20v	For the necessities of life	ለመፍቅዳተ ሕይወትየ	20v	For the necessities of my life

Appendix 1: Chart of Differences

(continued)

	Abb 215			Abb 234	
	Folio	Literal Translation		Folio	Literal Translation
ይደልወኒ አግብር ወአያም በኩሉ ከሂሎትየ ለረኪበ ኩሎን መፍቅዳተ ሕይወትየ ወኢይበቍዓኒ ጸሎት ባሕቲቱ ዳዕሙ	20v	I should work and toil with all my ability to obtain all the necessities of my life, and it is not enough for me only to pray. Nevertheless	ይደልወኒ ከመ ለልየ አግብር ዘይትከሀለኒ ለረከበ ዘንተ ኩሎ ዘይትፈቀድ ሊተ ወባሕቱ አስመ	20v	I, for my part, should work as I can to obtain everything that is necessary for me. Because
ተጋባርየስ እንበለ በርክትከ እግዚአ ኢይበቍዓኒ ወኢምንተኒ	20v–21r	My ability without your blessing, O Lord, will not benefit me at all	አስመ ተግባርየ እንበለ በርከትከ ኢይበቍዓኒ	20v	Because my ability without your blessing will not benefit me
ወአንት ባርክ ለሕሊናየ ወለተግባርየ ወለነብረትየ	21r	And you, blessed my mind, my handiwork, and my livelihood	አንት ኦፈጣርየ ባርክ ለሕሊናየ ወለተግባርየ	20v	You, My dear Creator, blessed my mind and my handiwork
ሚጥ ልበ ሰብእ እለ ሀለዉ ምስሌየ ለገቢር ሠናየ ሊተ አስመ ኩሉ ይከውን በፈቃድከ ቡሩክ	21r	Turn the hearts of people who live with me to do well by me, because everything happens according to your blessed will	ሚጥ ልበ ሰብእ ለገቢረ ሠናይ ሊተ	20v	Turn the hearts of people to do well by me
ልብነ ዘልፈ ውስተ እደ እግዚአብሔር	21r	Our heart is always in God's hand	ልብነ ውስተ እደ እግዚአብሔር	20v–21r	Our heart is in God's hand
ወ⟨ያ⟩ይትከሀሎ ለእግዚአብሔር ይረስየነ	21r	And God can make us	ወከመ ይትከሀሎ ለእግዚአብሔር ይረስየነ	21r	And that God can make us
ወአንተዝ ንሬኢ ኩሎ ዓሚረ	21r	And because of this, we see all day	በከመ ኩሎ አሚረ ንሬኢ	21r	As all day we see
ወእንዝ ንህህ ኢንፈቅድ ሐዘን ይሠርቅ ውስተ ልብነ	21r	While we don't desire sadness, it rises in our hearts	ወንሕነኒ እንዘ ኢንፈቅድ ይሠርቅ ሐዘን ውስተ ልብነ	21r	*Transposition*
ወይደልወነ ንጸሊ ኀበ እግዚአብሔር	21r	And we should pray to God	ወይደልወነ ንስአል እምኀበ እግዚአብሔር	21r	We should beseech of God

(continued)

	Abb 215			Abb 234		
		Folio	Literal Translation		Folio	Literal Translation
አንተ እግዚአየ ወፈጣሪየ		21v	You, my Lord and my Creator	አንተ እግዚአ ፈጣሪየ ወአቃቢየ	21r-21v	You, O Lord, my Creator and my Protector
ወዓዲ ዕፀወ ገዳም		21v	Moreover, the forest's trees	ዕፀው	21v	The trees
ይበቅሉ ይለመልሙ ወይጸግዩ ወያወጽኡ ፍሬ ዘርአሙ በበነገዶሙ እንበለ ስሕተት ወይመስሉ ዘቦሙ ሕነፍስ		21v	They grow, bud, bloom, produce fruit and their kind of seed without any mistakes, and they seem to have a soul	Minus	21v	
ወዓዲ አድባርኒ		21v	And also the mountains	አድባርኒ	21v	The mountains
ኩሉ ግብርከ ይሴብሓ ለስምከ		21v-22r	All your works glorify your name	ኩሉ ይሴብሖ ለስምከ	21v	Everything glorifies your name
ጥቀ ዓቢይ ግብረ አደዊከ		22r	How great is the work of your hands!	ጥቀ ዐቢይ ስምከ እግዚአ	21v	How great is your name, O Lord!
ወነቅዕ ሕይወት ዓለም		22r	And the spring of the life of the world	ወነቀዐ ሕይወት	21v	And the spring of life
ወነበርኩ ከመዝ ጽዓመተ እንዘ አነክር		22r	I lived like this for two years, marvelling	ወነበርኩ ጽዓመተ እንዘ አነክር ኩሎ ፍጥረት	21v–22r	I lived for two years, marvelling at all creation
ጥቀ ሠናይ		22r	Very good	ጥቀ ዐቢይ	22r	Very great
ይሐሉ ወይቤ ወተፈነውኩ አምኀበ እግዚአብሔር ከመ አክሥት ለሰብእ ጥበበ ወጽድቀ		22r	He lies and said, 'I was sent from God to reveal his wisdom and righteousness to humankind'	ይመጽእ ኀቤነ ወይብለነ መጻእኩ ኀቤክሙ ከመ አክሥት ለክሙ ጥበበ እግዚአብሔር	22r	He comes to us and says to us, 'I came to you to reveal the wisdom of God to you'
ወአይከሥት		22r	And he doesn't reveal anything	ወባሕት [sic] ኢይከሥት	22r	But he doesn't reveal anything
ዘይደልወኒ አአምር በእንቲአከ		22v	What I should know about you	ዘይደሉ ትለቡ ለባዊት ፍጥረት ከማየ	22r	What a rational creation like me should understand

(continued)

	Abb 215			Abb 234	
	Folio	Literal Translation		Folio	Literal Translation
Chapter 11			Abb 234		
ወነግሠ ወልደ ፋሲላደስ ህየንቴሁ	22v	And Fasiladas son ruled in his place	ወነግሠ ወልዱ ፋሲለደስ	22r	And his son, Fasiladas, ruled.
ኀበ አክሱም	22v	To Aksum	አክሱም	22r	[to] Aksum
እምኀበ [እግዚአብሔር]	22v	By {God}	አምኀበ እግዚአብሔር	22v	By God
ብሔረ እንፍራዝ	23r	[To] the country of Enferaz	ኀበ ብሔረ እንፍራዝ	22v	To the country of Enferaz
ፍና በዘእሴሰይ	23r	A way by which I could eat	ፍና ከመ እሴሰይ	23r	A way to eat
እንበለ ይጽልዑኒ ያስተዋድዩኒ ወይሰድዱኒ	23r	Without hating me, accusing me, or persecuting me	እንበለ ያስተዋድዩኒ ወይሰዱኒ	23r	Without accusing me, or persecuting me
ወአብድር ፍሬ ግማየ እሴሰይ ወእትገደፍ በኀበ ሰብእ	23r	And I would prefer to eat the fruit of my labour and to be forgotten by people	ወአብደርኩ እሴሰይ እምግብር እደውየ ወእትገደፍ	23r	And I prefer to eat from the work of my hands, and to be forgotten
መመሁቡኒ አልባሰ ወአጣሌ፣ ወጼው ወእክለ	23v	And they gave me clothes, and goats, and salt, and grain	ወየሁቡኒ አልባሰ ወአጣሌ፣ ወጼው	23v	And they were giving me clothes, and goats, and salt
ወአነሰ ሁብከ ዓስበ ሲሳየ ዘየአክለከ	24r	And I will give you your wage in enough food to feed yourself	ወአነ ሁብከ ዘትበልዕ	23v	And I will give you what you can eat
Chapter 12			Abb 234		
ወአአመርኩ ከመ ኢይደልዎ ለብእሲ ይንበር ባሕቲቶ እንዘ አልቦቱ ብእሲት	24r	And I knew that it's not fitting for a man to live alone without a wife	ወአአመርኩ ከመ ኢይኄይሥ ለብእሲ ይንበር ባሕቲቱ እንበለ ብእሲት	23v	I knew that it is not good for a man to live alone without a wife
እስመ ዝንቱ ፍና ይስሕብ ኀበ አበሳ	24r	Because this path draws one into sin	እስመ ዝንቱ ይስሕብ ኀበ አበሳ	23v	Because this draws one into sin
በዘኢኮነ ፍጥረቶሙ	24r	In a way that is not according to their nature	እንበለ በሥርዓተ ፍጥረቶሙ	23v	Except by their established created order

(continued)

	Abb 215			Abb 234	
	Folio	Literal Translation		Folio	Literal Translation
በከመ ተብህለ ለቀደምት ኢይሄኒ ይንበር ብእሲ ባሕቲቱ እስመ ይትፈቀድ ሎቱ ብእሲት	24r	As it was said for the ancients 'it is not good for a man to live alone. For a wife is needed for him'.	*Minus*	23v	
ኢኮንኩ	24r	I am not	አንስ ኢኮንኩ	23v	As for me, I am not
ገበሩ ለእግዚአ	24r	A servant of Lord	ገበሩ ለእግዚአ ሀብቱ	24r	A servant of Lord Habtu
ወእሉ እቤላ ትሥምሪኑ ትኩኒኒ ብእሲትየ	24v	And I asked her 'Would you agree to be my wife?'	ወእቤሌ ትፈቅድኑ [sic] ትኩኒኒ ብእሲትየ	24r	And I asked her, 'Would you like to be my wife?'
ወይእቲስ ትቤለኒ ወሠናይ ሊተ ወአይቴ እረክብ ዘይኄይሰኒ እምኔከ	24v	And she said to me, 'It's good with me, and where will I find one better than you?'	ወይእቲ ትቤ ሠናይ ሊተ እረክብት ዘይኄይሰኒ እምኔከ	24r	And she said, 'It's good with me. Will I find one better than you?'
ወንቤሎ ለእግዚአ ሀብቱ	24v	We said to Lord Habtu	ወንቤሎ ለሀብቱ	24r	We said to Habtu
ወሰብአ ቤቱ አሕመምዎ ዘልፉ	24v	And the people of his house had always made her suffer	ወሰብአ ቤቱ ያስተሐምሞዋ	24r	And the people of his house troubled her
ዘሀለው ህየ	25r	Who were there	ዘሀለው ዝየ	24v	Who were here
ወእግዚአ	25r	And the Lord	ወሀብቱስ	24v	And Habtu
ወልደ	25r	A child	ውሉደ	25r	Children
Base hand: አምፐ{ለ}ጥቅምት በዕለተ ሰኑይ	25r	*Base hand:* When it was the 10th of Teqemt on Monday	አም ፲ለጥቅምት በዕለተ ሠኑየ ሰኑይ	25r	When it was the 10th of Teqemt on <Monday> Monday
Secondary hand: አምፐ{፩}{ለ}ጥቅምት በዕለተ ሰኑይ		*Secondary hand:* When it was the 1{1}th {of} Teqemt on Monday			
አቡነ እፎንስ ሐረ	25v	Bishop Efons went	ሐረ እፎንስ	25r	Efons went. *Minus of* አቡነ *occurs twice on this folio*
መሰልክዎሙ ለሰብአ	25v	I seemed to the people	አመስሎሙ ለሰብአ	25r	I seem to the people

(continued)

Abb 215			Abb 234		
	Folio	Literal Translation		Folio	Literal Translation
አልብየ ጸላዒ ወአልብየ ፍቁር	25v	I have no enemies, and I have no friends	አልብየ ፀር ወኢፍቁር	25r	I have no adversary nor a friend
ወሊተ ኢይከውነኒ አትመየጥ ኀቤክሙ	25v	But I will not return to you	ወሊተስ ኢይትከሀለኒ አትመየጥ ኀቤክሙ	25v	But it is not possible for me to return to you
ሐረ አቡነ ኤፎንስ	25v	Bishop Efons had gone	ሐረ አቡነ ኤፎንስ ብሔሮ	25v	Bishop Efons had gone to his country
ዓዒ ያስተዋድየኒ	26r	He again began to make accusations against me	እንዘ ያስተዋድየኒ	25v	He was making accusations against me
መምህረ ፍራንጅ ውእቱ	26r	He is a foreign teacher	እስመ መምህረ ፍራንጂ ውእቱ	25v	For he is a foreign teacher
ዘይሜህር {በኀቡዕ}	26r	Who {secretly} teaches	ዘይምህር በኀቡእ	25v	Who secretly teaches
በእንተ ጽልሑቱ እስመ ቅድመ ይቤ በእንቲአየ	26r	Because of his malice for previously he had said of me...	በእንተ እኩዩ እስመ ቅድመ ይቤ	25v	Because of his evil for previously he had said...
Chapter 13			**Abb 234**		
እስመ {እለ} ተወክፉ	26v	Because {those who} welcomed	እስመ እለ ተወክፉ	26r	Because those who welcomed
ወእለ ተሰዱስ ፈደዮሙ ድኅረ በአጽራሪሆሙ ምስብዒተ	26v	Those who were persecuted later paid back their enemies sevenfold	ወድኅረ እለ ተሰዱ ፈደዩ ምስብዓት ላዕለ አፅራሪሆሙ	26r	*Transposition and a changed preposition*
ወይትዋጎጡ በበይናቲሆሙ ከመ ብልዓተ አክል	26v	And they devoured one another like they were eating a meal	*Minus*		
ወውእቱ ፋሲለደስ ኮነ ሐነባሬ እኪይ በኵሉ ወቀተለ ሰብአ እንበለ ፍትሕ	27r	This Fasiladas became a doer of wickedness in every respect. He unjustly killed people	ወኮነ ገባሬ ዓመፃ ወቀተለ ሰብአ ዘአልቦሙ ኍልቍ እንበለ ፍትሕ	26v	He became a violent man. He unjustly killed innumerable people
እስመ ጸንዑ በዕበዶሙ ወጽልዖሙ	27r	Because they persisted in their foolishness and their hatred.	*Minus*	26v	
ወመንፈቆሙ	27r	And half of them	እስመ መንፈቆሙ	26v	For half of them

(continued)

	Abb 215			Abb 234	
	Folio	Literal Translation		Folio	Literal Translation
ወአርኵስክሙዋ ለቤተ ክርስቲያን	27r	And defiled the Church	*Minus*	26v	
ወተዓደዉ ሥርዓተ ጽድቅ ዘእግዚአብሔር ዘሥርዓ ለኵላ ፍጥረት	27r-27v	And they had transgressed God's order of righteousness, which God had established for all creation	ወተዐደዉ ትእዛዘ እግዚአብሔር	27r	And they had transgressed God's command
ወሠዓሉ ሕገ ጠባይዊተ በእንተ ሕገጋተ ሰብአ	27v	They had violated natural law due to human laws	ወሠዓሉ ቃሎ ለእግዚአብሔር ዘይብለነ (ውስተ) ልቡናነ ኢትቅትል ወኢትግበር ለካልእከ ዘኢትፈቅድ ይግበሩ ለከ በእንተ ሥርዓቶሙ	27r	They had violated the word of God which says (in) our minds, 'do not kill, do not do to others what you do not want them to do to you', due to their precepts
ሃይማኖታቲሆሙ	27v	Their beliefs	ሃይማኖት	27v	Belief
ሤጥነ አልህምቲነ ወአልባሲነ ወስብሐት ለእግዚአብሔር	27v-28r	We sold our cows and clothes. And, praise be to God	ሤጥነ አልህምተ ወአልባሰ ወባቱ ስብሐት ለእግዚአብሔር	27v	We sold cows and clothes. But, praise be to God
ዳዕሙ	28r	Rather	አላ	27v	*Synonym, no difference in meaning*
ወተፈጸመ ብነ	28r	And it was fulfilled in us	ወተፈጸም [sic] ላዕሌነ	27v	And it was fulfilled over us
Chapter 14			**Abb 234**		
ወምትኩ አአመረ ዓዲ	28v	And Meketu had learned also	ወምትኩ ዓዲ አአመረ	28r	And Meketu also had learned
ወሰዋሰወ ወመጻሕፍት	28v	And the grammar and the scriptures	ወሰዋሰወ	28r	And the grammar
ወአልቦ ዘኅባዕኩ ሎቱ	28v	And there was nothing that I hid from him	*Minus*	28r	
ጸሐፍኩ ዘንተ ንስቲተ እምድኃር ሰአለኒ ብዙኃ ጊዜ	28v	I wrote this small work following his repeated requests.	እምድኃረ ሰአለኒ ብዙኃ ጊዜ ጸሐፍኩ ዘንተ ንስቲተ	28r	Following his repeated requests, I wrote this small work
Chapter 15			**Abb 234**		
ወሰበ ኮነ ዕደሜሁ መጠነ ፩ ዓመት	28v	And when he was 1 year old	ወሰበ ኮነ ዕደሜሁ መጠነ ፳ ዓመት	28r	And when he was 20 years old

(continued)

	Abb 215			**Abb 234**	
	Folio	Literal Translation		Folio	Literal Translation
ይኤብስ በኢያእምሮ አበሳ እንተ ትኤምር ኀበ መፍቅደ አውስቦ ሐዊወ ዘ...›	28v	He was sinning in ignorance of sin, which indicates the desire of marriage <spilling seed ...>	ይኤብስ በሥጋሁ በከዒወ [sic] ዘርእ በእንተ ጣዕም ዘይረክብ ቦቱ	28r	He was sinning in his flesh by spilling seed because of the pleasure that he would get from it
እስመ ይነስት ሥርዓት ዘሠርዓ ለነ ፈጣሪ	28v	Because it violates the rules which the Creator established for us	እስመ ይነሡት ሥ(ር)ዓተ ፈጣሪ	28r-28v	Because it violates the Creator's rules
ወንበር በሥርዓተ ፍጥረትነ	28v	And live according to the rules of our nature	ወንበር በከመ ይደሉ	28v	And live as is proper
ዘእምብሔረ ላምጌ	29r	Who was from the region of Lamge	Minus	28v	
ይትባረክ ይትባርክ እግዚአብሔር ብሂልያ	29r	Yetbarak, meaning, 'May God be blessed!'	ይትባርክ	28v	Yetbarak
ወለእም ከሠትኩ	29r	And if I reveal	እስም ለእም እከሥት	29r	For if I reveal
እንበለ ይድርፉኒ	29v	Rather they will insult me	እንበለ ይጽርፉ ላዕሌየ	29r	Rather they will insult against me
Minus	29v		እንበለ ዳዕሙ እከዮሙ	29r	Except for their evil deeds
እጽሐፍ ዘንተ	29v	I wanted to write this	እጽሐፍ ዘንተ ንስቲተ	29r	I wanted to write this short text
ለባዊ ብእሲ ወሐታቲ	29v	A wise and inquisitive person	ለባዊ	29r	A wise person
ናሁ ወጠንኩ አነ ሐቲትየ ዘኢተሐተተ ቅድመዝ ወእንተ ፈጸም ዘወጠንኩ አነ ‹ባሕቲትየ› ከመ ሰብእ ብሔርነ ይጥበቡ በረድኤተ እግዚአብሔር ወይብጽሑ ኀበ አእምሮ ጽድቅ	29v	Look, I began my inquiry, which has not been explored before this. Complete what I have begun <alone>, so that our nation's people might gain wisdom with God's help and arrive at the knowledge of truth	ወከመዝ ኵሎ ሰብእ ለእመ ይትከሀል ይብጽሑ በበንቲት ኀበ አእምሮ ጽድቅ	29r	In the same way all people, if they are able, should arrive gradually at knowledge of the truth

(continued)

	Abb 215			Abb 234	
	Folio	Literal Translation		Folio	Literal Translation
ይለብዉ ጽድቅ	29v	They might understand truth	ይለቡ ጥበበ ፈጣሪ ወይሰፈዉ ሳህሎ ወጽድቆ ወይጸልዩ ኃቤሁ በልብ ንጽሕ አመ ምንዳቤሆሙ	29r-29v	They might understand the Creator's wisdom, and set their hope on his mercy and truth, and pray to him with a pure heart when they suffer
ወያፍቅሩ አኃዊሆሙ	29v	And love their brothers	ወያፍቅሩ አኃዊሆሙ ከመ ነፍሰሙ	29v	And love their brothers as themselves
ወኢይትበአሱ እንከ	29v	And they would not fight with one another anymore	ወኢይትበዓሱ	29v	And they would not fight with one another
ዘይሌቡ ዘንተ ወዘይሤኒሂ እምዝንቱ ወይመህር ወይጽሕፎ	29v-30r	Who understands this and things even more excellent than this, and teaches and writes	ዘይሌቡ ከማየ	29v	Who understands like me
ዘአልቦ መሥፈርት	30r	Which is limitless	ዘአልቦ ኍልቋ	29v	Which is innumerable
ይጸርዉ ላዕሌየ በእንተ ዝንቱ መጽሐፍየ	30r	He slanders me because of this book	ይጸርዉ ላዕሌየ ወላዕለ መጽሐፍየ	29v	He slanders me and my book
ወኢይፈቅድ ይለቡ ከመ ይሠኒ	30r	And does not want to understand how to be better	Minus	29v	
አመ ነግሠ {ሞተ} ፋሲለደስ	30r	When Fasiladas <reigned> {died}	አመ ሞተ ሱሱንዮስ ፋሲለደስ ንጉሥ	29v	When <Susenyos> King Fasiladas died
ጸሐፈ ዘንተ መጽሐፈ	30r	He wrote this book	ጸሐፈ ዘንተ	29v	He wrote this
እንዘ ያፈቅሮ ለእግዚአብሔር ፈጣሪ ወይሴብሖ	30r	Loving God our creator and glorifying him	እንዘ ያፈቅር ወይሴብሖ ለእግዚአብሔር ፈጣሪ	29v	Loving and glorifying God our creator
ወኮነ ክቡረ ጥቀ	30r	And he became very honourable	ወኮነ ክቡረ	30r	And he became honourable
ዘተሰመይኩ ምትኩ	30v	Who is known as Metekku,	ዘተበህልኩ ምትኩ	30v	Who is called Metekku,

Appendix 1: Chart of Differences — **187**

(continued)

	Abb 215			Abb 234	
	Folio	Literal Translation		Folio	Literal Translation
ወሰኩ ዘንተ ንስቲተ ላዕለ መጽሐፈ መምህርየ ከመ ታአምሩ ድኃሪቶ ሠናየ	30v	I added this little bit to my teacher's book, so that you may know the beautiful end of his life	ወሰኩ ዝየ ዘንተ ንስቲተ	30v	I added this little bit here
ወዘሀረኒ {ዘርዐ ያዕቆብ ፶ወ፱ ዓመተ ናሁ ጸሐፍኩ አነሂ ካልአ መጽሐፈ ለአእምሮ ወለተግሣጽ [sic] ውሉደ ኢትዮጵያ}	30v	And what {Zara Yaqob} taught me {for 59 years. Behold I too, wrote another book for knowledge, and reprimand of Ethiopia's children}	ወዘመሐሉ(ሀ)ረኒ ዘርአ ያዕቆብ ፶ወ፱ ዓመት ናሁ ጸሐፍኩ ወአነሂ [sic] ካልአ መጽሐፈ ለአእምሮ ወለተግሣጽ ውሉደ ኢትዮጵያ	30v	And what Zara Yaqob taught me 59 years, behold I too, wrote another book for knowledge, and reprimand of Ethiopia's children
{የሀቦሙ እግዚአብሔር ልቡና ወጥበ ወፍቅረ ወይባርኮሙ ለዓለመ ዓለም አሜን}	30v	{May God give them understanding and wisdom and love, and may he bless them forever and ever. Amen!}	የሀቦሙ እግዚአብሔር ልቡና ወፍቅረ ወይባርኮሙ ለዓለመ ዓለም አሜን	30v	May God give them understanding and love, and may he bless them forever and ever. Amen!
{ተፈጸመ ዛቲ መጽሐፍ} [sic]	30v	{The end of this book}	ይባርክ እግዚአብሔር በበረከት ዘርአ ያዕቆብ ለገብሩ ወልደ ጊዮርጊስ ዘአጽሐፎ ለዝንቱ መጽሐፍ ከመ በረከተ እግዚአብሔር የሀሎ ም[ስ]ሌሁ ዘልፈ ወለጸሐፊሁ ወልደ ዮሴፍ ለዓለመ ዓለም አሜን ለይኩን ለይኩን	30v	May God bless, with the [same] blessing [as] Zara Yaqob, his servant Walda Giyorgis, who enabled this book to be written down so that God's blessing would always be with him, and also bless his scribe Walda Yosef, forever and ever. Amen! Let it be, let it be.

Jeremy R. Brown and Wendy Laura Belcher
Appendix 2: Scribal Intervention in Abb 215 and Abb 234

Both manuscript witnesses to the *Hatata Zara Yaqob* and the *Hatata Walda Heywat* demonstrate a considerable amount of scribal intervention. The techniques utilized by the Ethiopian scribe in Abb 215 are typical of Ethiopian scribal culture: interlinear insertion of text; insertion of text in the upper margin and located with an *ancora* symbol; text marked for erasure with lines, dots, or circles; and text that has been erased or washed away. Giusto da Urbino's techniques in Abb 234 are more idiosyncratic. To learn more about the manuscripts as a whole, see the Manuscripts of the Texts section.

Abb 215

Abb 215 has two separate layers of text insertion interventions (see Figure 7). The first layer consists of those proposed by the same scribe who copied the base text, Gabra Maryam. Gabra Maryam wrote his interventions in dark ink, the same ink as the base text. The second layer consists of insertions written by a second, unknown scribe in a different hand and in a much lighter ink. These two layers are distinguished in the chart below. Regarding the text erasure interventions, one cannot detect the hand that erased material and so they are treated together in the chart.

Almost three quarters of the scribal interventions in Abb 215 move the text into alignment with the text that appears in Abb 234 (see the discussion in Manuscripts of the Texts section). This suggests a proofreading pass through the manuscript, comparing Abb 215 with MS β (see Figure 4). Of the scribal interventions that do not move Abb 215 towards alignment with Abb 234, half are just single letter spelling corrections. The remaining changes, about a tenth of all the changes, do not align the text with Abb 234 but rather are small substantive corrections. They are as follows:

1. F. 5r: Insertion of the particle እም 'if' by the base hand. This is likely the scribe Gabra Maryam clarifying the text.
2. F. 9r: Addition of the grammatically required word መሀመድ (Mohammed) by the secondary hand.
3. F. 11r and f. 21r: Removal of the erroneous negation particle ኢ..

4. F. 16r: Addition of the grammatically required word 'Creator' in the phrase ፈቃደ {ፈጣሪ} (will of {the Creator}) by the secondary hand. Abb 234 reads almost alike: ፈቃደ እግዚአብሔር (will of God).
5. F. 25r: Editing the date to be the 11th rather than the 10th of the month by the secondary hand. For discussion of this correct intervention, see The Authorship of the *Hatata Inquiries* section.
6. F. 28v: Erasure of a line of text about masturbation. For a discussion of this, the largest substantive intervention, see Manuscripts of the Texts. For an image of it, see Figure 6.
7. F. 29v: Marking for erasure the word ባሕቲትየ (I alone).
8. F. 29v: Marking for erasure the word በእንተ (about). This is the lone example of a word attested in Abb 234 being marked for erasure in Abb 215, thus moving the text of Abb 215 away from the text of Abb 234. However, it is possible that this word was mistakenly marked for erasure by a reader falsely believing that the phrase በእንተ በእንተ was a case of dittography, as they appear quite similar in this scribal hand.

	Number	Percent
Total interventions	71	100%
Total base hand insertion interventions	10	14%
-7 letters written interlineally		
-3 words written interlineally		
Total secondary hand insertion interventions	31	44%
-13 letters written interlinearly		
-14 words written interlinearly		
-4 words written in the upper margin		
Total erasure interventions	30	42%
-27 letters or words marked for erasure		
-3 letters or words that have been erased		
Interventions aligning with text of Abb 234	52	73%
Base hand interventions	6	60%
Secondary hand interventions	26	84%
Erasures	20	67%
Interventions not aligning with Abb 234	19	27%
Simple spelling corrections	10	53%
Substantive corrections (see list above)	9	15%

Figure 7: Scribal Interventions in Abb 215.

Abb 234

The scribal interventions in Abb 234 are different from those in Abb 215 (see Figure 8). First, only one scribe seems to be at work. The nature of the hand and the ink suggests that the same scribe who copied the base text, Giusto da Urbino, made the insertion interventions. Second, two types of intervention are not typical of Ethiopian scribal culture but seem to be peculiar to Giusto da Urbino. Likely this is because he produced Abb 234 on paper not parchment, the medium usually used by Geʿez scribes. Paper limits a scribe's erasure options because it is thin and porous. A penknife that easily scrapes away ink on parchment cuts through paper. Water that easily washes away ink on parchment leaves an unsightly smudge on paper.

One type of unusual intervention Giusto da Urbino made was marking a letter for erasure and then immediately following it with an interchangeable letter. This is a form of spelling correction. Yet the spellings that Giusto da Urbino was amending were not misspellings, but rather acceptable alternate spellings. The Ethiopic script has many letters that no longer have discernible sound differences and have become interchangeable. Thus, Giusto da Urbino is changing an accepted and clear alternate spelling toward a common lexical form. This systematic emendation of interchangeable letters towards the lexical form does not occur in manuscripts copied by Ethiopian or Eritrean scribes. It seems likely that MS β had the alternate spelling and Giusto da Urbino amended the spelling towards the lexical form in Abb 234.[1] Giusto da Urbino laboured to create a Geʿez lexicon during his stay in Ethiopia and so may have been motivated to document lexical forms in his own scribal work.

Giusto da Urbino used this unusual technique to mark interchangeable letters seventeen times (20 percent of the interventions in this manuscript). For example, on f. 6v, he crossed out the letter ሐ (ḥa) and then followed it with the letter ሀ (ha): ሐሀያይማኖትዎ. On f. 15r, he marked for erasure the letter ዐ (ʿ) and followed it with the letter አ (ʾ): ኃጥዐአ. In two-thirds of the cases, both characters fit on the line; neither is added above or below the line, and neither is squeezed in. This evidences that many of the changes were made immediately in the process of the original copying and not added later.

The other type of unusual intervention is related to the first: marking a whole word for erasure and then immediately following it with a 'correct' word.[2] This occurs in four instances in Abb 234. On f. 2v, he marked for erasure the word ዓሙት

---

[1] This also suggests that Giusto da Urbino was copying MS β letter-by-letter rather than word-by-word or even phrase-by-phrase.
[2] Of the 63 total erasure interventions in Abb 234, 61 are marked for erasure, one character is washed away, and one character is crossed out and obscured.

(years) and followed it with the correct word አውራኅ (months). On f. 3v, he marked for erasure the word ዐቢይ (great) followed it with a verbal form of the same root: አዐቢ. (I was greater). On f. 25r, he marked for erasure the word ሠኑይ (Monday) and followed it with a different spelling: ሰኑይ (Monday). (This fits the first type; he merely did not notice the substandard lexical form until he had completed copying the word.) Finally, on f. 29v, he marked for erasure the king's name ሱሱንዮስ (Susenyos) and followed it with the correct historical figure, the king ፋሲለደስ (Fasiladas). Again, these words fit the line perfectly, neither is added above or below the line nor squeezed in, evidencing that the change was made immediately.

As for the four occurrences of whole words marked for erasure and followed by a correction, it is important to note that the corrected reading is shared with Abb 215 in all four occurrences. Given that Abb 234 and Abb 215 do not have a directly shared exemplar, this suggests that Giusto da Urbino introduced these four errors copying from MS β and immediately caught them and corrected them. Again, he could not erase the error because of the writing medium.

Total interventions	86	100%
Total insertion interventions	23	27%
-17 letters written interlinearly -5 words written interlinearly -1 word written in the upper margin		
Total erasure interventions	63	73%
-61 letters or words marked for erasure -1 letter washed away -1 letter crossed out and obscured		

Figure 8: Scribal Interventions in Abb 234.

Contributors

Dr. Ralph Lee has been a teaching associate in World Christianities at the School of Oriental and African Studies, UK, since the summer of 2018. He lived and worked in Ethiopia for over sixteen years, teaching theology in Ethiopia, including teaching at the EOTC's Holy Trinity Theological College from 2008 to 2014. Lee's book *Symbolic Interpretations in Ethiopic and Early Syriac Literature* (published by Peeters Louvain) is a comparison of symbolic motifs on the Ark of the Covenant, the Cross, and Paradise in Ethiopic and early Syriac literature. Since 2017, Lee has been a member of the team updating and improving the cataloguing of Ethiopian manuscripts in the largest online resource of this material at the Hill Museum and Manuscript Library at St. John's University in Minnesota. He is also a Research Associate and doctoral supervisor at the Institute of Orthodox Christian Studies, Cambridge. Lee has published extensively on Ethiopia for the last two decades, for example in *The Encyclopedia of Christianity in the Global South* (2018), *Textual History of the Bible* (Vol. 1, 2016), *Journal of Ecclesiastical History*, and *Journal for the Study of the Pseudepigrapha*.

Mehari Worku is completing his doctorate in the study of the Christian Near East in the Department of Semitic and Egyptian Languages and Literatures at The Catholic University of America in 2023. An Ethiopian raised in the EOTC and schooled in its traditional system of education, he is an expert on Geʽez language and literature. At Addis Ababa University, he received a BA in Ethiopian Languages and Literature and a master's in African Languages and Applied Linguistics. He went on to teach in the AAU Department of Ethiopian Languages and Literature for eight years, until 2015. He has published his research on Ethiopian language politics, the Amharic philosophy of culture, Christian theology, and the Taʾammera Maryam (Miracles of Mary). The title of his dissertation is 'The Fifteenth-Century Ethiopian Orthodox Ecclesiology of Giyorgis of Sagla's መጽሐፈ፡ ምሥጢር (Mäṣḥafä Məsṭir, The Book of Mystery).' In his position as Researcher, Cataloger, and Translator for the Princeton Ethiopian, Eritrean, and Egyptian Miracles of Mary (PEMM) project, he has cataloged over 30 manuscripts of the Taʾammera Maryam and translated over 150 of its stories from Geʽez into English. He holds a position as Visiting Assistant Professor of Church History and Ethiopic Christianity at Agora University.

Dr. Wendy Laura Belcher is Professor of African literature with a joint appointment in the Princeton University Department of Comparative Literature and the Department for African American Studies. She is working to bring attention to early African literature and African language literature, especially that in Geʽez (classical Ethiopic), through scholarship and translation. She has many books and articles and is the co-translator (with Michael Kleiner) of perhaps the first biography of an African woman, originally written in Geʽez, *The Life and Struggles of Our Mother Walatta Petros: A Seventeenth-Century African Biography of an Ethiopian Woman* (Princeton University Press 2015), for which they received the Society for the Study of Early Modern Women award for the best Scholarly Edition in Translation of 2015 and the Paul Hair Award for Best Critical Edition or Translation into English of Primary Source Materials on Africa in 2015–2017. She also has several books in progress. One is related to the PEMM project, funded by two substantial NEH grants, and is titled *Ladder of Heaven: The Miracles of the Virgin Mary in African Literature and Art*.

Dr. Jeremy R. Brown is Cataloger of Ethiopic Manuscripts at the Hill Museum and Manuscript Library (HMML). He is also senior researcher on Princeton Ethiopian, Eritrean, and Egyptian Miracles of Mary (PEMM) project and was a visiting assistant professor in the Department of Semitic and Egyptian Languages and Literatures at The Catholic University of America, where he taught courses on Geʽez and Syriac. He is an expert on ancient and medieval Ethiopian history and religion broadly, with specialties in Ge'ez manuscripts, philology, biblical tradition, and hagiographies. He is coauthor of several volumes in the *Catalogue of the Ethiopic Manuscript Imaging Project* series. He was the director of digitization for the six-month British Library's Endangered Archives program to complete the digitization of the manuscript collection of the Institute of Ethiopian Studies in Addis Ababa.

Dag Herbjørnsrud is a global historian of ideas with a *candidatus philologiae* degree from the University of Oslo, Norway. He is a former reporter and op-ed writer at Norway's largest non-tabloid newspaper *Aftenposten* (1995–2005) and the former Scandinavian columnist for Al Jazeera's English website (2004–05). In 2015, Herbjørnsrud established the Center for Global and Comparative History of Ideas (SGOKI) with support from the Arts Council Norway. SGOKI has become a partner of Centre for Global Knowledge Studies (Gloknos) at the University of Cambridge and the Quantum Bio Lab at Howard University. He was guest editor of the journal *Cosmopolis* (Brussels) special issue on 'Decolonizing the Academy'. He has published several books, including *Globalkunnskap* (*Global Knowledge. Renaissance for a New Enlightenment*, Scandinavian Academic Press, second edition 2018). His journal article 'Beyond decolonizing: global intellectual history and reconstruction of a comparative method' in *Global Intellectual History* (May 2019) is one of its most downloaded and cited articles.

Bibliography

Abbadie, Antoine d'. 1859. *Catalogue raisonné de manuscrits éthiopiens*. Paris: Editions.

Abdullahi, Ali Arazeem, and Bashir Salawu. 2012. 'Ibn Khaldun: A Forgotten Sociologist?' *South African Review of Sociology* 43 (3):24–40. doi: 10.1080/21528586.2012.727543.

Abraham, William E. 2004. 'Amo's Critique of Descartes' Philosophy of Mind'. In *A Companion to African Philosophy*, edited by Kwasi Wiredu, 200–215. Malden: Blackwell.

Adamson, Peter. 2022. 'The Place of Ethiopian Philosophy in the History of Philosophy'. Paper presented at the *In Search of Zara Yaqob* Conference, Oxford University, 29 April.

Alaka Imbakom Kalewold. 1970. *Traditional Ethiopian Church Education*. New York: Teachers College Press.

Alemayyehu Moges. 1968. 'Hatata Zer'a Ya'ekob'. PhD diss., Haile Selassie I University (Addis Ababa University).

Alemayyehu Moges. 1970. 'Geez and Amharic Study Without Qene Is Incomplete'. In *Proceedings of the Third International Conference of Ethiopian Studies*, 99–116. Addis Ababa: Institute of Ethiopian Studies.

Amo, Anton Wilhelm. 1968. *Antonius Guilielmus Amo: Translation of His Works [into English]*. Translated by Dorothea Siegmund-Schultze. Halle: Martin Luther University Halle-Wittenberg.

Amo, Anton Wilhelm. 2020. *Anton Wilhelm Amo's Philosophical Dissertations on Mind and Body*. Translated by Stephen Menn and Justin E. H. Smith. Oxford: Oxford University Press.

Amo, Anton Wilhelm, and T. Uzodinma Nwala. 1990. *Anton William Amo's treatise on the art of philosophising soberly and accurately (with commentaries)*. Nsukka: William Amo Centre for African Philosophy, University of Nigeria.

Amsalu Aklilu. 1961. 'ዜርእ ያዕቆብ ፈላሳፊው (Zera Yacob the Philosopher)'. *Tarik: gazette d'information archeologique, historie et litteraire (published by the Institute of Ethiopian Archaeology)* 1:11–13.

Amsalu Aklilu. 1984. 'አጭር የኢትዮጵያ ሥነ ጽሑፍ ታሪክ (Aççär yä-'Ityopya śännä ṣaḥuf tarik; A Short History of Ethiopian Literature)'. MA thesis, Department of Ethiopian Languages and Literature, Addis Ababa University.

Annesley, Viscount Valentia George. 1809. *Voyages and Travels to . . . Abyssinia . . . in the Years 1802, 1803, 1804, 1805, 1806*. 3 vols. Vol. 3. London.

Anonymous, ed. 1906. *Vitae sanctorum indigenarum I: Acts s. Eustathii*. Edited by Carlo Conti Rossini. *Corpus scriptorum Christianorum orientalium, v. 32. Scriptores Aethiopici v. 15*. Paris: E Typographeo Reipublicae.

Anonymous. 1961. እንጋረ ፈላስፋ *(The Sayings of the Philosophers)*. Translated by Mogas Equba Giyorgis. Asmara.

Anonymous. forthcoming 2025. *The Kebra Nagast: A New English Translation of the Ancient Book about Glorious Monarchs, including the Ethiopian Queen of Sheba, King Solomon, and Their Son Menilek*. Translated by Wendy Laura Belcher and Michael Kleiner. Princeton: Princeton University Press.

Asale, Bruk A. 2016. 'The Ethiopian Orthodox Tewahedo Church Canon of the Scriptures: Neither Open nor Closed'. *The Bible Translator* 67 (2):202–222. doi: 10.1177/205167701665148

Bahru Zewde. 1968. 'Consolidator, Zera Yacob: Ethiopian Philosopher'. *The Ethiopian Herald* (10 January):3. Accessed 14 June 2023. https://gpa.eastview.com/crl/ean/newspapers/ethe19680110-01.1.2.

Bailey, Moses. 1921. 'The Philosophy of Zar'a Ya'kob'. *The Moslem World* 11 (1):281–295. doi: 10.1111/j.1478-1913.1921.tb01863.x.

Barbour, Bernard, and Michelle Jacobs. 1985. 'The Mi'raj al-Su'ud: A Legal Treatise on Slavery by Ahmad Baba'. In *Slaves and Slavery in Africa: Volume One: Islam and the Ideology of Enslavement*, edited by John Ralph Willis, 125–159. London: Frank Cass & Co.

Baumstark, Anton. 1911. *Die christlichen literaturen des Orients*. Leipzig: G.F. Goschen'scher Verlagshandlung.

Belcher, Wendy Laura. 2000. 'Out of Africa: Why Do So Many Travel Books about Africa Start the Same Way?'. In *Salon.com's Wanderlust: Real-Life Tales of Adventure and Romance*, 214–226. New York: Villard Books.

Bell, Richard H., and Jan Fernback. 2015. *Understanding African Philosophy: A Cross-cultural Approach to Classical and Contemporary issues*. New York and London: Routledge.

Bezold, Carl. 1907. Review of 'Philosophi Abessini. Edidit et interpretatus est Enno Littmann'. *Deutsche Literaturzeitung* 28 (20):1242–1244.

Binns, John. 2016. *The Orthodox Church of Ethiopia: A History*. London: I. B. Tauris.

Bonus, Albert. 1905. 'An Abyssinian Christian Freethinker'. *The Expository Times* 16 (10):453–455.

Bourgade, Francois. 1847. *Soirées de Carthage ou Dialogues entre un prêtre catholique, un muphti et un cadi*. Paris: Firmin-Didot.

Browder, Laura. 2000. *Slippery Characters: Ethnic Impersonators and American Identities*. Chapel Hill: University of North Carolina Press.

Budge, E. A. Wallis, ed. 1928. *The Book of the Saints of the Ethiopian Church: A Translation of the Ethiopic Synaxarium: Made from the Manuscripts Oriental 660 and 661 in the British Museum*. 4 vols. Cambridge: Cambridge University Press.

Cerulli, Enrico. 1926. 'Nuove idee nell'Etiopia e nuova letteratura amarica'. *Oriente Moderno* 6 (3):167–173.

Chemeda Bokora. 2004. Zar'a Ya'eqob's Argument for the Existence of God. *Meskot: An Ethiopian Online Journal*. Accessed 14 June 2023. www.meskot.com/Ethio_Philosophers3.pdf.

Chernetsov, Sevir. 2005. 'Education: Traditional Church Education'. In *Encyclopaedia Aethiopica: D-Ha: Vol. 2*, edited by Siegbert Uhlig, 228–230. Wiesbaden: Harrassowitz.

Cleaveland, Timothy. 2015. 'Ahmad Baba al-Timbukti and His Islamic Critique of Racial Slavery in the Maghrib'. *The Journal of North African Studies* 20 (1):42–64. doi: 10.1080/13629387.2014.983825.

Cohen, Leonardo. 2007. 'Mendes, Afonso'. In *Encyclopaedia Aethiopica: He-N: Vol. 3*, edited by Siegbert Uhlig, 920–921. Wiesbaden: Harrassowitz.

Conti Rossini, Carlo. 1912. *Catalogue des manuscrits éthiopiens de la collection Antoine d'Abbadie, Paris*. Paris: Imprimerie nationale.

Conti Rossini, Carlo. 1916. *Vicende dell'Etiopia e delle missioni cattoliche ai tempi di ras Ali, deggiâc Ubié e re Teodoro secondo un documento abissinio*. Rome: Tipografia della R. Accademia dei Lincei.

Conti Rossini, Carlo. 1918. 'L'autobiografia di Pawlos, monaco abissino del secolo XVI'. *RRAL (Rendiconti della Reale Accademia dei Lincei)* series 5 (27):279–296.Conti Rossini, Carlo. 1920. 'Lo Ḥatatā Zar'a Yā'qob e il Padre Giusto da Urbino'. *RRAL (Rendiconti della Reale Accademia dei Lincei)* series 5 (29):213–223.Conti Rossini, Carlo. 1935. 'L'Etiopia è incapace di progresso civile'. *La Nuova Antologia* (16 September):171–177.

Conti Rossini, Carlo. 2022. 'The Hatatā Zar'a Yā'qob and Father Giusto Da Urbino'. Translated by Lea Cantor. Unpublished. Original publication, 1920.

Conti Rossini, Carlo, and Bibliothèque nationale Département des manuscrits BNF. 1914. *Notice sur les manuscrits éthiopiens de la collection d'Abbadie*. Paris: Imprimerie nationale.

Contri, Siro. 1957. 'Zar'a, Yā'qob'. In *Enciclopedia FIlosofica*, col. 1818. Rome: Istituto per la Collaborazione Culturale.

Cowley, Roger W. 1974. 'The Biblical Canon of the Ethiopian Orthodox Church Today'. *Ostkirchliche Studien* 23 (4):318–323.
Crummey, Donald. 2007. 'Jacobis, Giustino De'. In *Encyclopaedia Aethiopica: He-N: Vol. 3*, edited by Siegbert Uhlig, 263–265. Wiesbaden: Harrassowitz.
da Sessano, Carmelo. 1951. 'GIUSTO da Urbino (Cortopassi)'. *Enciclopedia cattolica* 6:col. 863.
Damon-Guillot, Anne. 2014. 'Zema'. In *Encyclopaedia Aethiopica: Y-Z: Vol. 5*, edited by Alessandro Bausi and Siegbert Uhlig, 174. Wiesbaden: Harrassowitz.
Daniel Kibret. 2019. የሌለውን ፈላስፋ ፍለጋ እና ሌሎች *(Yelewun Felasfa Filega ena Leloch)*. Addis Ababa: Agios Printers.
Dawit Worku, Kidane. 2012. *The Ethics of Zara Yaqob: A Reply to the Historical and Religious Violence in the Seventeenth-Century Ethiopia*. Rome: Editrice Pontificia Università Gregoriana.
Dege-Müller, Sophia. 2020. 'The Manuscript Tradition of the Betä Ǝsraʾel (Ethiopian Jews): Form and Content; A Preliminary Analysis'. *COMSt Bulletin* 6 (1):5–40.
Delamarter, Stephen. 2022. 'Analysis of Vatican Ethiopic Psalter, Shelf mark Borg.et.8'. Email, 25 December.
Descartes, René. 1911 [1641]. *Meditations On First Philosophy*. In *The Philosophical Works of Descartes*, translated by Elizabeth S. Haldane. Cambridge: Cambridge University Press.
Dillmann, August. 1899. *Grammatik der äthiopischen Sprache*. Leipzig: Chr. Herm. Tauchnitz.
Dore, Gianni. 2003. 'Identity and Contemporary Representations: The Heritage of Alberto Pollera's Monograph 'I Baria ei Kunama''. *Northeast African Studies* 10 (3):71–99. Doi: 10.1353/nas.0.0018.
Egid, Jonathan, Lea Cantor, and Fasil Merawi. 2022. *In Search of Zara Yaqob Conference*, Worcester College, University of Oxford, 29–30 April. Ephraim Isaac. 2012. *The Ethiopian Orthodox Täwahïdo Church*. Lawrenceville: Red Sea Press.
Eyasu Berento. 2022. 'Zera Yacob and Wolde Hiwot: Seventeenth-century Ethiopia Freethinkers: Exceptionality and Situated-ness of the 'Hatetas' in the Ethiopian Intellectual Tradition'. Paper presented at the *In Search of Zara Yaqob* Conference, Oxford University, 30 April.
Eze, Emmanuel Chukwudi. 2008. *On Reason: Rationality in a World of Cultural Conflict and Racism*. Durham: Duke University Press.
Fasil Merawi. 2022. 'Examining the Hatetas as a Foundation of Ethiopian Philosophy'. Paper presented at the *In Search of Zara Yaqob* Conference, Oxford University, 30 April.
Fiaccadori, Gianfranco. 2005. 'Ewosṭatewos'. In *Encyclopaedia Aethiopica: D-Ha: Vol. 2*, edited by Siegbert Uhlig, 469–472. Wiesbaden: Harrassowitz.
Fisseha Taddese. 2014. 'Zara Yaqob Was Not Ethiopian [Hatata Debates]'. *On Shegar Cafe Podcast* by Zelalem Kibret. Addis Ababa, Ethiopia. 40:47 minutes. Accessed 14 June 2023. https://soundcloud.com/zelalem-1/zara-yaqob-was-not-ethiopian.
Fraser, Chris. 2002. Mohism. *Stanford Encyclopedia of Philosophy*. Accessed 14 June 2023. https://plato.stanford.edu/entries/mohism/
Gälawdewos. 2015. *The Life and Struggles of Our Mother Walatta Petros: A Seventeenth-Century African Biography of an Ethiopian Woman*. Translated by Wendy Laura Belcher and Michael Kleiner. Edited by Wendy Laura Belcher and Michael Kleiner. Princeton: Princeton University Press.
Getatchew Haile. 1983. 'The Cause of the Estifanosites: A Fundamentalist Sect in the Church of Ethiopia'. *Paideuma* 29:93–119.
Getatchew Haile. 2004. ደቂቀ እስጢፋኖስ 'በሕግ አምላክ' *(Däqiqä Ǝsṭifanos 'Bä-ḥeggä Amlak'; Children of Stephen: 'For the Sake of the God of the Just Law!')*. Collegeville: Saint John's University, Hill Museum and Manuscript Library.
Getatchew Haile. 2005. 'The Works of Ras Səmʿon of Hagärä Maryam'. *Journal of Ethiopian Studies* 38 (1/2):5–95.

Getatchew Haile. 2017. 'The Discourse of Wärqe. Commonly Known as Ḥatäta zä-Zär'a Yaəqob'. In *Ethiopian Studies in Honour of Amha Asfaw*. New York: Getatchew Haile.
Getatchew Haile. 2018. ስለ ግዕዝ ሥነ ጽሑፍ የተሰበሰቡ አንዳንድ ማስታወሻዎች *(A Few Notes Collected about Gəʿəz literature)*. New York: Getatchew Haile.
Gizaw Belayneh. 2005. 'Ethiopian Philosophy on Women: A Critical Analysis'. BA thesis, Department of Philosophy, Addis Ababa University.
Gobezayehu Baye. 2005. 'A Critical Analysis of the Two Classical Philosophers of Ethiopia: Zera Yacob and Wolde Heywot in Terms of Their Metaphysical and Moral Philosophy'. BA thesis, Department of Philosophy, Addis Ababa University.
Gokhale, Pradeep P. 2015. *Lokāyata/Cārvāka: A Philosophical Inquiry*. Oxford: Oxford University Press.
Grébaut, Sylvain. 1926. 'Recherches philologiques en Éthiopie pour la bibliothèque Vaticane'. *Journal asiatique* 209:170–172.
Grébaut, Sylvain. 1935. *Édition des spécimens poétiques recueillis par Juste d'Urbin et ajoutés à sa grammaire éthiopienne*. New York: Alma Egan Hyatt Foundation.
Grébaut, Sylvain, and Eugène Tisserant. 1935. *Codices Aethiopici Vaticani et Borgiani*. Rome: Biblioteca Apostolica Vaticana.
Gribbin, John, and Mary Gribbin. 2022. *On the Origin of Evolution: Tracing 'Darwin's Dangerous Idea' from Aristotle to DNA*. Lanham: Prometheus Books.
Guidi, Ignazio. 1932. *Storia della letteratura etiopica*. Rome: Istituto per l'Oriente.
Habtemichael Kidane. 2007a. 'Mäṣḥaf bet'. In *Encyclopaedia Aethiopica: He-N: Vol. 3*, edited by Siegbert Uhlig, 834. Wiesbaden: Harrassowitz.
Habtemichael Kidane. 2007b. 'Nəbab bet'. In *Encyclopaedia Aethiopica: He-N: Vol. 3*, edited by Siegbert Uhlig, 1159–1161. Wiesbaden: Harrassowitz.
Habtemichael Kidane. 2010. 'Qəne'. In *Encyclopaedia Aethiopica: O-X: Vol. 4*, edited by Siegbert Uhlig, 283–285. Wiesbaden: Harrassowitz.
Habtemichael Kidane. 2014. 'Zema Bet'. In *Encyclopaedia Aethiopica: Y-Z: Vol. 5*, edited by Alessandro Bausi and Siegbert Uhlig, 175. Wiesbaden: Harrassowitz.
Harden, John Mason. 1926. *An Introduction to Ethiopic Christian Literature*. London: Macmillan.
Herbjørnsrud, Dag. 2020. 'The Untold History of India's Vital Atheist Philosophy'. *Blog of the American Philosophical Association (APA)*. Accessed 14 June 2023. https://blog.apaonline.org/2020/06/16/the-untold-history-of-indias-vital-atheist-philosophy/.
Herbjørnsrud, Dag. 2021a. 'The Quest for a Global Age of Reason. Part I: Asia, Africa, the Greeks, and the Enlightenment Roots'. *Dialogue and Universalism* 31 (3):113–131. doi: 10.5840/du202131349
Herbjørnsrud, Dag. 2021b. 'The Quest for a Global Age of Reason: Part II Cultural Appropriation and Racism in the Name of Enlightenment'. *Dialogue and Universalism* 31 (3):131–155. doi: 10.5840/du202131349.
Hobbes, Thomas. 1968 [1651]. *Leviathan (The Pelican Classics)*. London: Penguin.
Hopfmann, Jürgen 1992. *Altäthiopische Volksweisheiten im historischen Gewand: Legenden, Geschichten, Philosophien*. Frankfurt am Main: Lang.
Isocrates. 1966. *Isocrates: With an English Translation in Three Volumes*. Translated by George Norlin. 3 vols. Vol. 3. London: William Heinemann.
Jasnow, Richard, and Karl-Theodor Zauzich. 2005. *The Ancient Egyptian Book of Thoth: A Demotic Discourse On Knowledge and Pendant to the Classical Hermetica: Vol. 1: Text*. 2 vols. Vol. 1. Wiesbaden: Otto Harrassowitz.
Kamil, Murad. 1945. 'Ethiopian Philosophers of the 17th Century'. *The Ethiopian Herald* (14 July):3. Accessed 14 June 2023. https://gpa.eastview.com/crl/ean/newspapers/ethe19450714-01.1.3

Kiros, Teodros. 2001. 'Zara Yacob: A Seventeenth Century Ethiopian Founder of Modernity in Africa'. In *Explorations in African Political Thought: Identity, Community, Ethics*, edited by Teodros Kiros, 69–79. London: Routledge.
Kiros, Teodros. 2004. 'Zera Yacob and Traditional Ethiopian Philosophy'. In *A Companion to African Philosophy*, edited by Kwasi Wiredu, 183–190. Oxford: Blackwell.
Kiros, Teodros. 2005a. 'Zara Yacob and Descartes'. In *African Philosophy at the Threshold of the New Millennium. Papers of the Annual Conference of the International Society for African Philosophy and Studies*, edited by Bekele Gutema and Daniel Smith, 25–32. Addis Ababa: Addis Ababa University Press.
Kiros, Teodros. 2005b. *Zara Yacob: Rationality of the Human Heart*. Lawrenceville: Red Sea Press.
Kiros, Teodros. 2022. 'Zara Yacob and the Rationality of the Human Heart'. *Intellectus: The African Journal of Philosophy* 1 (1):108–111.
Knibb, Michael A., and Edward Ullendorf. 1978a. *The Ethiopic Book of Enoch: A New Edition in the Light of the Aramaic Dead Sea Fragments: Vol. 1: Text and Apparatus*. 2 vols. Vol. 1. Oxford and New York: Clarendon Press and Oxford University Press.
Knibb, Michael A., and Edward Ullendorf. 1978b. *The Ethiopic Book of Enoch: A New Edition in the Light of the Aramaic Dead Sea Fragments: Vol. 2: Introduction, Translation and Commentary*. 2 vols. Vol. 2. Oxford and New York: Clarendon Press and Oxford University Press.
Kostadinov, Boyan. 2013. 'Simulation insights using R'. *PRIMUS* 23 (3):208–223. Doi: 10.1080/10511970.2012.718729
Krackovskii, Ignati Iulianovic. 1924. 'Zara-Jacob ili Džusto da Urbino'. *Izvestija Rossiskoj Akademii Rauk* Series 6(1–11):195–206.
Krause, Andrej. 2003. 'Spezielle Metaphysik in der Untersuchung des Zara Jacob (1599–1692)'. *Archiv für Geschichte der Philosophie* 85:331–345. Doi: 10.1515/agph.2003.016
Krause, Andrej. 2006. 'Zar'a-Jacob und Walda-Heiwat über die Rationalität religiöser Aussagen'. *Beiträge der Österreichischen Ludwig Wittgenstein Gesellschaft* 14:153–155.
Krishnakumar, Anita S. 2011. 'Passive-Voice References in Statutory Interpretation'. *Brooklyn Law Review* 76 (3):941–952.
Kropp, Manfred. 1992. 'Statistischer und stilistischer Ansatz zur Lösung des Problems der Urheberschaft von Hatata Zar'a-Yaqob' (A statistic and stylistic approach for resolving the problem of authorship of Hatäta Zär'a-Ya'qob). Academia.edu. Accessed on 15 June, 2023. https://www.academia.edu/2605547/A_Statistic_and_Stylistic_Approach_for_Resolving_the_Problem_of_Authorship_of_Hat%C3%A4ta_Z%C3%A4r_a_Ya%CA%BFqob.
Littmann, Enno, ed. 1904. *Philosophi abessini; sive, Vita et philosophia magistri Zar'a-Yā'qōb eiusque discipuli Walda-Ḥeywat philosophia [Vol 1: Textus; Vol. 2: Versio]*. Corpus scriptorum christianorum orientalium. Scriptores aethiopici volumes 18 & 19. Paris: E Typographeo reipublicae.
Littmann, Enno. 1909. 'Geschichte der athiopischen Literatur'. In *Geschichte der christlichen Litteraturen des Orients*, edited by Carl Brockelmann, 185–270. Leipzig: Amelang.
Littmann, Enno. 1916. *Zar'a Jacob, ein einsamer Denker in Abessinien, mit einter Einleitung von Benno Erdmann*. Berlin: Karl Curtius.
Littmann, Enno. 1930. 'Compte rendu de *Ethiopica & Amharica* de George F. Black' (Review of *Ethiopica & Amharica: A List of Works in the New York Public Library* by George F. Black, 1928). *Orientalistische Literaturzeitung Monatsschrift für die Wissenschaft vom ganzen Orient und seine Bezlehungen zu den angrenzenden Kulturkreisen* 23 (8/9):653–656.
Lochner, Norbert. 1958. 'Anton Wilhelm Amo: A Ghana Scholar in Eighteenth Century Germany'. *Transactions of the Historical Society of Ghana* 3:169–179.

Luam Tesfalidet. 2007. 'Rezeptionsgeschichte der Ḥatäta Zär'a Ya'əqobs und Wäldä Ḥəywät'. MA thesis, Hiob Ludolf Centre for Ethiopian and Eritrean Studies, Universität Hamburg.

Maiocchi, Roberto. 2015. 'Italian scientists and the war in Ethiopia'. *Rendiconti Accademia Nazionale delle Scienze detta dei XL Memorie di Scienze Fisiche e Naturali 133* 39 (Part II, Tome I):127–146.

Mallette, Karla. 2011. *European Modernity and the Arab Mediterranean: Toward a New Philology and a Counter-Orientalism*. Philadelphia: University of Pennsylvania Press.

Marchiotto, Lino. 1964–1965. 'Gli Hatata Zar'a Ya'qob, Walda Heywat e la loro filosofia'. PhD thesis, Universita di studi di Napoli, Facolta Lettere e filosofia.

Martínez d'Alòs-Moner, Andreu. 2010. 'Səmʿon'. In *Encyclopaedia Aethiopica: O-X: Vol. 4*, edited by Siegbert Uhlig, 617–618. Wiesbaden: Harrassowitz.

Matthewson, Amy. 2021. 'Cui Malo? Cui Bono? Reflections on a Literary Forgery: The Case of The Memoirs of Li Hung Chang'. *Partial Answers: Journal of Literature and the History of Ideas* 19 (1):19–34. doi: 10.1353/pan.2021.0001.

Meley Mulugeta. 2010. 'Säwasəw'. In *Encyclopaedia Aethiopica: O-X: Vol. 4*, edited by Siegbert Uhlig, 562–564. Wiesbaden: Harrassowitz.

Maimire Mennasemay. 2009. 'The 'Dekike Estifanos': Towards an Ethiopian critical theory'. *Horn of Africa: An Independent International Journal* 27:64–118.

Maimire Mennasemay. 2010. 'A Critical Dialogue Between Fifteenth and Twenty First Century Ethiopia'. *International Journal of Ethiopian Studies* 5 (1):1–37.

Fasil Merawi. 2018. 'Zera Yacob's Hatata and the Vitality of an Indigenous Ethiopian Philosophy'. *Ethiopian Journal of Social Sciences* 3 (2):1–9. Doi: 10.20372/ejss.v3i2.87

Fasil Merawi, and Setargew Kenaw. 2019. 'Is There an Ethiopian Philosophy? Rereading the Hatetas of Zara Yaecob and Walda Hewat in the Context of Knowledge Production'. *Ethiopian Journal of the Social Sciences and Humanities* 15 (1):59–75.

Mittwoch, Eugen. 1934. 'Die amharische Version der Soirees de Carthage: mit einer Einleitung: die angeblichen abessinischen Philosophen des 17. Jahrhunderts'. In *Abessinische Studien, Volume II*. Berlin and Leipzig: Walter de Gruyter.

Mo Zi. 2013. *The Book of Master Mo*. London: Penguin Classics.

Mohammed Seid. 2005. 'Ethiopian Philosophy: Its Roles for Development'. BA thesis, Department of Philosophy, Addis Ababa University.

Mudimbe, Valentin-Yves. 1988. *The Invention of Africa: Gnosis, Philosophy, and the Order of Knowledge*, *African Systems of Thought*. Bloomington: Indiana University Press.

Molla Bekalu Mulualem,, Alemayehu Bishaw Tamiru, and Asrat Dagnaw Kelkay. 2022. 'Educational Practices of Indigenous Qene Bet Schools and Its Implications to The Modern Educational Practices'. *Cogent Education* 9 (1):2158673. Doi: 10.1080/2331186X.2022.2158673.

Nöldeke, Theodor. 1905. 'Zwei abessinischen Deisten'. *Deutsche Rundschau* 9:457–459.

Nöldeke, Theodor. 1925. 'Die äthiopische Literatur'. In *Die Kultur der Gegenwart ihre Entwicklung und ihre Ziere*, edited by Paul Hinneberg. Leipzig, Berlin: B. G. Teubner.

Pankhurst, E. Sylvia. 1955. 'The Enquiries of Zara Yakob: Thoughts of an Ethiopian Philosopher'. In *Ethiopia: A Cultural History*, Chap 20. Addis Ababa: Lalibela House.

Pankhurst, Richard. 1969. 'A Preliminary History of Ethiopian Measures, Weights and Value: Part II'. *Journal of Ethiopian Studies* 7 (2):99–164.

Park, Peter K. J. 2013. *Africa, Asia, and the History of Philosophy: Racism in the Formation of the Philosophical Canon, 1780–1830*. Albany: SUNY Press.

Parkyns, Mansfield. 1853. *Life in Abyssinia: Being Notes Collected During Three Years' Residence and Travels in that Country*. 2 vols. Vol. 2. London: John Murray.

Perry, Ben Edwin. 1964. *Secundus, The Silent Philosopher: The Greek Life of Secundus, critically edited and restored so far as possible, together with translations of the Greek and Oriental versions, the Latin and Oriental texts, and a study of the tradition*: Chapel Hill: American Philological Association.

Petros Solomon. 2018. 'The Gəʾəz Acts of Abunä Filəp̣os of Däbrä Libanos: Critical Edition and Annotated Translation'. PhD, Philology, Addis Ababa University.

Pietruschka, Ute. 2005. 'Fälasfa ṭäbiban: Mäṣḥafä fälasfa ṭäbiban [The Book of the Wise Philosophers]'. In *Encyclopaedia Aethiopica: D-Ha: Vol. 2*, edited by Siegbert Uhlig, 485–486. Wiesbaden: Harrassowitz.

Pietruschka, Ute, and Alessandro Bausi. 2010. 'Urbino, Father Giusto da'. In *Encyclopaedia Aethiopica: O-X: Vol. 4*, edited by Siegbert Uhlig, 1043–1045. Wiesbaden: Harrassowitz.

Plato. 1947. *Phaedrus*. Translated by Harold N. Fowler. *Plato in Twelve Volumes*, Vol. 9. Cambridge: Harvard University Press.

Poetsch, Christoph. 2021. 'Das Thothbuch: eine ägyptische Vorlage der platonischen Schriftkritik im Phaidros?' *Archiv für Geschichte der Philosophie* 103 (2):192–220. doi: 10.1515/agph-2018-0043.

Portenger, Hendrick, and R. De May. 1819. *Narrative of the Sufferings and Adventures of Henderick Portenger, A Private Soldier of the Late Swiss Regiment De Mueron, Who Was Wrecked on the Shores of Abyssinia, in the Red Sea*. London: Sir Richard Phillips and Co.

Portilla, Miguel León. 2002. *Bernardino de Sahagún, first anthropologist*. Norman: University of Oklahoma Press.

Prijac, Lukian. 2014. 'Freemasonry'. In *Encyclopaedia Aethiopica: Y-Z: Vol. 5*, edited by Alessandro Bausi and Siegbert Uhlig, 328–329. Wiesbaden: Harrassowitz.

Relf, Simon. 1999. 'Exploring the 'Birthdays Problem' and Some of Its Variants through Computer Simulation'. *International Journal of Mathematical Education in Science and Technology* 30 (1):81–91. doi: 10.1080/002073999288120.

Ricci, Lanfranco. 1964. 'Le ultime fortune di Giusto da Urbino'. In *Studi Orientali pubblicati a cura della scuola orientale*, edited by Giovanni Bardi. Rome: Università di Roma.

Ricci, Lanfranco. 1969. 'Letterature dell' Etiopia'. In *Storia delle letterature d'Oriente*, edited by Oscar Botto, 801–936. Milan: Vallardi.

Ricci, Lanfranco. 2003. 'Conti Rossini, Carlo'. In *Encyclopaedia Aethiopica: A–C: Vol. 1*, edited by Siegbert Uhlig, 791–792. Wiesbaden: Harrassowitz.

Rutherford, Ian, ed. 2016. *Graeco-Egyptian Interactions. Literature, Translation, and Culture, 500 BC–AD 300*. Oxford: Oxford University Press.

Ruthven, Kenneth Knowles. 2001. *Faking Literature*. Cambridge: Cambridge University Press.

Ryan, Judith, and Alfred Thomas. 2003. *Cultures of Forgery: Making Nations Making Selves*. New York and London: Routledge.

Sahagún, Fray Bernardino de. 1969. *Florentine Codex. General History of the Things of New Spain: Translated from the Aztec into English*. Translated by Charles E. Dibble and Arthur J. O. Anderson. Salt Lake City: University of Utah Press.

Serequeberhan, Tsenay. 1994. *The Hermeneutics of African Philosophy: Horizon and Discourse*: Psychology Press.

Simon, Jean. 1936. 'Le Hatata Zar'a Ya 'qob et le Hatata Walda Heywat'. *Orientalia Christiana Periodica* Series 2 (5):93–101.

Sokolinskaia, Evgenia. 2010. 'P̣awlos ' In *Encyclopaedia Aethiopica: O-X: Vol. 4*, edited by Siegbert Uhlig, 125. Wiesbaden: Harrassowitz.

Solomon Ghebre Ghiorghis. 1972. 'Ethiopian Philosophy (Part 1)'. *Ethiopian Herald* 29 (26 March):10. Accessed 14 June 2023. https://gpa.eastview.com/crl/ean/newspapers/ethe19720102-01.1.3

Srivastava, Neelam. 2022. 'Italian Colonialism and Orientalism in Ethiopia: The Hatata and the 'Scholar-Functionary' Carlo Conti Rossini'. Paper presented at the *In Search of Zara Yaqob* Conference, Oxford University, 30 April.

Stern, Henry Aaron. 1862. *Wanderings among the Falashas in Abyssinia; Together with a Description of the Country and Its Various Inhabitants*. London: Wertheim, Macintosh, and Hunt.

Stoffregen-Pedersen, Kirsten, and Tedros Abraha. 2003. 'Andəmta'. In *Encyclopaedia Aethiopica: A–C: Vol. 1*, edited by Siegbert Uhlig, 258–259. Wiesbaden: Harrassowitz.

Sula, Chris Alen, and Heather V Hill. 2019. 'The Early History of Digital Humanities: An Analysis of Computers and the Humanities (1966–2004) and Literary and Linguistic Computing (1986–2004)'. *Digital Scholarship in the Humanities* 34 (Supplement 1):i190-i206. doi: 10.1093/llc/fqz072.

Sumner, Claude. 1974. *Ethiopian Philosophy: Vol 1: The Book of the Wise Philosophers*. 5 vols. Vol. 1. Addis Ababa: Addis Ababa University.

Sumner, Claude. 1976. *Ethiopian Philosophy: Vol 2: The Treatise of Zär'a Ya'əqob and of Wäldä Heywat: Text and Authorship*. 5 vols. Vol. 2. Addis Ababa: Addis Ababa University.

Sumner, Claude. 1978. *Ethiopian Philosophy: Vol 3: The Treatise of Zär'a Ya'əqob and of Wäldä Heywat: An Analysis*. 5 vols. Vol. e. Addis Ababa: Addis Ababa University.

Sumner, Claude, and Samuel Wolde Yohannes. 2002. *Perspectives in African Philosophy: An Anthology on 'Problematic of an African Philosophy: Twenty Years After (1976–1996)'*. Addis Ababa: Addis Ababa University Printing Press.

Taddesse Tamrat. 1966. 'Some Notes on Fifteenth Century Stephanite 'Heresy' in the Ethiopian Church'. *Rassegna di Studi Etiopici* 22:103–115.

Taddesse Tamrat. 1972. *Church and State in Ethiopia, 1270–1527*. Oxford: Oxford University Press.

Taei, Payman. 2018. 'Do Humans Have Mating Seasons? This Heat Map Reveals the Surprising Link Between Birthdays and Seasons'. *Towards Data Science*. Accessed 14 June 2023. https://towardsdatascience.com/do-humans-have-mating-seasons-a723cad43500

Takla Haymanot. 1914. *Abouna Yacob, ou, Le vénérable de Jacobis: Scènes de sa vie d'apostolat, racontées par un témoin*. Paris: À la procure des Lazaristes.

Tarducci, Francesco. 1899. *P. Giusto da Urbino, missionario in Abissinia, e le esplorazioni africane*. Faenza: G. Montanari.

Tasfa Gabra Selasse, ed. 1996. *Tä'ammärä Maryam bä-Gəʿəz ənna bä-Amarañña [The Miracles of Mary in Ethiopic and Amharic: Part Two: 402 /381/ Miracles]*. Addis Ababa: Tasfa Gabra Selasse Printing Press.

Tassew Asfaw. 2004. 'The Contribution of Native Ethiopian Philosophers, Zara Yacob and Wolde Hiwot, to Ethiopian Philosophy'. *Meskot: An Ethiopian Online Journal*. Accessed 14 June 2023. http://www.meskot.com/Ethio_Philosophers2.pdf.

Tesfaye Debesay. 1970. 'In Search of Truth, Zera-Yacob the Philosopher of Yore'. *The Ethiopian Herald* (11 January):2. Accessed 14 June 2023. https://gpa.eastview.com/crl/ean/newspapers/ethe19700111-01.1.2.

Tewalda Madhen. 2006. *The Gəʿəz Acts of Abba Ǝṣṭifanos of Gʷəndagʷəndé*. Translated by Getatchew Haile. Edited by Getatchew Haile. 2 vols. *Corpus scriptorum christianorum orientalium 620*. Leuven, Belgium: Peeters.

Turayev, Boris Alexandrovich. 1903. 'Абиссинские свободные мыслители XVII века (Abbisinskiye svobodnyye mysliteli XVII veka; Ethiopian Freethinkers of the Seventeenth Century)'. *Журнал Министерства Народного Просвещения (Zhurnal Ministerstva Narodnavo Prosveshcheniya; Journal of the Ministry of Education)* December:443–447.

Turayev, Boris Alexandrovich. 1905. 'Hatata Zar'a Yae'qob: Izledovaniye Zarya Yakoba: Ispoved abissinskavo Svobodnavo myslitelya XXVII veka'. *Imperatorskoy Russkoye Arkheaologischeskoye Obshchestvo: Zapisi Vostochanvo Otdeleniya* 16:1–62.

Turayev, Boris Alexandrovich. 1920. 'Абиссинская литература (La littérature d'Abyssinie)'. *Литература Востока* 2:152–161.

Ullendorff, Edward. 1945. *Exploration and Study of Abyssinia: A brief Survey, with an Appendix on the Obelisk of Matara*. Asmara: Il Lunedi dell' Eritrea.

Ullendorff, Edward. 1960. *The Ethiopians: An Introduction to Country and People*. Oxford: Oxford University Press.

Ullendorff, Edward. 1987. 'The Confessio Fidei of King Claudius of Ethiopia'. *Journal of Semitic Studies* 32 (1):159–176.

United Nations Statistics Division. 2022. 'Demographic Statistics Database: Live births by month of birth'. UNData: A World of Information. Accessed 12 September 2022. http://data.un.org/Data.aspx?d=POP&f=tableCode%3A55#POP

Van Norden, Bryan William. 2017. *Taking Back Philosophy: A Multicultural Manifesto*. New York: Columbia University Press.

Voigt, Rainer. 2007. 'Mittwoch, Eugen'. In *Encyclopaedia Aethiopica: He-N: Vol. 3*, edited by Siegbert Uhlig, 981–982. Wiesbaden: Harrassowitz.

Weninger, Stefan. 2005. 'Fisalgos'. In *Encyclopaedia Aethiopica: D-Ha: Vol. 2*, edited by Siegbert Uhlig, 549–550. Wiesbaden: Harrassowitz.

Weninger, Stefan. 2010. 'Secundus'. In *Encyclopaedia Aethiopica: O-X: Vol. 4*, edited by Siegbert Uhlig, 590–591. Wiesbaden: Harrassowitz.

Wey, Wilhelm. 1906. 'Ein äthiopischer Philosoph'. *Beilage zur allgemeine Zeitung* 195:361–364.

Windmuller-Luna, Kristen D. 2016. 'Building Faith: Ethiopian Art and Architecture during the Jesuit Interlude, 1557–1632'. PhD Thesis, Department of Art and Archaeology, Princeton University

Wion, Anaïs. 2013a. 'L'histoire d'un vrai faux traité philosophique (Ḥatatā Zarʾa Yāʾeqob et Ḥatatā Walda Ḥeywat). Episode 1: Le temps de la démystification et la traversée du désert (de 1916 aux années 1950) [Full text]'. *Afriques: Débats, méthodes et terrains d'histoire*. Accessed 14 June. https://doi.org/10.4000/afriques.1063

Wion, Anaïs. 2013b. 'L'histoire d'un vrai faux traité philosophique (Ḥatatā Zarʾa Yāʾeqob et Ḥatatā Walda Ḥeywat). Épisode 2: Le temps de la démystification et la traversée du désert (de 1916 aux années 1950)'. *Afriques: Débats, méthodes et terrains d'histoire*. Accessed 14 June. https://doi.org/10.4000/afriques.1316.

Wion, Anaïs. 2021a. 'The History of a Genuine Fake Philosophical Treatise (Ḥatatā Zarʾa Yāʾeqob and Ḥatatā Walda Ḥeywat). Episode 1: The Time of Discovery. From Being Part of a Collection to Becoming a Scholarly Publication (1852–1904)'. *Afriques: Débats, méthodes et terrains d'histoire*. Accessed 14 June. https://doi.org/10.4000/afriques.3178.

Wion, Anaïs. 2021b. 'The History of a Genuine Fake Philosophical Treatise (Ḥatatā Zarʾa Yāʾeqob and Ḥatatā Walda Ḥeywat). Episode 2: The Time of Debunking, The Time in the Wilderness (from 1916 to the 1950s)'. *Afriques: Débats, méthodes et terrains d'histoire*. Accessed 14 June. https://doi.org/10.4000/afriques.3188.

Wion, Anaïs, and Aïssatou Mbodj-Pouye. 2013. 'L'histoire d'un vrai faux traité philosophique (Ḥatatā Zarʾa Yāʾeqob et Ḥatatā Walda Ḥeywat). Introduction: Enquête sur une enquête'. *Afriques: Débats, méthodes et terrains d'histoire*. Accessed 14 June. doi:https://doi.org/10.4000/afriques.1060.

Yonas Zerfu. 2005. 'The Idea of Natural Law in the Philosophy of Zarayacob and Waldahaywat'. BA thesis, Department of Philosophy, Addis Ababa University.

Za-Manfas Qeddus Abreha. 1955. ኢትዮጵያውያን ፈሎሶፋዎች፤ ሐተታ ዘዘርዓ ያዕቆብ አክሱማዊ መወልደ ሐይወት እንፍራዛዊ (Ethiopian Philosophers: The Hatäta of Zärʾa Yaʿəqob of Aksum and Wäldä Həywät of Ennfraz). Asmära. Arti Grafichi Eritree.

Zara Yaqob. 1992. *The Mariology of Emperor Zärʾa Yaʿəqob of Ethiopia: Texts and Translations*. Translated by Getatchew Haile. Edited by Getatchew Haile. Rome: Pontificium Institutum Studiorum Orientalium.

Zitelmann, Thomas. 2005. 'd'Abbadie, Antoine and Arnauld d". In *Encyclopaedia Aethiopica: D-Ha: Vol. 2*, edited by Siegbert Uhlig, 25–26. Wiesbaden: Harrassowitz.

Index

Abb 215 manuscript
– colour digital copy 13
– origin and transmission 12
– scribal intervention 192
– stemma 10
– wording differences from Abb 234 187
Abb 234 manuscript
– as superior to Abb 215 15–16
– colour digital copy 13
– origin and transmission 12
– scribal intervention 192
– stemma 10
– wording differences from Abb 215 187
abortion 151
adultery. *See* sex
Afonso Mendes, Jesuit 64, 101–104
African philosophy VII, 1, 22–23, 44
Aksum, city of 2, 38–39, 62, 64–66, 97–98, 100–101, 118
Alemayyehu Moges 21
Amhara province 19, 66, 97
andemta (commentary) 6–7
angels, existence of 116, 126
animals
– as different 115
– difference from 79, 123, 140
– similarity to 95
– soul of 96, 116, 129
Antiochus, King 157
Antoine d'Abbadie, patron 9, 19
Apophthegmata Patrum (Collection of the Desert Fathers) 142
asceticism
– celibacy 35, 76, 84, 144–147
– fasting 79, 81, 84, 140

Begemder district 97
Beta Lehem, town 19
Betsega Habta Egziabher, son of Zara Yaqob 101, 106, 108
BnF Éthiopien d'Abbadie 215 manuscript . *See* Abb 215 manuscript
BnF Éthiopien d'Abbadie MS 234 manuscript. *See* Abb 234 manuscript

Catholic faith 30, 64, 118
– in Ethiopia XXIII, 2, 65, 67, 71, 82, 91, 97, 102–103
celibacy. *See* asceticism
Christian faith 83, 112
– fasting laws 79, 81
– laws 77
Colossians, Book of 114, 120, 132, 138
Conti Rossini, Carlo 20, 27, 30
Coptic (Egyptian) faith 65, 67, 97, 118
1 Corinthians, Book of 130, 139, 141
2 Corinthians, Book of 119, 131

Dabra Tabor, town 19
Daniel, Book of 125
da Sessan, Carmelo, biographer of Giusto da Urbino 21
death
– fear of 90, 158–159
– life after 85–86, 88, 95, 158
– saved from 63
debate on authorship
– case for Ethiopian authors 53
– case for European author 42
– history of 23
Dembiya province 102
Descartes IX, 4
Deuteronomy, Book of 75–76, 131, 135

Ecclesiastes, Book of 73, 132, 141, 154
Efons. *See* Afonso Mendes
Enfraz district 97, 102
1 Enoch, Book of 40, 126, 151
Ephesians, Book of 130, 132, 135–136
epistemology (theory of knowledge) 118, 120
equality
– of all human beings 79, 81, 121, 131, 133
– of men and women 100
erotapokriseis genre 7
Estifanos, Abba X, 48
Ethiopian Herald, English language newspaper 21
Ethiopian Orthodox Church 2, 35, 67, 101, 104
– educational system 5
Ewostatewos, Abba X

Exodus, Book of 69, 75–76, 135, 144

famine 103–104
Fasiladas, King 2, 97, 102–103, 108
– wickedness of 103
fasting. *See* asceticism; Christian faith; Islamic faith
fortune telling and astrology 74

Gabra Maryam, scribe 10, 12, 189
gadl (hagiography) genre 7
Galatians, Book of 130–131
Ge'ez language 57
– fidal (syllabary) 57
– Simplified spellings XIX
Genesis, Book of 78, 99–100, 115, 123–124, 130, 138, 146–147
Getatchew Haile 13
Giusto da Urbino 13
– as scribe 9, 191
– birth date 24, 28
– birth name 18, 24, 27
– Catholic faith 35, 51
– collector 12
– Ge'ez skills 25, 31
– life XXIV
– personality 25
– works by 19
God, existence of 69–70, 82, 89, 114, 120
Gojjam province 97
Guidi, Ignazio 20

Habtu, patron of Zara Yaqob 97–98, 102, 105
hatata genre 7
Hatata, scholarship on XXV
Himyarite peoples of Yemen 118
Hirut, wife of Zara Yaqob 100
human
– as fallen angels 127
– soul of 116, 121, 126

Indian (south Asian) religions 81, 118
In Search of Zara Yaqob conference 23
Isaiah, Book of 104, 122, 127, 139, 160
Islam. *See* Muslim faith
Italian colonialism 19

James, Book of 125, 142
Jewish faith 71, 75, 81, 112, 118
– fasting laws 81
– laws 77
John, Gospel of 71, 77, 122, 130, 133, 151
1 John, Book of 104–105, 133
Jubilees, Book of 147

Littmann, Enno 14, 18
Luam Tesfalidet 23
Luke, Gospel of 64–65, 78, 87, 89, 119, 122, 131, 135, 139, 159

Maccabees, book of 157
Maccabees, Ethiopic book of 157
Malachi, Book of 130
Mark, Gospel of 65, 87, 100, 104, 122, 132, 135, 146, 148
marriage 76–78, 80, 84, 100, 144–148, 151–152
– divorce 148–149
Matsehaf Bet, house of exegesis 6, 64
Matthew, Gospel of 65, 78, 86–88, 99–100, 104, 119, 122, 127, 131, 135, 148, 157, 159
Medhanit, daughter-in-law of Zara Yaqob 106
Mittwoch, Eugen 20
Mohammed, prophet 76–77, 79, 118
Moses, prophet 75–76, 78, 81, 118
Muslim faith 71, 79, 81, 112, 118
– fasting laws 80–81
– laws 77, 79

Nebab Bet, house of reading 5
non-European philosophy VII
nostalgia, problems with 154

parables
– cause of conflicts 142
– old man and his son 135
– robber and his father 152
– thrice-married man 149
– wife and lion 150
1 Peter, Book of 124, 127, 132, 134, 149, 155
Physiologus X, 49
plague 104–105

Plato VIII, X, 4, 49
Proverbs, Book of 23, 111, 127, 132, 153–154
Psalms, Book of 2–3, 5, 34, 43, 45–47, 59, 61–63, 66–70, 72, 77, 79, 81, 83–86, 88–98, 102–103, 105, 108–109, 113, 119–125, 128–134, 136–139, 141–142, 144–145, 147, 151–152, 155
Psalter 2, 5–6, 41, 45–47, 63, 66, 99, 106, 125, 129, 144, 160

Qene Bet, house of poetry 6, 63

rationalist philosophy 3–4, 22
reason (rationality) 64, 70, 72–73, 75, 79, 112, 116–118, 137
religion. *See* individual religions
religions, problems with 118
religious belief, as false 82
Romans, Book of 74, 103, 122, 130–132, 138

Sabean peoples of Yemen 118
1 Samuel, Book of 104, 129
Sayings of the Philosophers X, 34, 143, 155
Secundus, philosopher X, 49
sex 75–76, 80
– adultery 79, 82, 84, 87, 103, 143, 146–148, 152
– ensuring women's satisfaction in 3, 147
– masturbation 106
– moderation 148
– pleasure in 146–147
Shewa region 66
Sirach, Book of 124, 139
slavery IX, 38, 79, 156
Soirées de Carthage book 26, 33, 38
soul. *See* animals; human
South Arabian religions 118
stars, distance of 96

Sumner, Claude 21–22
Susenyos, King XXIII, 2, 64–66, 91, 97, 102–103, 192

Takkaze River 66
Takla Haymanot 24, 29–30
Ten Commandments 87
Teodros Kiros 22
1 Thessalonians, Book of 130, 136, 155
2 Thessalonians, Book of 141
1 Timothy, Book of 132, 151
2 Timothy, Book of 106, 119
Turayev, Boris Alexsandrovich 18

Walda Heywat, author and philosopher XXIV, 10, 111
– as disciple of Zara Yaqob 106
– as Habtu's son 99
– later life 109
– purpose in writing 112
Walda Michael, Habtu's son 98
Walda Yohannes, enemy of Zara Yaqob 65, 91, 102
Walda Yosef, scribe 12
Wion, Anaïs 23, 26
wisdom literature 4

Yaqob I, King 62
Yohannes I, King 108

Zara Yaqob, author and philosopher
– as not a Christian 107
– later life 109
– life XXIV, 2, 67, 107
– purpose in writing 107
Zema Bet, house of music 5, 63

www.ingramcontent.com/pod-product-compliance
Lightning Source LLC
Chambersburg PA
CBHW020229170426
43201CB00007B/368